Publications

of

𝕿𝖍𝖊 𝕮𝖔𝖑𝖔𝖓𝖎𝖆𝖑 𝕾𝖔𝖈𝖎𝖊𝖙𝖞 𝖔𝖋 𝕸𝖆𝖘𝖘𝖆𝖈𝖍𝖚𝖘𝖊𝖙𝖙𝖘

VOLUME LXXII

The
Colonial Church Records

of the First Church of Reading (Wakefield)
and the First Church of Rumney Marsh (Revere)

Reading Meeting House, built 1688

Rumney Marsh Meeting House, built 1710

The
Colonial Church Records

of the First Church of Reading (Wakefield)
and the First Church of Rumney Marsh (Revere)

Editors

James F. Cooper, Jr.
Oklahoma State University

Kenneth P. Minkema
Yale University

Boston   THE COLONIAL SOCIETY OF MASSACHUSETTS   2006
Distributed by the University of Virginia Press

DEDICATED TO

Harold Field Worthley

Printed from the Income of the Sarah Louise Edes Fund

Contents

Acknowledgements

The editors wish to thank a number of individuals and institutions that made possible the publication of this volume. First, we wish to thank Jane Wilkins, Herbert Leafquist, and Alma Leafquist of the First Parish Congregational Church of Wakefield, for their friendliness and their assistance in locating and duplicating the long lost church record book. We also wish to thank the staff of the Reading Public Library for providing the Works Projects Administration's typescript of the volume. Thanks are also owed to the staff of the Museum of Fine Arts in Boston, which provided us with access to the Rumney Marsh records, and assisted us in microfilming them. The New England Historic Genealogical Society of Boston provided a useful nineteenth-century handwritten transcription of the Rumney Marsh records; in particular we wish to thank Timothy G. X. Salls. Financial assistance for this project was provided by the Center for Religion and American Life at Yale University and the Department of History at Oklahoma State University. Brian Harrison and Joel Halcomb assisted in entering and proofreading the transcribed text; the latter benefited from a research scholarship endowed by Thomas Steele. Harold Field Worthley and Harry S. Stout provided valuable comments on drafts of the introduction. Finally, we would like to acknowledge John Tyler of the Colonial Society of Massachusetts, who shepherded us through the publication procedure with his usual aplomb, from initial proposal of the idea to final production.

This volume is dedicated to Harold Field Worthley, who served as Librarian and Executive Director of the Congregational Library in Boston and its parent American Congregational Association from 1977 until his retirement in 2004. All scholars interested in colonial Massachusetts church records and in Congregational history are indebted to Dr. Worthley, not only for his 27 years of service at the Congregational Library, but for the three years of effort and 28,000 miles of travel (all within Massachusetts, and mainly at his own expense) that he devoted during the 1960s to hunting down and inventorying the hundreds of local church manuscripts that, for the most part, still remain scattered throughout the state. But for these Herculean efforts and the now-famous 716-page "Worthley Inventory" of early Congregational church records that emerged from them, our project, and many others, would have been impossible.

The
Colonial Church Records

of the First Church of Reading (Wakefield)
and the First Church of Rumney Marsh (Revere)

Introduction

*F*ew topics have dominated the attention of colonial American historians more than the establishment and development of the first Congregational churches in early Massachusetts. From the early Congregationalists themselves, who regarded their form of church organization as a major step in the Protestant Reformation, to later Congregational historians, who saw their church "ordinances" as the root of American democracy, to modern historians, who have tied church developments to the Great Awakening and even the American Revolution, Congregationalism has held a prominent place in virtually all significant interpretations of early Massachusetts's unique political and religious culture.[1]

Traditionally, almost all of the literature on Congregationalism and early church life in Massachusetts had been based on ministerial writings. But this approach began to shift several decades ago, owing to greater emphasis upon social history and "history from the bottom up." In recent years, historians have begun to focus more specifically on popular or "lived" religion and the history of religious practice.[2] Yet, not surprisingly, scholars are only now turning their full attention to arguably the most useful sources for examining the social, cultural, and political implications of popular religion: church records.[3] Virtually every church in early Massachusetts kept records of the minutes of church meetings, lists of baptisms and memberships, records of disciplinary proceedings and, at times, larger debates that surrounded a wide variety of church decisions. Formerly the province largely of genealogists and denominational historians, these documents are now recognized as indispensable for any study on topics such as the early development and implementation of church government, church practices, lay and clerical interchanges on the principles behind church government, and the general evolution of Congregationalism over the course of the colonial period. Beyond religion, these records reveal ancillary information on topics such as patterns of speech, patterns of urban negotiation, demographics, economics, community development, social mores, judicial proceedings, and day-to-day life. These records, in short, provide the most direct means toward achieving an understanding of church life in colonial Massachusetts and of religious culture in colonial New England.

While virtually every Massachusetts church kept records, some record keepers were far more careful than others. Many remaining church records consist mainly of sketchy, line-a-day entries. An unfortunate number of records have been lost to fire or theft, or have simply been misplaced. Remarkable quantities of useful records remain from some periods in early Massachusetts history, such as the first years of founding. Yet for other periods, such as the mid- to late seventeenth century, surprisingly few sets of records remain extant, even though more churches had been established by that time.

Presented in this volume are two of the finest sets of church records from the colonial era of Massachusetts history that remain unpublished. Culled from a survey of hundreds of sets of church records, both of these documents are a testament to the commitment that some ministers and lay members maintained in keeping careful and detailed accounts of church affairs. Both are remarkable for their chronological breadth, their depth, or both, and reveal an extraordinary amount of information on church life over the course of the colonial era. The Reading church records, in particular, are unique insofar as they cover the entire colonial era, while the Rumney Marsh book casts unprecedented light on the neglected period of 1715 through 1757.

Despite their obvious usefulness to religious and social historians, both sets of records have gone largely unnoticed, but for good reasons. The Rumney Marsh record book has remained obscure because of its unlikely location in Boston's Museum of Fine Arts. The story behind the extraordinary records of the First Church of Reading is even more remarkable. For decades, the early record books were missing and presumed lost. Only a useful but flawed typescript of the records (completed in the 1930s by the Works Projects Administration) had been available before. But a new search in the church vaults during the summer of 2001 by Professor Cooper and the historians of the Wakefield First Congregational Parish Church turned up a treasure trove. The original documents have now been rediscovered and transcribed, and are presented here. We are pleased to make both of these documents available to historians and interested scholars for the first time.

A Primer of Early New England Congregationalism

In order to fully grasp the purpose, meaning, and significance of these documents, it is important to achieve a general understanding of the basic principles and practices of Congregationalism in early Massachusetts. The most fundamental goal of the Congregationalists, as expressed in their written "covenants," was to operate their churches in strict accordance with scriptural warrants. The Reading church vowed in their covenant of 1644 to "give up our-selves to yᵉ Lᵈ Lord Jesus Christ, to be ruled & guided by him in yᵉ mattʳˢ of his worship, & in our whole conversation."[4] In matters of church government, the doctrine of "sola scriptura," or dependence on the direction of the Bible, stood in contrast to Catholic practices and those in the Church of England, which, the early Congregationalists believed, had been corrupted with "humane inventions" not found in the Scripture.[5]

The Congregationalists expended tremendous time and energy in the 1630s and 1640s discussing larger principles and hammering out specific provisions of their form of church organization, formally codifying their practices in the Cambridge Platform of 1648, a document composed by ministers and lay delegates from throughout Massachusetts and ratified by every local church in the colony.[6] Churches repeatedly reviewed and affirmed their commitment to the Cambridge Platform in the colonial era, and frequent references to the document are found in the records presented in this volume. At the suggestion of the "Reforming Synod" of 1679, for example, the Reading church "had Some time of perusing the Booke Called the platforme of Discipline" and they unanimously reconfirmed that the church "approved of it for the substance of it to be the word of God."[7] Originally, the Congregationalists intended the Platform to be a simple description of church practices as they had evolved over the first two decades of settlement. Some issues of greater import, such as baptism, as well as many lesser procedural details, would continue to evolve over the course of the seventeenth and eighteenth centuries. In time, the Platform took on increasingly greater significance as a document that not only established and justified, through Scripture, the duties and privileges of church officers and lay members, but even defined the larger Congregational mission in the New World. Eventually, the Platform gradually became vested with a sacred "constitutional" status.

Within local churches, the Platform confirmed the Congregationalists' efforts to establish a "mixed form" of government, in which decision-making authority was shared by the members and the church officers. Congregationalism limited voting in church meetings and affairs to male members in full communion, that is, those converted "saints" who had been admitted to partake of the sacraments. Lay full members elected all of their church officers (later, all churchgoers, in addition to those who qualified for full church membership, would have a say in the selection of ministers). Typically, the minister served as the moderator in church meetings, setting agendas, supervising debates, and guiding the decision-making process. Ministers enjoyed positions of considerable authority: candidates for church admission, for instance, could not stand "propounded" before the church for membership until they had demonstrated their "election" or spiritual conversion in private before their local minister. Similarly, as we shall see, ministers typically decided whether disciplinary complaints among churchgoers ought to be resolved privately, or whether they were "ripe" for a more formal hearing before the church.

The Congregationalists also believed in strict limitations on human authority; consequently, they allowed ministers to conduct little church business entirely on their own. Indeed, ministers enjoyed almost nothing in the way of unilateral church power. Congregationalism thus included a sophisticated system of checks and balances that granted specific powers, liberties, and duties to lay officers and voting members in addition to the "authority" granted to ministers.

Every church, for instance, elevated a small number of "worthy laymen" whom they elected as lay officers to assist their ministers in matters of church government (see Table 1). At first these figures often served as "ruling elders," who had the power to perform nearly every ministerial function except administer the sacraments. This office eventually fell largely (though never entirely) into disuse in the Congregational churches, partly due to clergy who questioned its scriptural basis. More commonly, ministers received assistance in governing their churches from deacons. Among other duties, deacons accompanied ministers in witnessing lay conversion testimonials and assisted ministers in determining whether disciplinary cases ought to come before the entire church.

The Congregationalists sought to balance these "managing powers" of the church officers with the "liberties" of the brethren. Churches allowed members to vote on virtually all church decisions and no formal church action became "official" without the approval of the membership. For example, though ministers and lay officers determined who stood before the church as candidates for admission, Congregational provisions required candidates to offer their conversion

Table 1: Deacons and Ruling Elders of Reading and Rumney Marsh, 1648-1769

Reading			Rumney Marsh		
Name	*Appointed*	*Died*	*Name*	*Appointed*	*Died*
Zechariah Fitch	1645	1662			
John Pierson	1645	1679			
Thomas Kendall	1645	1681			
Thomas Parker	1645	1683			
William Cowdrey	1645	1718			
Benjamin Fitch	1690	1713			
Thomas Bancroft	1690	1718			
John Damon	?	1708			
Nathaniel Lawrence	1715	?			
Thomas Boutell	1707	1737			
Thomas Nichols	1712	1737			
John Pearson	1712	?	John Tuttle	1715	1723
John Goodwin	1722	1757	Jacob Hasey	1715 resigned	1749
Francis Smith	1722	1744	John Chamberlane	1720 resigned	1749
Raham Bancroft	1737	1758	Samuel Tuttle	1720	1742
Nathaniel Stow	1737	1737	Samuel Watts*	1735	?
Kendall Parker	1738	1755	William Hasey*	1735	1753
Thomas Nichols Jr.	1738	1745	David Watts	1749	?
Brown Emerson	1746	1774	Benjamin Brintnal	1749	?
Jonathan Temple	1746	after 1767			
Benjamin Brown	1753	?			
Samuel Bancroft	1758	1782			

(*=ruling elder)

testimonials before the entire congregation. Members could—and sometimes did—"veto" the applications of candidates of questionable character.

The same balance and limits extended to church discipline, which required the carefully coordinated participation of both ordinary members and church officers. As both the Reading and Rumney Marsh records make clear, the Congregationalists sought to resolve most complaints over misbehavior among churchgoers privately, meaning that ordinary lay people conducted much church discipline on their own. One provision found in every local church covenant obligated members to enter into a system of "mutual watch," which required them to privately admonish one another when aware of transgressions. In Reading, churchgoers offered the "promise by yᵉ help of Christ to walk with our brethren & Sisters of yᵉ Congregation, in yᵉ spirit of brotherly love, watching over them & caring for them . . . yet seasonably Admonishing & restoreing them by a Spirit of meekness; And Sett them in Joynt again that have been thrû infirmity overtaken in any fault among us." Even when more serious or irresolvable complaints came to the attention of the church officers, efforts were made to avoid formal hearings. In 1659, Reading's George Davis suffered a formal censure from his church but, the records show, it occurred only after efforts to rectify the matter in private had failed.[8] In general, the Reading records are unusually valuable for their numerous references to mutual watch and private disciplinary hearings, topics that ministers often omitted from their church records in order to keep them private. Conscious of the public nature of the records, they undoubtedly left out certain information—such as the names of the parties or the exact natures of the complaints—in order to safeguard the reputations of the individuals involved.

The records also demonstrate that some disciplinary cases, because of their seriousness, their public nature, or because of an offender's "obstinacy," inevitably required formal church hearings. Ministers and lay officers generally determined whether unresolved cases were "ripe" for consideration by the entire church.[9] In formal church disciplinary hearings, the officers and lay witnesses laid out the case before the members. Typically, the pastor then invited the membership to debate matters and to discuss disciplinary alternatives. As with nearly all formal church decisions, discipline was thus a negotiated process. Often ministers weighed in with their views, and congregations typically took very seriously the suggestions of their officers. But frequently, ministers simply presented the issues before the congregation and stood back while the members decided a course of action (or inaction) on their own. Usually, after a full hearing of the case, ministers attempted to determine the "mind of the church" or a "sense of the meeting," and they then called for a vote. The Congregationalists believed in the ideal of unanimous consent, and most votes, whether disciplinary or otherwise, passed without dissent. But as the passage of time brought greater diversity of opinion and complexity of issues, churches increasingly rendered decisions by majority vote.

The 1653 disciplinary case of Elizabeth Hart in Reading nicely illustrates both the mechanics of church disciplinary procedures and the nature of the larger decision-making process. Hart faced disciplinary charges for "Sundry offences" such as "Contempt of Authority" and "Evil surmising." According to witnesses, Hart had boasted that "all ye wit ye church had could not keep hir out nor beigin [to] cast hir out" of the church and that "she never had ye worst of it befor^e Minister or church." She only made matters worse for herself by expressing her determination to "teach old fooles more wit." Numerous churchgoers labored with her in private, but she failed to display contrition—to the contrary, she put on a "shew of much hotienesse" and demonstrated a "proud high spirit." The officers consequently haled Hart before the entire church for a formal hearing. She offered only a weak apology for her offenses, forcing the church to decide whether or not to formally admonish her. Debating their alternatives, pastor Samuel Haugh observed, "one or two [members] Exp^{r}ssed themselves Content to Sit down" and drop the matter. "[B]ut others," he noted, "thought y^{m}selves unsatisfied." The pastor and membership concluded that "without fully Understanding ye churches mind," or in the absence of a sufficient degree of unanimity, they had best defer the case. A week later the church reached a general consensus that Hart had shown "Little signs of Repentance" and administered a censure, which denied her access to the Lord's Supper and required other church members to avoid her.[10]

The ultimate disciplinary penalty a church might administer was excommunication, which churches generally reserved for cases of great public scandal or incorrigible stubbornness on the part of the offender. Excommunication barred offenders from communion and subjected them to ostracization in the hope that the offender would see the error of his or her way, repent, and return to the church. In 1750, the Reading Church had to execute the awful sentence of excommunication "in face of ye Congregat^n" upon Ebenezer Parker for his "habitual Drunkenness." The church did not find any of Parker's particular offenses outrageous; rather, the problem rested with his ongoing refusal to repent and to reform himself. The members resorted to the drastic measure of excommunication only after twelve years of trying to reclaim him.[11]

Churches rendered these sorts of decisions entirely at the local level and without outside interference. Another central tenet of the Congregational system—one which lasted throughout the colonial era—was the concept of congregational independence. In contrast to churches with hierarchical structures, such as those found in the Roman Catholic, Anglican, or Presbyterian systems of organization, Congregationalists vested final decision-making authority within each local church. In local, internal affairs, no neighboring church, group of churches, or body of church elders maintained binding authority over any local congregation. This understanding meant that, theoretically, each church was free to develop and practice its own form of Congregationalism, and historians have generally made much of the variability of practices from church to church. Still, as the records in this volume demonstrate, Congregational churches harmonized their practices by communicating regularly with one another about issues of church government. Even more, all of the churches attempted to adhere to the Cambridge Platform as a general blueprint for practice—including many in Connecticut, even after the institution of the Saybrook Platform in 1709, which attempted to establish a distinct and more hierarchical ecclesiology for that colony. While Congregationalism was by no means static, and while some variability did exist from church to church, larger surveys of Congregational government point to the similarity of practices in the churches of colonial Massachusetts, especially during the first several decades of settlement.[12]

The Evolution of Colonial Massachusetts Congregationalism

While continuity represented one major theme of Congregationalism in colonial Massachusetts, many settlers of the founding generation would scarcely recognize some aspects of church government practiced by their successors in the later seventeenth and eighteenth centuries. Indeed, early seventeenth-century churchgoers vilified one another for suggesting modest changes in Congregationalism that pale before some of the innovations evident a century later. Some of these changes were narrowly procedural, but others were more fundamental. By the third and fourth decades of the seventeenth century, for instance, the vast majority of churches practiced the "Halfway Covenant," a significant revision in church admissions requirements. This innovation, recommended to local churches by the "Halfway Synod" of 1662, allowed adult, non-scandalous, unconverted children of full church members to "own" the church covenant and have their children baptized. This arrangement thus brought "Halfway" members into the system of church discipline and under mutual watch, though the new requirements did not extend voting privileges or participation in the sacrament of the Lord's Supper. Many churchgoers, long accustomed to traditional practices, resisted this change, and historians have closely studied the internal church struggles that accompanied efforts to adopt the Halfway Covenant. The innovation may indeed have represented the most significant church controversy of the colonial era in Massachusetts.

The actions of the Reading and Rumney Marsh congregations confirm the churches' varying responses to the Halfway Covenant, as well as increasing variety in church practices. During the long pastorate of Thomas Cheever, which extended from 1715 to 1749, the Rumney Marsh church was one of a significant minority of churches that refused to implement the Halfway Covenant. Indeed, the Halfway Covenant failed to stimulate much even in the way of debate among the members. Only one churchgoer member offered protest to the church's refusal to implement the innovation. In 1717 one Edward Tuttle was called before the church because, Pastor Cheever noted, he "absented [himself] from the Lords-supper three several times one after the other." A full member himself, Tuttle justified his behavior, explaining that "he was dissatisfied" because Cheever "refused to baptize one of his Grand Children" in accordance with the Halfway Covenant. Cheever simply reminded the dissenter that the church had decided to maintain traditional admissions requirements at its gathering in 1715, and that the minister "had openly & fully declared my judgment in that matter before we Signed our Church-Covenant." Tuttle acknowledged the "irregularity & disorder of his former absence," and the matter "was lovingly ended." The Halfway Covenant first appears the Reading records, in contrast, decades earlier, in 1665. Pastor John Brock carefully reviewed the innovation and its justifications before the congregation prior to taking a vote. The measure passed unanimously and, again, no evidence remains in the records to suggest that the change even occasioned debate, much less acrimony.

Virtually all churches that adopted the Halfway Covenant still required regenerate membership. But many began to adjust their policies toward relations, owing to the fact that churchgoers—especially women—found it increasingly difficult to offer their experiences of grace in public, before their entire congregation. Increasingly, churches allowed candidates to provide written relations. Others did away with public relations all together, requiring only that candidates for admission satisfy the minister and lay officers in private. (Reading was not among these; the church still required "a written or oral relation of Christian experience" as late as 1877.) In 1681, Pastor Brock urged his Reading congregation to address the issue of "the weake that say they can't speake their Experience of grace before many (according to the [Cambridge] platforme)." The church decided to allow shy members to testify in private, before the elders. But the members also refused to permit the elders to exercise unilateral control of the admissions process. They voted to "have some Brethrin Joyned with ye Elders to heare & Judge & represent the Brotherhood; whither the season Calls for it, or ye person must Speake before sufficient witnesses for ye Churches safety & the persons admonition to learne the feare of God."[13]

Changes in church discipline accompanied those in church admissions. Innovations in church discipline reflected ongoing cultural developments in New England. During the seventeenth and early eighteenth centuries, New England society experienced a growing population and changing economy and demographics. Religious culture was affected by shifting assumptions about gender, the public versus private spheres, the growing taste for finer goods, competing sites of discourse such as the tavern and the political arena, toleration of different (Protestant) religions, negotiation of clerical and lay prerogatives, and a rising spirit of individualism.[14] These factors, among others, gradually undermined a Congregational system that depended heavily upon communitarian values. Both sets of records in this volume contain hints pointing toward the increasing internal friction within eighteenth-century Congregational churches, and sometimes between them, as congregations battled among themselves, ministers argued with other ministers, and individual churchgoers bickered with one another over a seemingly unending range of issues.

As early as 1661, Lydia Dastin's employment of mutual watch in Reading seemed much more motivated by neighborly aggression than the "spirit of meekness" or "brotherly love" described in the original church covenant. Leaving the meetinghouse one Sunday, she saw several young men laughing and chatting and concluded that they "laughed and jeered at the minister that had then been dispencing the word to them." Rather than approaching the men in private to clarify matters, she tattled on them. A brief investigation into the matter revealed that, in fact, the men had not been laughing at the minister at all, but only at a "Senseless Jest put forth by S.G.: concerning one who at ye meeting broke wind." The young men dealt with Dastin privately for "blemishing their names," but Dastin "denyed y^t she had particularly named any of them." At length, Dastin apologized for provoking this squabble. The members accepted her confession even though Pastor Samuel Haugh believed the apology lacked "the freedom and willingnesse as was to be desired."[15]

The records presented in this volume reveal that another problem increasingly bedeviling the churches was disorder within the ministerial community itself. Both the Reading and Rumney Marsh churches found themselves drawn into numerous eighteenth-century controversies involving neighboring pastors. A 1729 division in the Leicester church over pastor David Parsons exemplifies the struggles that sometimes erupted between ministers and their congregations. The Leicester members brought up their pastor on no less than nineteen charges, including "Male administration," "Delinquency," "Immorality," "Slander," "fraudulent dealing" and "lying." According to the account left in the Rumney Marsh records, events in Leicester several times nearly broke down into complete pandemonium: the pastor "command[ed] the Deacon out of his seat" during one church service, and publicly denounced one church meeting as a "cabal" and another as a "mob." A deacon made off with "the Churches Vessels from the Use of the Reverend Mr. Parsons" and later the members even physically "opposed Mr Parsons his going into his Pulpit on the Lords day." In a fit of rage, the Leicester church took the extraordinary step of deposing their minister from office. Ministers and lay delegates from no less than fourteen churches in the area brokered a peace agreement in Leicester, but the church formally dismissed Parsons five years later.[16]

Parsons's case was hardly an isolated incident. One Robert Sturgeon from Ireland sought to "irregularly" set up a church in Watertown. In another episode, Peter Thatcher's Weymouth church saw his departure for the Fifth Church of Boston as a breach of covenant (they accused him of seeking more prestige and a higher salary); many Bostonians agreed, and an ugly brawl punctuated the minister's ordination.[17] The Reading church received numerous complaints about neighboring ministers in the late 1740s and early 1750s; many of the objections concerned doctrine, a topic that was rarely a matter of controversy in the seventeenth century. Even Jonathan Edwards's noted dismission, which culminated in June 1750, found its way into the Reading church record book. Indeed,

Edwards's effort to enforce stricter membership requirements in Northampton may have had an effect in Reading; after Rev. William Hobby's death, a division rose in the church, apparently over this very issue, and celebration of the Lord's Supper was suspended.[18] Not until 1768 did the church, having "for a considrable time Past Lived in a neglect of the Lords Supper by means of Some perplexing Circumstances which have attended our affairs," finally vote to "attend the holy Supper with all Convenient Speed."[19]

Throughout the colonial era, Massachusetts churches struggled to police one another in response to this increasing internal and interchurch contention, but provisions of Congregational independence presented major obstacles to these efforts. Minorities within local churches that complained of unfair treatment from majorities, for instance, discovered that under Congregational provisions they enjoyed little in the way of formal recourse. Similarly, if any local church violated traditional practices, there was nothing, technically, or by way of binding authority, that neighbor churches could do to intervene.

With varying success, the Congregationalists attempted to address these difficulties by establishing a non-binding system of mutual supervision. On several occasions during the seventeenth and eighteenth centuries, lay and clerical representatives gathered together in synods and passed along resolutions or recommendations to all of the churches in the colony. These resolutions—the Halfway Covenant was the most famous—were non-binding. In matters of more local concern, mutual supervision was exercised most commonly through the implementation of ecclesiastical councils. Divided congregations were urged to call upon several neighbor churches to send their officers and lay representatives to hear cases and render written opinions on the controversy at hand. Ecclesiastical councils expected local congregations to take seriously their decisions (or "results") and to abide by their recommendations. Nevertheless, these councils enjoyed no binding authority over local churches; their decisions only represented "advice."

The Congregationalists gradually discovered that this system of local oversight was fraught with weaknesses. Both sets of records in this volume demonstrate the struggles that Congregational churches suffered in trying to maintain mutual supervision, particularly during the first half of the eighteenth century. The Rumney Marsh records, in particular, contain perhaps the most complete and illuminating accounts extant in the entire body of Massachusetts church records concerning the nature, frequency, and difficulty of attempts to employ ecclesiastical councils to address controversies within and between churches.

Oftentimes, councils succeeded according to the ideal: divided parties within local churches mutually consented to seek outside assistance, stood in agreement on the specific neighbor churches to call, received a unanimous decision from the council, and then heeded the council's advice. In 1745, the Reading church received a letter from the pastor and membership of the First Church of Grafton, indicating that "a number of Brethren there were and for a long time had been Uneasy" over doctrinal issues. Both sides were "now Desirous y^t Matters of Diff[erence] might be Accomodated" through the intervention of a council. Importantly, "Every of ye Chhes of S^d Councill" was "Acceptab: to & agreed upon by Each party," that is, both sides in the dispute agreed on the specific churches to call upon for help—yet another issue over which divided churches often fought. The Reading church voted to send both its deacons and another prominent member to accompany the pastor to the Grafton council. The Reading records do not contain the fulsome accounts of council results found in the Rumney Marsh records; few church books do. But there is little doubt that the Grafton council met with success. The Reading pastor concluded his entry in the church records by observing, with apparent relief, "NB: Every Person Came in to Receive Councill given. Glory to G^d. peace on Earth."[20]

Many councils did not meet with such happy results. Earlier in the colonial period, individuals, as opposed to entire churches or significant church minorities, asserted and won the right to convene councils. The first council to appear in the Rumney Marsh records concerned a dispute between the church of Wenham led by pastor Joseph Gerrish, and one William Rogers whom the church suspended unanimously for offering "words of Opposition" and an "injurious charge" against his minister. Rogers appealed for outside assistance as a lone member.[21] A council was convened by Ipswich pastor John Wise, the immensely popular minister of Chebacco Parish, who insisted that most eighteenth-century church disorder stemmed from aristocratically minded ministers who attempted to subvert the Cambridge Platform and trample upon lay rights. Given Wise's lay sympathies, the council ruled in favor of Rogers and against the Wenham church.

Even when fully justified in their actions, councils that overturned decisions of local churches in this fashion threatened to undermine the entire disciplinary process: members subject to disciplinary measures, for example, soon began to refuse to abide by the decisions of their local churches, instead demanding hearings before a council. Church discipline eventually began to create so much friction that many churches simply threw up their hands and paid noticeably less attention to it. Churchgoers exercised mutual watch less frequently. As one minister ruefully noted, "[w]hen particular members undertake to make enquiry" for the purpose of exercising mutual watch, "they are charged either with prejudice, or doing what is none of their business."[22] Many churches thus began to adjust their understanding of the sorts of cases that legitimately fell under church purview, involving themselves mainly with non-controversial and clear-cut sorts of cases like public drunkenness or premarital pregnancy, offenses that were far less likely to divide a church and create the demand for a council.

Finally, it bears repeating that council results only represented advice. The controversies described in the Rumney Marsh record book demonstrate that it was hardly unusual for churches to ignore the strong expectation that council results would be regarded with reverence. During the Gerrish-Rogers dispute, the Wenham church, which had never requested a council in the first place, paid no heed to John Wise's admonitions. It similarly ignored a formal council of five churches that repeatedly condemned the Wenham church for its "Obstinacy" in "slighting & rejecting the Process, & method taken with them," which "thereby put high contempt upon the Constitution of these Churches."[23]

The boldness that local churches displayed in ignoring council results became a matter of continual and growing frustration for the Congregationalists, ministers and laity alike. The North Reading church found itself divided into two sides in 1723 and formally requested the aid of a council. Fully aware of churches' tendencies to ignore the advice of councils, the neighboring clergy attempted a preventive strike: they announced that they would hear a case only if all parties in the North Reading dispute agreed, in advance, to accept the council's decision, whatever it might be. Both sides agreed to these conditions, "The Rev^{d}: Mr Putnam, & the whole Church, before the Opening of the Council, laying themselves under Obligation to sit down satisfied by the Judgment of this Council."[24] Once the council justified pastor Putnam, however, the minister's opponents ignored the council's advice and continued to wreak havoc in the church for another two years.[25]

Churches could, in concert, condemn offending local churches and withdraw from communion with them. But the "third way of communion" acted as an effective deterrent only in cases that found large numbers of churches united in their opinions about a particular case—an increasingly rare occurrence indeed. In fact, as the eighteenth century progressed, local churches that found themselves condemned by a council increasingly went so far as to convene "anti-councils" of handpicked allies, whose mission was to contradict the conclusions of the initial council. William Gerrish, for example, convened a council of sympathizers in 1719, which "Justifyed the whole Processe of the Church in Wenham" in its treatment of William Rogers while refuting the actions and conclusions of Wise and his earlier council of five churches.[26]

At length, churchgoers and pastors alike generally came to recognize that the Congregational system threatened to unravel if local churches were free to ignore any supervisory advice. Such "contempt" for council decisions, John Wise warned Rumney Marsh and other churches, "if not check't & stopt in time, tends to the utter ruine and subversion of the Noble frame & constitution of these famous, ancient, & flourishing Churches."[27] Equally ominous was the lack of success neighboring churches and elders had in bringing offending pastors to heel. The Rumney Marsh records contain a meticulously detailed account of one of the most notorious eighteenth-century cases of alleged ministerial malfeasance, involving Salem pastor Samuel Fiske, who in 1734 stood accused of "interpolating" or forging into the record book a vote concerning his salary, which, many Salem members insisted, had never been raised (much less passed) in a church meeting. Determined to take a united stand on clerical misbehavior, neighboring ministers assembled dozens of representatives from around the colony to convene in Salem. This huge council itself soon broke down into chaos. Representatives bickered endlessly over countless procedural issues, angry delegates departed or refused to vote, and those resolutions that the largely emasculated council did pass had little effect in remedying the controversy. Eventually an unrepentant Fiske and his supporters split from the Salem church to form the Salem Third (or "Tabernacle") Church.

The Salem controversy brought into sharp focus the failing efforts to enforce standards of behavior upon local churches and ministers. It also forced congregations to reconsider lay-clerical relations within local churches. Congregations called for more careful lay supervision over ministers, leading some in the early eighteenth century to suggest the reinstitution of the office of lay or "ruling" elder. Most churches did not respond to the crisis in any institutional fashion, but the Fiske affair had an immediate effect upon government in the Rumney Marsh church, which had been following the controversy with rapt attention. In

1736, shortly after the First Church of Salem parted ways with Samuel Fiske and his adherents, the remaining members of the Salem congregation elected two ruling elders. The Rumney Marsh church followed suit, electing Captain Samuel Watts to the ruling eldership and elevating deacon William Hasey to the same position. The move confirmed, as we shall see, that no minister was more committed than Rumney Marsh pastor Thomas Cheever to principles of lay participation and limits on authority—even his own.

The Reading church found itself dragged into the Fiske affair as well. Shortly after the church division, the Reading church received a letter from the lay leaders of the "Antient place of worship in Salem; Signifying y^r Desires y^t: we woud by our Elder & Messengers Assist in ye Ordinat^n of M^r <u>John Sparhawk</u> to ye Pastoral Care over y^m." Reading pastor Hobby then immediately produced and read a letter from Samuel Fiske and his allies who, at this point, also claimed to be the First Church of Salem, "protesting ag^n our Assistance in Afores^d: Ordinat^n." The church voted unanimously to support Fiske's opponents and to assist in the ordination of Sparhawk. The matter, pastor Hobby recorded wryly in the record book, required only "a very short Debate."[28]

The records in this volume, in sum, demonstrate that by the eighteenth century, churches like Rumney Marsh and Reading often saw their attention dominated by events in other churches. Rumney Marsh pastor Thomas Cheever served almost constantly on ecclesiastical councils, a testament to the high esteem he held among his ministerial peers but also to the degree of strife in the churches. In many instances, Cheever served as moderator and scribe for these councils as well. The Reading church, on the other hand, manifested far less patience with the contentious state of church affairs in the first half of the eighteenth century. In 1722, the church received a request for council delegates from the First Church of Worcester, which was divided over its choice of pastor. In response, Reading's "Lt Briant affirmd, ye Counsel y^t [had convened] last y^r unanimously agreed, y^t Mr Gardener's call & Settlem^t to & in Woster w^s right, & y^rupon advised ye dissenting party to fall in." Why convene another council, the Reading church asked, when the Worcester church had simply ignored the unanimous advice of the first? Two decades later, the Reading church received council requests from Framingham, Hopkinton, the second Church of Bradford, and Dorchester, all within a three-month period. The church flatly refused to provide assistance in the last two councils. As pastor Hobby explained, "y^e Main Reason of Such Refusals" was "Our being so frequently Engag'd in y^e Affairs of Other Chhes."[29]

Parker-Cheever House, Rumney Marsh, 1640-1904

Thomas Cheever and "Traditional" Congregationalism in Eighteenth-Century Rumney Marsh

The Rumney Marsh and Reading church records demonstrate that contention and the convening of ecclesiastical councils and anti-councils at times threatened to engulf the eighteenth-century Congregationalists. But these records also make clear that not all local churches witnessed this gradual disintegration of the Congregational Way. If the churches were not a "peaceable kingdom," neither were they a scene of unremitting discord. It is important for us to consider the significance of the fact that the Rumney Marsh church—no matter how entangled it may have grown with disputes wracking neighboring churches—suffered virtually no internal strife itself. Similarly, while most Congregational churches saw their practices and procedures evolve and diversify over the course of the eighteenth century—sometimes in dramatic ways—some churches remained largely unaffected by change, something that has scarcely been recognized by historians. Rumney Marsh stands out as a remarkable example of an eighteenth-century church whose practices demonstrate strong continuities with those of the previous century. Indeed, in its procedures of admissions, discipline, dismissions, and interchurch relations, the Rumney Marsh church seems almost a "throwback" to the practices of the first generation of churches. In their careful accounts of neighboring church controversies, in short, the Rumney Marsh records illuminate for us the sorts of developments that generally affected local Congregational churches in the eighteenth century. At the same time, these records provide a glimpse at church life in a congregation largely unaffected internally by those changes.

In seeking reasons for this combination of circumstances in Rumney Marsh, one needs look no further than the church's committed minister, Thomas Cheever. Throughout the colonial era, churches stood a far better chance of maintaining harmony when blessed with a skilled and respected pastor; lay-clerical relations within local churches often directly reflected the deference earned by such individuals. And ministers, such as John Wise, often won respect and deference by strongly adhering to Congregational provisions and by recognizing the importance of respecting lay "liberties." In the charged political atmosphere of provincial Massachusetts in the early eighteenth century, when elected deputies in the House of Representatives clashed with the governor and his appointed officials over gubernatorial prerogatives and royal supervision, the question of traditional rights and liberties enjoyed by New Englanders was hotly defended.[30] No one agreed more fully with Wise than Thomas Cheever. The publication of the Rumney Marsh records establishes Cheever as an important figure in northeastern Massachusetts religious affairs and shows that Wise was not alone in his principles. Cheever's success in Rumney Marsh presents us with an interesting eighteenth-century representation of a seventeenth-century model: a ministerially established ecclesiastical culture based heavily upon lay participation.

Born in 1658, Cheever's remarkable career spanned no less than sixty-eight years. He graduated from Harvard College in 1677 at the age of nineteen, and began preaching in Malden in 1680. His strong commitment to Congregationalism may have been owing in part to his coming of age during and after the convening of the Reforming Synod of 1679, at which the ministers and lay leaders of the colony performed a powerful and public recommitment to Cambridge Platform, and urged every local church to do the same. Cheever's roots, at least by extension, can be traced all the way back to the founding generation; the First Church of Malden ordained him in 1681 as a colleague to longtime pastor Michael Wigglesworth, who had been with the church since 1656.

Cheever's five-year stay in Malden was turbulent. In 1686, he found himself barred from church communion and then haled before a council of ministerial and lay delegates for "scandalous breaches" of the third and seventh commandments. The specific charges remain cloudy, beyond that he offered "light and obscene expressions (not fit to be named) in an Ordinary at Salem" and "as he was travailing on the Rode." Cheever acknowledged guilt before the council, condemning himself for "expos[ing] Religion and ye ministry to Reproach." Impressed with Cheever's "humble and penitent" demeanor, the council recommended that the Malden church "grant him a Loving Dismission to some church according as himself shall desire."[31]

Even in the absence of complete documentation, the case against Cheever seems to have been less than clear-cut. Although he added his assent to the council's decision, Cotton Mather nevertheless expressed reservations about the outcome, noting that this "poor *young minister*" had been "terribly stigmatized for his Misdemeanors." Mather seems to have believed that the affair should have been resolved quietly and privately; in response to the controversy he tellingly vowed personally to avoid "uttering any Reproachful Thing" unless it "bee not only *True* in itself but also *proper* and *useful* to be mentioned." Mather also undoubtedly recognized that the Maldenites were a fractious lot: members of the Cheever council condemned the Malden church for "that want of Love, and for that bitterness of Spirit which appears in sundry of them."[32]

Finally, Cheever's relationship with Wigglesworth had likely been stormy, as was Wigglesworth's relationship with his own congregation. Events in the aftermath of the council suggest that Wigglesworth may have opposed his colleague's ordination in the first place, and that many Malden members clearly opposed Cheever's dismissal. In response to Cheever's dismission, Wigglesworth gloated that his church "had cause to condemn themselves, as for other sins, so their sudden laying Hands on Mr. Cheever." A second council was eventually convened in Malden to address not only an angry salary dispute involving Wigglesworth but the fact that overtures had been made to rehire Cheever. The second council ordered "that no further disturbance or offer be made . . . to restore the said Cheevers [sic] to the service of the Ministry in that place."[33]

The next thirty years of Cheever's life remain something of a mystery. He probably served as a schoolteacher and he is on record as having taught "reading, writing, and ciphering" at Rumney Marsh from 1709 to 1719. Apparently, his early indiscretions were not brought up when he was hired to serve as pastor of the newly gathered church in 1715, nearly three decades after his dismission for scandal.

From the outset, Cheever and his congregation together made clear their intention to follow traditional Congregational practices, pledging in their covenant not only "to endevour to keep ourselves pure from the sins of the times" but to adhere strictly to principles and practices of the Cambridge Platform, mutual watch, careful observation of discipline, oversight of the elders, and communion with neighboring churches:

> We do give up our selves to one another in the Lord, engaging to walk by faith as a Church of Christ in the faith & Order of the Gospel, so far as the Lord hath or shall reveal unto us (& particularly as is held out in the Platform sett for by these Churches unto which for the substance we declare our adherence) promising in brotherly love to watch over one another & to avoid all sinfull stumbling blocks, and contentions as much as possible; and to submit our selves to the Discipline & Government of Christ in this his Church; and to the Ministerial teaching, guidance, & Oversight of the Elder, or Elders thereof, in all things agreable to the Rules of Christ in his word, and conscienciously to attend the Seals & censures, and all the holy Institutions of Christ in Communion with one another, desiring also to walk with all Regular & due Communion with other Churches.[34]

Five years later the church again confirmed their commitment to the Congregational way and its "mixed" form of government.

> A Church meeting, in which the Church Covenant was read, showing that we fixed upon Congregational principles, according to the Platform sett forth by these Churches, in which both the power of the Elders, and the liberty of the Brethren are so sett out, as that no Church act is compleat & perfected without the consent of both: when it was put to Vote, whither the Church did consent to and were willing to abide by the s^d first settlement & Covenant, there was an unanimous consent manifested by lifting up the hand.[35]

Cheever thus ably managed church affairs by institutionalizing for his followers the principle of government by consent and by carefully adhering to the Congregational procedures and provisions to which he and the members mutually agreed. The Rumney Marsh membership debated and voted on virtually every issue facing the church from the important (such as the establishment of ruling elders) to the mundane (such as the specific seating location in the church for the ruling elders and psalm setters).[36]

Throughout Cheever's thirty-four year pastorate, Rumney Marsh continued to adhere to "traditional" Congregationalism in its handling of both internal and interchurch affairs. As mentioned, the church refused to implement the Halfway Covenant. Though over three-quarters of Massachusetts churches had relaxed admissions by 1690, and nearly all churches followed suit in the early decades of the eighteenth century, Rumney Marsh did not adopt the Halfway Covenant until 1749, shortly after Cheever's death. The small number of full members—usually less than a hundred—shows that the church's resistance to the Halfway Covenant was a matter of principle and not a concern about the size of its membership rolls.

Church disciplinary hearings do not dominate the Rumney Marsh church records. But this observation does not suggest that the church shied away from controversy or church watch, as neighboring churches increasingly began to do in the eighteenth century. Possibly the community generally suffered less in the way of contention than other towns. Perhaps more likely, Cheever simply enjoyed more success in convincing members to resolve their disputes privately.

In any event, the records make clear that, in contrast to developments in many contemporary Congregational churches, discipline and church purity remained matters that the church took seriously in the eighteenth century. Prior to the admission of Abraham Skinner in 1719, for example, the church discovered that years earlier Skinner had been charged with "stealing or carrying off a post from the parsonage land in Maldon."[37] The church launched a full investigation, appointing several prominent members to contact authorities in Malden to authenticate the charge. After gathering testimony from numerous witnesses, the church concluded that the charges had been fabricated; Skinner's membership owed considerably to the close attention to procedural detail exercised by the Rumney Marsh church and its pastor.

Decades into the eighteenth century, when most churches were drifting away from mutual watch, the Rumney Marsh church still regarded private behavior as resting entirely within its purview. In 1730, Elisha Tuttle and his wife were charged with "abusive carriage" to their mother and sister, and the church required them to "give satisfaction" to the church for their behavior.[38] The church then disciplined Tuttle again the following year for withdrawing from communion. The church admonished one William Tuttle for drunkenness, but even in this case the church's action cannot be characterized as perfunctory. The records make clear that Tuttle had been guilty of multiple offenses, and that the church had long been exercising mutual watch over the errant "brother." Several members labored with Tuttle in private, where the offender offered many "promises" of reformation. Eventually, Tuttle was restored to the church.[39]

The Tuttle case also indicates that while much changed throughout the eighteenth century, another continuity in the Rumney Marsh church, and in other churches as well, was the emphasis—even a growing emphasis—on lay participation. Toward the end of his career, Cheever began to refer to himself as the "moderator" of church meetings (a title usually given to the lay leader of a committee), whose charge was simply to present the agenda and maintain order until decisions could be reached by majority vote.

Decades of participation in church government left the church well-prepared when age and infirmity forced their minister from the pulpit. As Thomas Cheever neared the end of his life, the Rumney Marsh church prepared to ordain William McClanachan first to the office of colleague and later to the office of pastor—but not before first settling some critical issues of authority and church government. Prior to the ordination, the church voted that "The Ruling Elders, the rev.[d] W[m.] McClenachan, Mes[s.] Thomas Pratt and Hugh Floyd take the Ch[h] Covenant into Consideration, and make what additions or amendments agreeable to the substantials of the Platform that they think just and report thereon" to the church.[40]

The "worthy laymen" on the committee affirmed that McClanachan's church authority would be strictly limited—and that they would impose those limits personally. The committee thus reported: "They are of the Opinion that Ruling Elders are, agreeable to the Platform, Essential Oficers in a Congregational Church; and that no teaching Elder be admitted as Pastor of this Church unless he submit to such oficers in y[e] Ch[h]." They further disabused McClanachan of any notion that he would enjoy a veto power over any church decision, a right that some ministers attempted to assert in the eighteenth century. Any "negative power" over church decisions, the committee noted, "does not pertain to the teaching, or ruling Elders distinct but to a majority of the eldership."[41] The committee also recommended, at last, that the church adopt the Halfway Covenant. The members agreed to all of the committee's proposals.

Despite the limits on his power, McClanachan succeeded in convincing the Rumney Marsh church to embark upon a rapid course of liberalization. He introduced the Halfway Covenant, though the number of people who took advantage of it was so abysmally small that the measure did little to boost overall membership—if that indeed was McClanachan's goal. Also, McClanachan proposed, and the church accepted, the use of Isaac Watts's hymns in worship to supplement or replace traditional psalm-singing. These innovations alienated several prominent members of the church, including Nathan Cheever, son of the former pastor, and two of the deacons, who removed to another church. Even so, the remaining members registered surprisingly little consternation when McClanachan, continuing his history as a religious chameleon, announced he had converted to the Church of England and requested to be dismissed. In December 1754, the church voted not to allow him to depart. After the long pastorate of Cheever, the prospect of his successor lasting only a few years may have seemed incomprehensible. Alternatively, the congregation may have anticipated that they would have a difficult time finding another minister. If so, their fear turned out to be true. After McClanachan's unauthorized departure for England, two potential candidates turned them down, and it took three years before they found a replacement in Philips Payson.

Church Records and Religious Practice

Early Massachusetts church records contain great potential for scholars and practitioners interested in a newer area of historical inquiry: the history of religious practice.[42] Dorothy Bass, one of the most prominent American scholars in this field, writes that "Practices are those shared activities that address fundamental human needs and that, woven together, form a way of life." David D. Hall, who has been the most active in applying the study of practice to early America, points to a conception of practice as "culture in action." "As most of us use the term," Hall writes, "it encompasses the tensions, the ongoing struggle of definition, which are constituted within every religious tradition and that are always present in how people choose to act. Practice thus suggests that any synthesis is provisional. Moreover, practice always bears the marks of both regulation and what, for want of a better word, we may term resistance."[43]

A great number of practices that characterized the Congregational churches of colonial New England are reflected in the records of Reading and Rumney Marsh. Some have already been described in the "Primer" section above, but many others merit attention. For example, accounts of lay and clerical ordinations were carefully and proudly preserved, usually by the incoming minister. Clerical ordinations were especially important rituals in colonial life; churches or the new ordinands themselves sometimes expended the equivalent of a year's salary for an ordination "ball," which typically featured plenty of food, spirits, and even dancing. The records note meticulously the names of neighboring ministers who participated in the service, extended the right hand of fellowship (or gave the "charge"), and preached the ordination sermon. Congregationalists also honored the elevation of lay officers as an important tradition in their churches; those entrusted with such positions assumed high responsibilities in the church's worship and meetings, served as delegates in ecclesiastical councils, and generally helped to establish the tone of local religious life. Consequently, while the ordinations of lay elders and deacons were less celebrated affairs, churches carefully recorded the process of electing and ordaining these officers as well.

What historians term "regulatory" practices are also amply evident in the hundreds of pages of entries in these records. A complex of practices, generally covenantal in nature, reflected the Congregationalists' communal identity. In order to embody themselves as a church, as we have seen, a group of believers drafted and agreed upon a covenant that bound them together in common fellowship. When a person entered the church, he or she owned the church covenant, or consented to be bound by it. These covenants regulated individual behavior according to a literalistic reading of Scripture, including all but the ceremonial laws in the Old Testament, obligating members to participate in mutual watch and subjecting them to church discipline. It was not uncommon for family members—siblings and cousins, or extended kin—to present themselves for membership together, to symbolize a mutually supporting familial network of shared piety within the larger church community. Husbands and wives often presented themselves together as well, even though only one parent in full communion was required in order to have children baptized. This suggests that couples often went through significant religious episodes together. Occasionally, churches publicly and collectively re-affirmed their covenants, as both the Reading and Rumney Marsh congregations did.[44] Days of fast or humiliation, observed by civil proclamation, provided opportunities for the community as a whole to acknowledge its sins and covenant breaches and to seek God's favor.[45]

The churches incorporated these regulatory acts in accordance with general guidelines such as Scripture rules (especially Matthew 18, where steps for reclaiming offending fellow believers are laid out), the Cambridge Platform, more specific institutional expressions such as local committees and clerical councils, and sentences of admonition, suspension, and excommunication. But there were other, more subtle, interpersonal regulatory practices besides these codified or formal processes. Rendering confessions for offenses, whether in writing or orally, represented an established method for members to be received back into the good graces of the church. Both the Reading and Rumney Marsh records contain excerpts of such lay confessions.[46] But confessors did not always immediately meet with acceptance. Here they entered a realm in which they were subject to their fellow members' subjective interpretations of religious meaning and practice. We have already seen that members carefully scrutinized candidates for full membership and sometimes rejected them. Those in full membership who strayed could expect even more demanding treatment. The Reading church deemed Elizabeth Hart's 1655 confession unsatisfactory, "& some desired to deferre till another time." When given another chance, she again failed to convince her fellow members of her repentance. Only on the third try did she provide sufficient "Satisfaction" to remove her censure.[47]

The fact that members sometimes remained dissatisfied with offenders' confessions demonstrates the degree to which lay people took seriously their covenant obligations and the ways in which they interpreted their duties, and reaffirms the central role they played in implementing church practices. By involving themselves in cases of neighborly acrimony or family misunderstandings churchgoers actively regulated discourse and behavior. The regulation of speech, especially women's speech, has been examined as an important facet of early American religious and civic culture.[48] Church records reveal that regulation of discourse cut across gender lines. In 1683, "Brother Briant" of Reading was reported to have "spoken passionately in a Towne meeting"; some brethren, taking exception, "cast it into the church [as] disorderly & unseasonably." Fellow members even "helped" Briant in writing his "acknowledgment." George Davis was earlier heard to sing a portion of a "filthy song"; those at a church disciplinary meeting saw through his attempts to dodge the charge and suspended him. Nearly a century later, in 1747, Jonathan Eaton entered a complaint against William Bryant Jr. for "Some Slanderous & Vilifying Expressions." In this instance, however, the church ended up focusing its attention on the accuser rather than the accused, first for not sufficiently following "ye private Steps prescribed by Our Sav^r," and then for following only the letter of the law but not the "Charitable Design & End of ye Gospell w^ch: is to Reclaim an Offender." Thus, *Eaton's* "Conduct" was voted to be "Defective."[49]

As Hall notes, if certain practices constituted "regulation" of collective behavior, others reflected individual "resistance" to those regulations. In response, communities were forced to negotiate and define the larger covenantal identity in the face of resistive, delinquent, or unlawful acts, and then to enforce conformity to that evolving identity.

Let us look at drunkenness, a common problem for the Congregationalists in colonial New England, which had the highest alchohol consumption in American history.[50] In 1700, the Reading church without much debate cast Mary Salmon out of the church for habitual intemperance following a public admonition. Only a year had passed before the church resorted to excommunication. The same church's prolonged dealings with Ebenezer Parker Jr.'s alcoholism four decades later illustrate both the growing disinclination to employ excommunication and the patience with which a congregation could treat a fellow member. By the same token, the records reveal the absence of means for dealing with such a problem beyond the traditional punitive ones of censure, suspension of privileges, and, ultimately, excommunication. The community viewed the solemn penalties, publicly accepted and declared, as having enough rehabilatory power of their own for any person not thoroughly lost in iniquity. Parker no doubt agreed, notwithstanding his condition.

Such assumptions, however, did not apply to fornication, especially as the eighteenth century progressed. For the most part, a person or couple stood accused of fornication if their child was born less than seven months after marriage. In 1680, for example, the Reading church accused Mary Davis (though not her husband) of "having broken the seaventh Command of God before her marriage."[51] She admitted her sin "before the Church" (that is, the full members), which accepted her repentance. Her confession was then further "published" (possibly in written form, or else by word of mouth) to the wider congregation of members and non-members. Only after performing this public act of contrition was she allowed to own the covenant. In 1724, Daniel and Elizabeth Nichols were accused, and after witnessing their confession before the congregation and pleas for forgiveness of God, the church restored them to charity and communion. But the Nicholses were one of several couples simultaneously brought before the church on similar charges. By this time, premarital, and indeed promiscuous, sex were widespread in most New England communities and churches increasingly treated these cases in a pro forma manner.[52]

Another practice of "resistance" that increasingly vexed New England churches as the eighteenth century wore on was separatism. Ironically, the sophisticated knowledge of congregational practice among lay people paved the way for schisms and separations. The Rumney Marsh church was one of several represented in a 1722 council that criticized dissenting members of the Watertown church for taking the initiative to ordain Irish émigré Robert Sturgeon as their pastor. The council also sternly rebuked Rev. MacGregore of Nutfield for collaborating with the Watertown laity by single-handedly installing Sturgeon in a clandestine night meeting. In 1747, the Reading church assisted in remonstrating with the "Separating Breth^n" of Dorchester. And that same year, Reading dealt with a separatist in its midst in the person of John Dammon, who "had fallen into ye Depths of Enthusiasm," "enthusiasm" being a term used to deride the seemingly irrational behavior and speech of revival participants. Taking matters in stride, the church appointed a committee to deal with Dammon. For two full years the church endured Dammon's diatribes, including fulminations claiming that Reading church and all the churches in the land "were but Baals [Bel's] Chhes & ye Ministers, but ye Dragons Angels."[53] Incidentally, the Reading church found itself debating the separatist Dammon's fate at the same time as it was considering Parker's alcoholism. In the end, the church adjudged Dammon's transgressions less offensive than Parker's. Dammon seems never to have been excommunicated; after characterizing the separatist as temporarily insane, the church suspended the offender and his wife from communion. After this, they drop out of the records.

As the case of John Dammon illustrates, individuals sometimes resisted criticism and censures of their church despite all efforts to reclaim them. Refusal to bow before the will and advice of churches and councils was a recourse individuals increasingly took—some with conscientious motives, some with merely obstructionist ones. The controversies involving pastors Gerrish, Fiske, and Parsons demonstrate that clergymen, no less than ordinary churchgoers, were not above ignoring petitions from church members and advice from neighboring churches.[54] Therefore, in a church such as Rumney Marsh, whose first pastor had been so sensitive to his people's will, it must have been heartrending for some when, in 1749, several prominent members—including Cheever's son Nathan—objected to the new minister. The head deacon, Jacob Halsey, even declared he "wou'd not deliver the utensills of the Church" to an appointed committee.[55]

Church members who felt slighted or unjustly treated could make their feelings known in various ways. One avenue of expression, of course, was speaking out in a church meeting. Another was communion. The political dimension of communion, so evident in these records, has never been fully noted by scholars before. As we have seen, clergy and councils used communion as a device to impose conformity. But the laity could register grievances by absenting themselves from communion—exercising, on a personal level, a form of reverse admonishment that churches usually employed towards individuals. So in 1742, Elisha Tuttle of the Rumney Marsh church, charged with his wife for ill-treatment of family members, withdrew for "a considerable time." When asked to appear before a church meeting to explain his reasons, he stated that he felt "Slighted by the Church" and that several people were "prejudiced" against him. In this case, the church had to produce answers to a member's objections and criticisms. Once they had done so and the misunderstanding was cleared up, Tuttle "Owned that he had done wrong" and promised to return to communion.[56] Given the prescribed range of practices, we see that the responses to "resistance" and the general dynamics of applying religious precepts could be surprisingly complex.

Another realm of church practice was financial. Like all churches, the Rumney Marsh church kept careful accounts of the funds that it committed into the hands of the deacons, who provided periodic reports on their use.[57] These reports reveal that churches expended money for communion, for repairs, which might include fixing broken windows or installing new pews, and especially, for the needy.[58] Such practices represented extensions of worship, or supported some part of worship life such as the liturgy. Churchgoers regarded them as important opportunities to express their faith in the context of community and to draw members into concerted and collective action. At Rumney Marsh's founding, the congregation voted to purchase a set of "utensils," or communion vessels. The church also decided that the sacrament would be held three months apart and that "each Communicant should give six pence a time." Throughout the seventeenth and eighteenth centuries, congregants continued to give a regular "contribution" for the Lord's Supper, customarily observed once every month or two. The Reading church voted in 1734 to increase the contribution from two to three shillings "in Order to ye making a proper provision of Elements for ye L^ds Table," that is, wine and bread.[59]

Charity in colonial Massachusetts began at home. Massachusetts law required that every town take care of its indigent and impoverished. When a family's house burned down or when a widow was unable to support herself and her family because of illness, the local church stepped in. In 1727, for example, the Rumney Marsh congregation earmarked a contribution for one Mrs. Marble, whose daughter had been "for a considerable time under the Doctours hand having a dangerous humour in her Mouth & throat."[60] Another sort of charity evident in the records, perhaps unique to the often combative nature of the larger colonial setting, provided funds for "redeeming" individuals who had been taken captive by Indians.[61] Finally, members often left bequests or legacies to their church as an expression of faith and as a means of perpetuating their memory in the life of the church.[62]

Church Admissions and Membership Patterns

The records of the Reading and Rumney Marsh churches are remarkably useful in providing us with the number and names of people who "owned" the covenant and who were admitted to full membership. Ministers and deacons of both churches were especially conscientious about keeping track of new members of various levels. Reading did not accept the Halfway Covenant until 1670, twenty-two years after the church was gathered, and Rumney Marsh until 1748, thirty-three years after its foundation (and, more importantly, only after Thomas Cheever was no longer active). Consequently, until those dates, only full members are listed, usually by year and sometimes by month and day (Table 2).

The records demonstrate that, after formation, whether in 1648 or 1715, both churches witnessed an initial wave of members, followed by a period of few or no new admissions. This was the norm in most colonial New England churches.[63] In Reading, no new communicants came forward for a full decade from 1651 to 1661. Rumney Marsh saw a steady trickle, but seldom more than that, reflecting the small size of the community through the eighteenth century. The church seems never to have topped more than about 100 full members, whereas a tally of Reading members in 1721 by Pastor Richard Brown resulted in more

Table 2:
Church Admissions in Reading and Rumney Marish, Massachusetts, 1648-1769

Reading   Rumney Marish

Membership Level	Half-Way			Full			Half-Way			Full		
Year	Men	Women	Total	Men	Women	Full	Men	Women	Total	Men	Women	Total
1648	-	-	-	19	22	41						
1649	-	-	-	0	0	0						
1650	-	-	-	2	5	7						
1651	-	-	-	0	0	0						
1652	-	-	-	0	0	0						
1653	-	-	-	0	0	0						
1654	-	-	-	0	0	0						
1655	-	-	-	0	0	0						
1656	-	-	-	0	0	0						
1657	-	-	-	0	0	0						
1658	-	-	-	0	0	0						
1659	-	-	-	0	0	0						
1660	-	-	-	0	0	0						
1661	-	-	-	0	0	0						
1662	-	-	-	7	6	13						
1663	-	-	-	2	6	8						
1664	-	-	-	0	0	0						
1665	-	-	-	0	0	0						
1666	-	-	-	0	3	3						
1667	-	-	-	0	0	0						
1668	-	-	-	0	0	0						
1669	-	-	-	2	9	11						
1670	17	12	29	13	20	33[1]						
1671	3	2	5	0	0	0						
1672	3	2	5	0	0	0						
1673	4	9	13	0	0	0						
1674	0	0	0	0	0	0						
1675	0	0	0	0	0	0						

[1] The list on MS p. 20, cued after the list on MS p. 6 ending 1669, is undifferentiated and may identify all full admissions for 1670-1681.

Table 2 (Continued)

Reading   Rumney Marish

Membership Level	Half-Way			Full			Half-Way			Full		
Year	Men	Women	Total	Men	Women	Full	Men	Women	Total	Men	Women	Total
1676	1	7	8	0	0	0						
1677	6	3	9	0	0	0						
1678	0	2	2	0	0	0						
1679	2	0	2	0	0	0						
1680	1	3	4	0	0	0						
1681	6	2	8	0	0	0						
1682	5	3	8	2	1	3						
1683	1	3	4	10	17	27						
1684	10	7	17	7	6	13						
1685	4	0	4	14	14	28[2]						
1686	15	11	26	14	7	21						
1688	0	0	0	0	0	0						
1689	7	14	21	6	9	15						
1690	9	7	16	8	7	15						
1691	7	7	14	2	1	3						
1692	12	12	24	7	6	13						
1693	1	10	11	0	8	8						
1694	12	2	14	2	4	6						
1695	1	11	12	1	4	5						
1696	0	3	3	0	1	1						
1697	8	10	18	3	8	11						
1698	5	3	8	3	4	7						
1699	2	6	8	3	11	14						
1700	3	4	7	1	9	11[3]						
1701	10	13	23	2	7	9						
1702	8	14	22	5	9	14						
1703	5	13	18	4	6	10						
1704	0	12	12	3	9	12						
1705	12	7	19	3	14	17						
1706	0	12	12	6	15	22[4]						

[2] The lists from the bottom of MS p. 30 through MS p. 31 are undated; the breakdown of full admissions for 1685-86 is conjectural.

[3] Includes one admission of unknown gender.

Table 2 (Continued)

Reading

Runney Marish

Membership Level	Reading						Runney Marish					
	Half-Way			Full			Half-Way			Full		
Year	Men	Women	Total	Men	Women	Full	Men	Women	Total	Men	Women	Total
1707	5	4	9	2	6	8						
1708	3	6	9	4	5	9						
1709	0	4	4	0	1	1						
1710	0	0	0	0	0	0						
1711	0	0	0	0	0	0						
1712	6	4	10	11	12	23						
1713	9	9	18	9	5	14						
1714	0	4	4	4	4	8						
1715	4	10	14	7	7	14	-	-	-	40	45	95
1716	0	8	8	5	13	18	-	-	-	4	59	
1717	1	3	4	3	6	9	-	-	-	0	22	
1718	0	2	2	8	10	18	-	-	-	2	46	
1719	0	1	1	3	10	13	-	-	-	-	54	9
1720	0	0	0	3	20	23	-	-	-	3	14	
1721	0	0	0	4	12	16	-	-	-	0	00	
1722	0	1	1	2	7	9	-	-	-	3	14	
1723	0	0	0	5	7	12	-	-	-	0	11	
1724	0	2	2	8	3	11	-	-	-	2	24	
1725	0	0	0	1	4	5	-	-	-	0	11	
1726	0	0	0	12	11	23	-	-	-	0	00	
1727	16	37	53	20	29	49	-	-	-	1	23	
1728	7	16	23	14	28	42	-	-	-	4	26	
1729	0	1	1	0	2	2	-	-	-	0	00	
1730	0	2	2	3	4	7	-	-	-	1	12	
1731	0	0	0	2	4	6	-	-	-	0	00	
1732	0	0	0	2	2	4	-	-	-		11	2
1733	0	0	0	3	6	9	-	-	-		22	4
1734	0	0	0	6	5	11	-	-	-		22	4
1735	1	0	1	7	5	12	-	-	-		01	1
1736	1	1	2	9	10	19	-	-	-		00	0
1737	3	2	5	17	15	32	-	-	-		01	1

[4] Includes one admission of unknown gender.

Table 2 (Continued)

	Reading						Rumney Marish					
	Half-Way			Full			Half-Way			Full		
Membership Level	Men	Women	Total	Men	Women	Full	Men	Women	Total	Men	Women	Total
Year												
1738	2	3	5	6	7	13	-	-	-		10	1
1739	2	0	2	6	10	16	-	-	-		16	7
1740	1	0	1	8	7	15	-	-	-		01	1
1741	2	0	2	12	13	25	-	-	-		11	2
1742	1	0	1	8	10	18	-	-	-		12	3
1743	0	1	1	4	5	9	-	-	-		01	1
1744	0	0	0	5	5	10	-	-	-		00	0
1745	0	1	1	0	5	0	-	-	-		01	1
1746	0	0	0	0	0	0	-	-	-		01	1
1747	0	0	0	2	2	4	-	-	-		00	0
1748	0	0	0	1	2	3	1	0	1		11	2
1749	0	0	0	3	2	5	1	0	1		21	3
1750	0	0	0	4	2	6	0	0	0		00	0
1751	0	0	0	1	2	3	1	0	1		02	2
1752	0	0	0	1	8	9	0	0	0		00	0
1753	0	0	0	5	8	13	0	0	0		01	1
1754	0	0	0	2	3	5	0	0	0		00	0
1755	0	0	0	0	6	6	0	0	0		00	0
1756	0	0	0	2	8	10	0	0	0		00	0
1757	0	0	0	0	0	0	0	0	0		00	0
1758	0	0	0	1	7	8						
1759	0	0	0	0	2	2						
1760	0	0	0	0	0	0						
1761	0	0	0	5	5	10						
1762	0	0	0	1	8	9						
1763	0	0	0	1	8	9						
1764	0	0	0	0	4	4						
1765	0	0	0	1	2	3						
1766	0	0	0	2	5	7						
1767	0	0	0	0	4	4						
1768	0	0	0	0	0	0						
1769	0	0	0	2	2	4						

than twice that number (Table 3). In light of its small size, it is difficult to offer statistically significant conclusions about Rumney Marsh, but if we examine membership trends there and compare them with Reading and other churches for which studies have been done, some general patterns in our two subject churches emerge.

Table 3: List of Full Members in Reading Church, 1721

Residence	Men	Women	Total
Reading	69	115	184
Lynn-End	8	12	20
Malden	2	5	7
Charlestown	6	20	26
Total	85	152	237

FEMINIZATION

For some time now, scholars have posited a "feminization" of church membership in early America. During the eighteenth century, significantly more women than men joined the churches and became full, communing members.[64] One estimate suggests that as many as two-thirds of members in many churches were women.[65] The rise of genres of popular literature, such as female eulogies that praised the virtues of deceased women, and the proliferation of female religious societies, reflected the changing constituency of the churches.[66] Membership lists quantify the shift, which in Reading began in the 1690s—to be specific, in 1693. During the previous decade, sixty-eight men owned the covenant compared to sixty-one women; for full members, the ratio was sixty-nine to sixty-three. But in the decade beginning in 1693, the difference was fifty to seventy-six for half-way members, and twenty to sixty-six for full. By 1721, as Table 3 indicates, 64.1% of all the members in full communion were women, a figure very much in line with the "feminization" thesis.[67] In fact, beginning in 1693, more men were admitted to full membership in only nine out of the seventy-six years until 1769. For the period under examination, 1715-57, Rumney Marsh saw a total of seventy-seven men and ninety-six women—hardly a large disparity, but indicative of trends in larger churches like Reading.

"Awakenings"

Periodically, the church records document sharp, usually brief, increases in membership. These membership spikes often were due to any number of local factors, such as new families moving into town, re-drawing of boundaries, or discontent with one's minister. Once in a while, however, religious revivals ushered in unprecedented numbers of new members.

Two such points in the late seventeenth century that saw significant influxes of new members, both halfway and full, were 1675-76, during King Philip's War, and 1685-86, following the revocation of the Massachusetts Charter. Both of these crises generated great anxiety, both spiritual and temporal. King Philip's War was, relatively speaking, one of the bloodiest ever fought on American soil; nearly half of the existing settlements in Massachusetts were wiped out.[68] While the war fostered a crisis over physical survival, the charter controversy put the colony's political survival and its very identity into doubt. Like many of its neighbor churches, Reading registered a significant increase in members during both of these periods. In 1685-86 alone, for example, thirty joined the church in halfway status and forty-nine as full members.

The "earthquake revival" of 1727 was another instance of concern, this time stemming from a natural catastrophe. On October 29, a series of strong quakes rocked New England, toppling chimneys and terrifying the population. Thomas Paine of Weymouth recalled that "The motion of the earth was very great, like the waves of the sea."[69] Days of fasting and humiliation were held as hundreds of ministers preached imprecatory sermons threatening God's wrath. People flocked to the churches. In Reading's and Rumney Marsh's neighbor town, Lynn End, at least ten people were admitted in the wake of the event, and this in a church that previously totaled only thirty-six full members.[70] Other towns saw even more dramatic results. John Brown of Haverhill reported in late 1727 that "since the *Earthquakes*, I have admitted and propounded 154 Persons; 87 for the Lords Table, the rest for Baptism, or the Renewing the Baptismal Covenant."[71] Reading saw an influx of new full members comparable to Haverhill—ninety-one during 1727-28. In 1727 the number of people in Reading owning the covenant (being baptized or renewing their baptismal covenant) exceeded the number of new full members, fifty-three to forty-nine. Even tiny Rumney Marsh witnessed a spurt of nine new communicants during these two years, nearly a third of the total that had been admitted in the entire previous decade. Tellingly, the celebrated "Great Awakening" that was soon to come had less of an effect on Reading and Rumney Marsh, not to mention the Boston churches, than the earthquake.[72]

The late 1730s were a period of widespread revival, originating at Northampton in 1734 under the ministry of Jonathan Edwards and emanating up and down the Connecticut River Valley and beyond. Eastern Massachusetts churches are not usually noted for their involvement in this wave of revivals; Edwards does not mention any in his *Faithful Narrative of a Surprising Work of God* (1737). Yet the Reading and Rumney Marsh records do register respectable increases in full members. Beginning in 1736, Reading admitted nineteen new members, and the following year that amount nearly doubled to thirty-two. Though in each of the following three years the total dropped to half that amount or so, this was still higher than preceding averages. Rumney Marsh, a little late in the game, admitted seven members in 1739, its most productive single year since the first two years of its founding.

Simply put, the Great Awakening of the 1740s barely touched these churches. Rumney Marsh continued at its small but steady pace, perhaps a reflection of Cheever's increasing age and infirmity, or of his and the church's conservative policies. Reading, meanwhile, saw an increase of twenty-five full members in 1741, immediately after George Whitefield's first tour, and eighteen the following year. In 1744, the year of Whitefield's second tour, ten were admitted, but thereafter numbers dropped until nearly a decade later. These numbers hardly impress in light of reports in churches in western Massachusetts and southeastern Connecticut, which often admitted scores and even hundreds.[73] But if these churches did not enjoy the large increases in members, neither were they beset by the contention and division that plagued revival regions such as southeastern Connecticut and central Massachusetts.[74] Along with fairly normal growth, both churches continued in their relatively harmonious ways. In Reading, as we have seen, only John Dammon and his wife were brought before the church for advocating Separatist doctrines. Almost comically, however, they were treated as if they were *non compos mentis*—temporarily insane. Upon perusing the church records of Reading, Rumney Marsh, and others in the area, one would hardly guess that a "great and general awakening" transpired in New England, which suggests that the Great Awakening was, as some scholars have depicted it, a localistic and sporadic phenomena.[75] This does not render the revivals of the 1740s any less significant, but rather helps us to recognize their varying natures and contexts.

Another distinctive aspect of church admissions in both Reading and Rumney Marsh during the revival period of the mid- to late-eighteenth century was the baptism and membership of African slaves. As early as 1655 there were twenty slaves in Reading,[76] but it would be some time before free or enslaved Africans were allowed to join the church. Admission of blacks to baptism did not begin until 1727 with three women, followed by single men in both 1735 and 1736. The man baptized in 1736, Primus, was the next year the first black admitted to full communion in Reading. In all, from 1727 to 1762, at least twelve slaves were baptized (some mothers were recorded as having their children baptized as well) and seven admitted to the Lord's Supper. Rumney Marsh recorded its first admission of a black—Elder Watts's "negro woman," Phillis—to full communion in 1744. The following year, her three children were baptized. The revivals appealed to Africans, and itinerants happily reported a number of them among their converts. But as with black exhorters, admission of free and enslaved blacks into the standing churches was controversial, since membership implied some kind of equality as Christian brothers and sisters. Nonetheless, a racial hierarchy prevailed. While church discipline applied to blacks—several were brought up at Reading for neglecting sabbath worship—they were not allowed to vote in church meetings.[77]

Lacking systematic data on the births, marriages, and deaths of the members, it is beyond the scope of this introduction to explore other variables. But the lists provide the raw materials for further study on such factors, among many others, as age at baptism and admission, marital age and status at admission, gender, race, and family membership patterns. More generally, these records can tell us much about the nature of religious institutions in colonial Massachusetts, the development of communication networks, speechways, gender roles, deviance and punishment, and the relationship between written and unwritten belief systems and social behavior.

The Towns and Their Ministers

READING (WAKEFIELD)

The town of "Redding" was formed in 1639 on lands belonging to the Saugus tribe. However, the original purchase price of £10 was not paid until 1686, when there were virtually no Indians left to receive payment. While the

First Church of Reading and its first meetinghouse traditionally date from 1644, the church was officially gathered on November 5, 1645. A meetinghouse was built in 1648 and replaced in 1688. In 1713, residents in North Reading became a separate precinct, gathering their own church in 1720, while residents of Lynnfield followed suit in the same year. Half a century later, the inhabitants of southern Reading gathered themselves into a distinct church. In 1869, the remainder of Reading divided into two towns, Reading and Wakefield. The present-day Wakefield First Parish Congregational Church stands on the location of the ancient church and burying grounds, and is the institutional descendant of the original First Church of Reading.

READING PASTORATES, 1645-1765

Henry Green

The town's first minister, and one of its original settlers, was Rev. Henry Green. Born in Great Bromley, England, in 1619, he began his studies at Emmanuel College, Cambridge, in 1634 and, after migrating, attended Harvard College. Sought after because of his reputation as a scholar, he came to Reading in 1645, or possibly earlier, as a teacher. But he was soon elevated to the Reading pastorship. In that year, as Edward Johnson recounts, "The people ordained a minister from among themselves—a young man of good abilities and very humble behavior, by the name of Green."[78] Unfortunately, he died only three years later.

Samuel Haugh

Samuel Haugh was born in Boston, England, in 1620 and migrated to New England in 1634. Though a member of the first class of Harvard College, he did not graduate. His father, Atherton Haugh, a magistrate in the Massachusetts General Court, was a member of John Cotton's Boston (Massachusetts) congregation and was a disciple of Anne Hutchinson. His son, apparently free of the antinomian taint, began preaching at Reading in 1648; the church ordained him two years later. He died in 1662, in Boston, while attending the "Half-Way" synod.

John Brock

Only six months after Haugh's death, John Brock arrived to take his place, in more ways than one. He was ordained on November 13 of that year, and the day after married Haugh's widow. Born in Stradbrook, England, in 1620, and graduating from Harvard College in 1648, he first preached and taught school briefly at Rowley before completing graduate work in 1650. He then preached at the Isles of Shoals. In 1659 he was considered for a missionary position among the Indians in Maine because he was said "to be expert in the Indian toungue and fitly quallifyed for the purpose." Though this talent was relatively rare among the English colonists, Brock did not take up the post. Instead, he removed to Reading in 1662 to become the pastor there. His death in 1688 marked the end of the longest pastorate at Reading to date. Judge Samuel Sewall remembered him as a man who was "very laborious in Catechizing & instructing Youth."[79] Others remembered him for his abilities in "Christian Conference," or private counsel. The fact that Reading adopted the Halfway Covenant under him may be a testimony to his skill in this vein.

Jonathan Pierpont

Jonathan Pierpont was Reading's first New England-born minister. Born in Roxbury in 1664, he was a member of the Harvard class of 1685, after which he served as college tutor, taking his graduate degree in 1688. He was highly sought after; before coming to Reading, he received calls from Dedham, New London, Newbury, Northfield, and Roxbury, all of which he turned down because of a lack of unanimity among the congregations. Apparently, the deep affection that the people of Reading showed at the funeral of John Brock convinced Pierpont to settle there in 1689. He died in 1709 at the age of 44.[80]

Richard Brown

Born in Newbury in 1675, Richard Brown graduated from Harvard in 1697 and then, beginning in 1699, he served as a teacher and pulpit supply in his native town for eleven years. He was not on the best of terms with the folk of his hometown. One sermon he preached brought an attempted assault and death threats. Whenever Brown could, he took temporary jobs elsewhere as a schoolmaster or as a temporary preacher. When the offer came from Reading in 1711, he wrote in the town book that for all of his labor at Newbury, the town had rewarded him with nothing but "abuse, contempt and ingratitude." That Brown had something of a martyr's temperament, however, was indicated in his early appraisal of his situation at Reading, in which he lamented that he met with "many and great trials."

About a decade into his tenure at Reading, Brown tabulated 236 members in full communion (the actual amount was 237). This would represent an apex in the church's life during the colonial period, for within a few years two precincts broke off and formed their own churches. After serving for twenty years, Brown died in 1732.[81]

William Hobby

William Hobby was born in Boston in 1707, was a member of the Harvard class of 1725, and settled in Reading in 1733 until his death in 1765. Hobby's pastorate coincided with the age of revivals that accompanied the preaching tours of George Whitefield in the 1740s. Conscious of his superior position, he was ridiculed for his pompous manners and for his great wig and silver buckles.

When he went to hear Whitefield preach on the Reading green in 1741, Hobby was disposed to disapprove of him. But when the proud Hobby "went to pick a hole in Whitefield's coat, . . . the preacher picked one in his heart."[82] From that point on, he weighed in on the side of the revival party. In 1745, Hobby published a defense of Whitefield entitled *Inquiry into the Itinerancy, and the Conduct of the Rev. Mr. George Whitefield, An Itinerant Preacher*, which, in the predominantly "Old Light" region of northeastern Massachusetts, drew public criticism and mockery. One anonymous pamphlet aimed at Hobby was satirically dubbed *A Twig of Birch for Billy's Breech* (1745).[83] Hobby was undaunted. In response to widespread characterizations of revival converts and apologists as "enthusiasts," Hobby published in 1746 a series of sermons, *Self-Examination in It's Necessity and Advantages Urged and Applied*. Here, he pointed out that enthusiasm is "as little understood as it is admired," and that earnest, sincere believers were being unfairly tarred with the same brush as the deluded and irrational.

As a friend of Whitefield and of the revivals, Hobby found a friend and ally in the Rev. Jonathan Edwards of Northampton, the famous commentator on revival phenomena and one of New England's leading intellectuals. However, Edwards's views about reforming church admission policies in the late 1740s brought down the ire of his church upon him. In choosing members for the council that should decide whether he should be dismissed or not, Edwards selected two churches from outside his home county of Hampshire. One of those churches was Reading. Though Hobby could not prevent Edwards's dismissal, he and the Reading delegates did attend the council of June 22, 1750, and voted in favor of Edwards. When those who opposed Edwards's dismissal included their "protest" against the council's proceedings in the printed "result," they were attacked in the press by members of the Hampshire Association. Hobby replied with *A Vindication of the Protest against the Result of the Northampton-Council*.[84] The following year, Hobby again made the long trip to Northampton when a small contingent from Northampton wanted to explore the possibility of having Edwards pastor a second church in the town.

Hobby even sought to exert his influence over his parishioners from the grave. In an extraordinary letter to be read to his people after his death, he exhorted them, "Don't judge of a minister as you do of a bell, by mere sound; watch narrowly his preaching. Take heed what ye hear. Examine whether his preaching be close, pungent and particular . . . Take time, and you will not only do it better, but do it sooner. I solemnly charge you, as from eternity, that you do not lift up your hands suddenly for any man."[85] Apparently, the people of Reading took his advice, for it took them four years to find a suitable replacement.

RUMNEY MARSH (REVERE)

The area north of Boston originally known as "Rumney Marish" was part of the domain of the Pawtucket tribe. However, war with the neighboring Penobscots and epidemics brought over by Europeans devastated the natives in the early seventeenth century. Still, it was not until 1685 that the Pawtuckets finally surrendered their claim to Rumney Marsh and the surrounding areas. The town was first annexed to Boston in 1634, and allotments made the following year.[86] Original landholders included such worthies as John Winthrop, Henry Vane, and Robert Keayne. Approximately one-third of the original proprietors, including Vane, were implicated in the Antinomian Controversy of the 1630s and some were forced to leave the colony and give up their land. Over time, more of the original allottees sold their land until five or six families dominated the area, including the Newgates, Keaynes, Cogans, Tuttles, and Coles—names that populate the church records.

In his 1642 account of New England entitled *Plain Dealing*, Thomas Lechford wrote that "Where farmes or villages are, as at *Rumney-marsh* and *Marblehead*, there a Minister, or a brother of one of the congregations of *Boston* for the *Marsh*, and of *Salem* for *Marblehead*, preacheth and exerciseth prayer every Lords day, which is called prophesying in such a place." The inhabitants of "the *Marsh*," he added, came to Boston to receive communion.[87] When the North Church was built in Boston in 1650, most people of the Marsh attended services there, though others belonged to churches in Lynn and, later, in Malden. Prior to 1706, Rumney Marsh had a "meetinghouse" of some sort, possibly made of logs, which by 1750 had been torn down.

The first motion that Rumney Marsh establish its own church apparently came from Cotton Mather, pastor of the North Church. In 1693, noting in his diary how "Many Families of my Flock, residing on t'other side the water, putt themselves unto considerable Trouble, every *Lords-Day*, to attend upon my Ministry," he urged them to gather and settle their own distinct church. Sensing that "so *small a Village*" would not be able to maintain a minister, Mather offered to donate part of his salary for that purpose.[88] Rumney Marsh finally submitted a petition in 1705, which was ultimately approved four years later. On July 10, 1710, Judge Samuel Sewall of Boston recorded in his diary that he attended the raising of the new meetinghouse, where he "drove a Pin" and "gave a 5^s Bill."[89] The First Church of Rumney Marsh was gathered and Thomas Cheever ordained as its pastor on October 19, 1715, with Mather presiding as moderator over the ceremony and Rev. Richard Brown representing the church of Reading.

Rumney Marsh became part of the newly created town of Chelsea in 1739 and the church was reorganized as the First Church of North Chelsea in 1841. The area was incorporated as the town of Revere in 1871, when the church was renamed the First Church of Revere. Shortly after becoming the First Unitarian Society in 1888, the church became extinct.

RUMNEY MARSH PASTORATES, 1715-1757

Thomas Cheever

Born in 1658, Cheever's remarkable career spanned no less than sixty-eight years. [90] The son of the renowned schoolmaster Ezekiel Cheever, Thomas graduated from Harvard College in 1677 at the age of nineteen and began preaching in Malden in 1680. The First Church of Malden ordained Cheever in 1681 as a colleague to longtime pastor Michael Wigglesworth, who had been with the church since 1656. In a controversial decision, a clerical council recommended that the Malden church dismiss Cheever in 1686, after the minister suffered cloudy accusations of "scandal."

For the next thirty years after his dismissal, he probably served as a schoolteacher; he is on record as having taught "reading, writing, and ciphering" at

Rumney Marsh from 1709 to 1719. During this time Cheever apparently redeemed himself through industry and reformed behavior. His early indiscretions seem never to have been mentioned when he was hired to serve as pastor of the newly gathered church in 1715.

For more than three decades, Cheever was a successful pastor who earned the respect of his people and of area ministers. The frequency with which the Rumney Marsh church was contacted to help solve disputes, and the lack of contention within the parish, bear out a close relationship between minister and congregation. Towards the end of his life, Cheever was increasingly frail and eventually housebound, reliant on his slave Cuffee, but his people supported him nevertheless. He was still holding church meetings in his house up until the time of his death in 1749.[91]

William McClanachan

Born in Ireland in 1714 and educated at the University of Edinburgh, McClanachan came to New England sometime before 1734. He served in a series of short-lived positions over the next dozen years or so, at Congregational and Presbyterians churches in South Portland, Maine, and in Georgetown and Blanford, and as an army chaplain in the expedition on Cape Breton in 1745.

Called upon to replace Thomas Cheever in 1748, McClanachan quickly convinced the church to adopt the Halfway Covenant and several other innovations. The moves divided the church, which saw several key members depart. Unexpectedly, McClanachan announced his conversion to the Anglican Church to his Revere congregation in 1754, and shortly thereafter departed for England.

Note on the Texts

DESCRIPTION OF THE MANUSCRIPTS

Located in the vault of the First Parish Congregational Church in Wakefield, Massachusetts, the Reading First Church Records are contained in a leather-bound octavo volume of 169 leaves. Each leaf measures 6 in. x 7 1/2 in. Sewn into the front of the volume are sixteen duodecimo leaves, measuring 4 in. x 6 in. As is often the case in volumes of church records, the minutes of church meetings (beginning with those kept by Rev. Richard Brown in 1712) commence at the back of the book. The records presented in this edition of the Reading

church book are confined to the colonial era, and thus end with the church's calling of the Reverend Caleb Prentice to office in 1769. It should be noted that
the records of church meetings and vital statistics in the church book extend to
1845.

The Rumney Marsh church records are located in the Museum of Fine Arts
in Boston, Massachusetts (MS #84412). The front and back covers of Book I
are detached, and the front cover is inscribed, "Rumny-marish Church-book: /
1715." Thirty quarto leaves, measuring 6 3/8 in. x 9 3/4 in., constitute this volume, with the first leaf damaged along both margins. Our transcription is that
of the entire first book; the second starts in 1757.

Excerpts from the Reading and Revere records have been published in town
histories that are now out of print. Selections from the Reading records appear
in Lilley Eaton, *Genealogical History of the Town of Reading, Mass.* (Boston, 1874), pp.
138-41. The Revere records are excerpted in Benjamin Shurtleff, *The History of the
Town of Revere* (Boston, 1937), pp. 424-27, and cited variously in Mellen
Chamberlain, *A Documentary History of Chelsea, Including the Boston Precincts of
Winnisimmet Rumney Marsh, and Pullen Point, 1624-1824* (Boston, 1908).

The transcripts of the church records printed in this volume are presented as
faithfully to the originals as is possible within the constraints of typography.
Original line length, spelling, capitalization, and punctuation (or lack of it) are
retained, as are archaic contractions. Words or parts of words in square brackets
indicate an editorial interpolation for missing text due to manuscript damage or
scribal omission. Deletions are also retained as struck-through text. Dashes within square brackets indicate an illegible deletion, with each dash standing for a
character. Some words appear with a macron above the *m*, indicating an abbrevi-
ation, com̄on for common, com̄union for communion, rem̄ber for remember,
com̄itted for committed, frõ for from.

GLOSSARY OF COMMON ABBREVIATIONS

acc^t	account	**NAMES AND TITLES**	
ag^t	against	B^{rin}	Brethren
chh	church	B^r	Brother
cov^t	covenant	Capt	Captain
dep^t	depart	Deac^n/D^c	Deacon
meet^g	meeting	Eliz^a	Elizabeth
o^r	our	Jno	John
ov^r	over	Jon^a	Jonathan
p^r	per	Junr	Junior
rec^d	received	L^t	Lieutenant
s^d	said	Nathl	Nathaniel
ten^r	tenor (currency)	R^d	Reverend or Richard
w^c/w^{ch}	which	Sam^{ll}	Samuel
w^o	who	Senr	Senior
w^r	were	Tim^o	Timothy
w^{r}in	wherein	W^m/Willm	William
w^{r}of	whereof		
w^s	was		
wth	within		
y^e	the		
y^{es}	these		
y^m	them		
y^n	then		
y^{os}	those		
y^r	there		
y^t	that		
y^y	they		
X	Christ		

Notes

1. A vast number of studies have pointed to the importance of early Congregationalism and its development over the colonial era. See, for example, Joseph S. Clark, *A Historical Sketch of the Congregational Churches of Massachusetts from 1620 to 1858* (Boston, 1858), 12-13, who argued that American democracy "sprang up spontaneously from that system of church polity which our New England fathers deduced from the Bible." Patricia U. Bonomi, in *Under the Cope of Heaven: Religion, Society, and Politics in Colonial America* (New York: Oxford University Press, 1986), 186, observed that "all that has been said and written about the New England town as the 'school of democracy' can be applied with equal or greater force to the church congregation." Similar themes are explored in James F. Cooper Jr., *Tenacious of Their Liberties: The Congregationalists in Colonial Massachusetts* (New York: Oxford University Press, 1999). Historians have examined developments within Congregational churches to find evidence of a decline of religious spirituality; see, for example, Perry Miller, *The New England Mind: From Colony to Province* (Cambridge, Belknap Press, 1953), 3-146; Darrett B. Rutman, "God's Bridge Falling Down: 'Another Approach' to New England Puritanism Assayed," *William and Mary Quarterly*, 3rd ser., 19 (1962): 408-21; David D. Hall, *The Faithful Shepherd: A History of the New England Ministry in the Seventeenth Century* (Chapel Hill, N.C.: University of North Carolina Press, 1972), 176-226. Many have pointed to developments in the churches to call into question this concept of "declension"; see the summary in Cooper, *Tenacious of Their Liberties*, 133-50. Scholars have also examined Congregational developments in light of the emergence of the Great Awakening; see Harry S. Stout, *The New England Soul: Preaching and Religious Culture in Colonial New England* (New York: Oxford University Press, 1986), 185-211, and Cooper, *Tenacious of Their Liberties*, 170-214. Others, in turn, have focused on the Great Awakening within Congregational churches and its relationship to the American Revolution; see Alan Heimert, *Religion and the American Mind from the Great Awakening to the American Revolution* (Cambridge: Harvard University Press, 1966); William G. McLoughlin, "'Enthusiasm for Liberty': The Great Awakening as the Key to the Revolution," in *Preachers and Politicians: Two Essays on the Origins of the American Revolution*, ed. William G. McLoughlin and Jack P. Greene (Worcester, Mass.: American Antiquarian Society, 1977), 47-73; Stout, *The New England Soul*, 210-11, 216-18.

2. See, for example, David D. Hall, ed., *Lived Religion in America: Toward a History of Practice* (Princeton, N.J.: Princeton University Press 1997).

3. The indispensable source for studying Massachusetts church records is Harold Field Worthley, *An Inventory of the Records of the Particular (Congregational) Churches of*

Massachusetts Gathered 1620-1805 (Cambridge: Harvard University Press, 1970). Some of the finest church records currently available include *The Records of the First Church of Boston, 1630-1868*, ed. Richard D. Pierce, Colonial Society of Massachusetts *Collections*, vols. 39-41 (Boston, The Society, 1961); *Records of the First Church of Dorchester in New England, 1636-1734*, ed. Henry Pope (Boston, 1891); and *The Records of the Baptisms, Marriages, and Deaths and Admissions to the Church and Dismissals Therefrom, Transcribed from the Town of Dedham, Massachusetts, 1638-1845*, ed. Don Gleason Hill (Dedham, Mass., 1888). Early Congregational church records have been utilized most extensively in Cooper, *Tenacious of Their Liberties*, which employs the records of over one hundred colonial Massachusetts churches to explore the evolution of Congregationalism. Other studies have utilized limited numbers of church records to explore specific topics. See, for example, Emil Oberholzer Jr., *Delinquent Saints: Disciplinary Action in the Early Congregational Churches of Massachusetts* (New York: Columbia University Press, 1956), which employs church records to examine church discipline, and Robert G. Pope, *The Half Way Covenant: Church Membership in Puritan New England* (Princeton, N.J.: Princeton University Press, 1969), which utilizes church records to cast light on changing admissions requirements. Church records have also been fruitfully employed in a number of community studies, such as Kenneth A. Lockridge, *A New England Town: The First Hundred Years, 1636-1736* (New York: Norton, 1970); Christine Heyrman, *Commerce and Culture: The Maritime Communities of Colonial Massachusetts* (New York: Norton, 1984); and George W. Harper, *A People So Favored of God: Boston's Congregational Churches and Their Pastors, 1710-1760* (Lanham, Md.: University Press of America, 2004).

4. Reading Records, MS p. 50 (p. 122).

5. On "primitivism" in early Puritanism, see Theodore Dwight Bozeman, *To Live Ancient Lives: The Primitivist Dimension in Puritanism* (Chapel Hill, N.C.: University of North Carolina Press, 1988).

6. See the text of the Cambridge Platform in Williston Walker, *Creeds and Platforms of Congregationalism* (New York, 1893), 194-237.

7. Reading Records, MS p. 24 (p. 90); for another reference, see ibid, MS p. 26 (p. 94).

8. See ibid., MS p. 50 (p. 122) and MS p. 8 (p. 72) where George Davis is charged because he did not confront a fellow member who had offended him.

9. See ibid., MS p. 8 (pp. 72-73).

10. Ibid., MS pp. 6-7 (pp. 70-72).

11. Ibid., MS pp. A26, A30, A35, A37-38 (pp. 177, 183, 188-89, 191-93).

12. Lockridge, *A New England Town: The First Hundred Years, 1636-1736*; Michael Zuckerman, *Peaceable Kingdoms: New England Towns in the Eighteenth Century* (New York: Knopf, 1970); Stephen Foster, *Their Solitary Way: The Puritan Social Ethic in the First Century of Settlement in New England* (New Haven, Conn.: Yale University Press, 1971); Stout, *The New England Soul: Preaching and Religious Culture in Colonial New England*; Cooper, *Tenacious of Their Liberties*, 3-87.

13. Reading Records, MS p. 24 (p. 91).

14. On these changes, see, for example, Richard L. Bushman, *From Puritan to Yankee: Character and the Social Order in Connecticut, 1690-1765* (New York: Norton, 1967); Richard L. Bushman, *The Refinement of America: Persons, Houses, Cities* (New York: Knopf, 1992); David W. Conroy, *In Public Houses: Drink and the Revolution of Authority in Colonial Massachusetts* (Chapel Hill, N.C.: University of North Carolina Press, 1995); Cornelia Hughes Dayton, *Women Before the Bar: Gender, Law, and Society in Connecticut, 1639-1789* (Chapel Hill, N.C.: University of North Carolina Press, 1995); David H. Flaherty, *Privacy in Colonial New England* (Charlottesville, Va.: University of Virgina Press, 1972); Thomas S. Kidd, *The Protestant Interest: New England After Puritanism* (New Haven, Conn.: Yale University Press, 2004); Paul R. Lucas, *Valley of Discord: Church and Society Along the Connecticut River, 1636-1725* (Hanover, N.H.: University Press of New England, 1976); Jackson Turner Main, *Society and Economy in Colonial Connecticut* (Princeton, N.J.: Princeton University Press, 1985); Margaret Ellen Newell, *From Dependency to Independence: Economic Revolution in Colonial New England* (Ithaca, N.Y.: Cornell University Press, 1998); Lisa Wilson, *Ye Heart of a Man: The Domestic Life of Men in Colonial New England* (New Haven, Conn.: Yale University Press, 1999).

15. Reading Records, MS p. 10 (p. 76).

16. Rumney Marsh Records, MS pp. 26-28 (pp. 265-71).

17. Ibid., MS pp. 15-16 (pp. 245-48).

18. For entries on Edwards and Northampton, see Reading Records, MS pp. 39, 40; on contention after Hobby's death, see Charles R. Bliss, *Wakefield Congregational Church: A Commemorative Sketch, 1644-1877* (Wakefield, 1877), 15.

19. Reading Records, MS p. A58 (p. 212).

20. Ibid., MS p. A31 (p. 184).

21. Rogers's lone status is confirmed in the Wenham MS Church Records, unpaginated, "An account of the church of Wenham there proceeding with Mr. W. Rogers."

22. Halifax MS Church Records, 1734-1833, entry for Oct. 27, 1763, Halifax (Mass.) Town Hall.

23. Rumney Marsh Records, MS p. 9 (p. 235).

24. Ibid., MS p. 20 (p. 256).

25. *The Records of the First Church in Salem, Massachusetts, 1629-1736*, ed. Richard D. Pierce (Salem, Mass.: Essex Institute, 1974), 278-79 and n.

26. Ibid., 269; Rumney Marsh Records, MS p. 8 ff. (pp. 231ff.).

27. Rumney Marsh Records, MS p. 10 (p. 235)

28. Reading Records, MS p. A25 (p. 176).

29. On the Church of Worcester, see ibid, MS p. 9; and for Hobby's remark, ibid., MS p. 33.

30. On politics in colonial Massachusetts at this time, see Henry R. Spencer, *Constitutional Conflicts in Provincial Massachusetts: A Study of Some Phases of Opposition Between the Massachusetts Governor and General Court in the Eighteenth Century* (Columbus, Ohio, 1905); Richard L. Bushman, *King and People in Provincial Massachusetts* (Chapel Hill, N.C.: University of North Carolina Press, 1985).

31. Quoted in Mellen Chamberlain, *A Documentary History of Chelsea, Including the Boston Precincts of Winnisimmet Rumney Marsh, and Pullen Point, 1624-1824* (Boston, 1908), 192-93.

32. *The Diary of Cotton Mather*, ed. W. C. Ford (2 vols., New York: Ungar, 1957), I:126; Chamberlain, *A Documentary History of Chelsea*, 193.

33. Quoted in Chamberlain, *A Documentary History of Chelsea*, 193-94.

34. Rumney Marsh Records, MS p. 1 (p. 223).

35. Ibid., MS p. 13 (p. 242).

36. Ibid., MS p. 39 (p. 293).

37. Ibid., MS p. 6 (p. 229).

38. Ibid., MS p. 29 (p. 273).

39. Ibid., MS p. 35 (pp. 234-35)

40. Ibid., MS p. 46 (p. 307).

41. Ibid., MS p. 46 (p. 308).

42. Examples of current studies in this area include Leigh Eric Schmidt, *Consumer Rites:*

The Buying and Selling of American Holidays (Princeton, N.J.: Princeton University Press, 1995); Robert A. Orsi, *Thank You, St. Jude: Women's Devotion to the Patron Saint of Hopeless Causes* (New Haven, Conn.: Yale University Press, 1996); Colleen McDannell, *Religions of the United States in Practice* (2 vols., Princeton, N.J.: Princeton University Press, 2001).

43. Dorothy Bass, *Practicing our Faith* (San Francisco: Jossey-Bass, 1997), xi; Hall, introduction to *Lived Religion in America*, xi.

44. Reading Records, MS p. A14 (pp. 166-67); Rumney Marsh Records, MS p. 13 (p. 242).

45. Reading Records, MS pp. 26-28 (pp. 93-95).

46. See, for example, Reading Records, MS p. A28 (p. 180, Ebenezer Merrow); Rumney Marsh Records, MS p. 5 (p. 227, Edward Tuttle).

47. Reading Records, MS p. 7 (pp. 71-72); see also ibid., MS p. 22 (pp. 88-89).

48. For example, Jane Kamensky, *Governing the Tongue: The Politics of Speech in Early New England* (New York: Oxford University Press, 1997) ; Sandra Gustafson, *Eloquence Is Power: Oratory & Performance in Early America* (Chapel Hill, N.C.: University of North Carolina Press, 2000).

49. Reading Records, MS pp. A34-35 (p. 188).

50. Bruce C. Daniels, *Puritans at Play: Leisure and Recreation in Colonial New England* (New York: St. Martin's Press, 1995), 141-59.

51. Possibly her husband was not a member of the Reading church, or of any church, and therefore the church had no power to discipline him. The Reading Records (MS p. 23 [p. 90]) record her as "Mary Davis alias widdow Grover," which indicates that she was married.

52. By the Revolution, between 30 and 40 percent of New England women were pregnant at the time they were married. Richard Godbeer, *Sexual Revolution in Early America* (Baltimore: Johns Hopkins University Press, 2003), 33-38, 228-38.

53. Reading Records, MS p. A37 (p. 190).

54. Rumney Marsh Records, MS pp. 8-11 (pp. 231-38).

55. Ibid., MS p. 48 (p. 311).

56. Ibid., MS p. 40 (p. 296).

57. Ibid., MS pp. 14, 19, 22, 23 (pp. 243, 254, 258, 260).

58. Ibid., MS p. 4 (p. 226), MS p. 22 (p. 259).

59. Rumney Marsh Records, MS p. 4 (p. 226); Reading Records, MS p. A23 (p. 174).

60. On votes for charity, see Reading Records, MS pp. A41, A44, A47 (pp. 196, 198-99, 203); Rumney Marsh Records, MS pp. 21, 23, 24 (pp. 257, 260, 263).

61. In 1724 and again in 1754, the Reading church contributed, or considered contributing, ransom money. Reading Records, MS pp. 12, 43, 44.

62. Reading Records, MS p. A45 (pp. 199-200).

63. See Pope, *The Half Way Covenant*, ch. 8; and Gerald F. Moran, "Conditions of Religious Conversion in the First Society of Norwich, Connecticut, 1718-1744," *Journal of Social History* 5 (1971): 241.

64. Ann Douglas, *The Feminization of American Culture* (New York: Knopf, 1978); Richard D. Shiels, "The Feminization of American Congregationalism, 1730-1835," *American Quarterly* 33 (1981): 46-62; Barbara Welter, "The Feminization of American Religion, 1800-1860," in *Clio's Consciousness Raised*, ed. Mary Hartman and Lois Banner (New York: Octagon, 1974), 137-55; Philip J. Greven Jr., "Youth, Maturity, and Religious Conversion: A Note on the Ages of Converts in Andover, Massachusetts, 1711-1749," *Essex Institute Historical Collections* 108 (1972): 130-31; and Moran, "Conditions of Religious Conversion in the First Society of Norwich," 338.

65. With the exception of times of revival, when more men tended to join, other Boston area churches had a higher number of females in full membership than men consistently through the seventeenth century. See figures on Roxbury, Charlestown, Boston Third, and Dorchester, in Pope, *The Half-Way Covenant*, 279-86. This trend continued in the eighteenth century; see, for example, Harper, *A People So Favored of God*, 183.

66. Margaret Masson, "The Typology of the Female as a Model for the Regenerate: Puritan Preaching, 1690-1730," *Signs* 2 (1976): 304-15; Laurel Thatcher Ulrich, "'Vertuous Women Found': New England Ministerial Literature, 1668-1735," in *Puritan New England: Essays on Religion, Society, and Culture*, ed. Alden T. Vaughan and Francis J. Bremer (New York: St. Martin's Press, 1977), 215-31.

67. For five churches in southeastern Massachusetts that also fit the general trend, see Douglas L. Winiarski, "'All Manner of Delusions and Errors': Josiah Cotton and the Religious Transformation of Southeastern New England, 1700-1770," Ph.D. diss., Indiana University, 2000, 413-15.

68. See Jill Lepore, *The Name of War: King Philip's War and the Beginning of American Identity* (New York: Knopf, 1998).

69. Quoted in Stout, *The New England Soul*, 177.

70. Kenneth P. Minkema, "The Lynn End 'Earthquake' Narratives of 1727," *New England Quarterly* LXIX (Sept. 1996): 473-99.

71. John Brown, appendix to John Cotton, *A Holy Fear of God* (Boston, 1727), quoted in Stout, *New England Soul*, 179.

72. On admission trends in the Boston churches, see Harper, *A People So Favored of God*, 181-82.

73. Moran, "Conditions of Religious Conversion in the First Society of Norwich"; Winiarski, "'All Manner of Delusions and Errors'"; William F. Willingham, "Religious Conversion in the Second Society of Windham, Connecticut, 1723-1743: A Case Study," *Societas* 6 (1976): 109-19; Stephen R. Grossbart, "Seeking the Divine Favor: Conversion and Church Admissions in Eastern Connecticut, 1711-1832," *William and Mary Quarterly* 46 (1989): 719, 721.

74. David S. Lovejoy, *Religious Enthusiasm and the Great Awakening* (Englewood Cliffs, N.J.: Prentice Hall, 1969); C.C. Goen, *Revivalism and Separatism in New England, 1740-1800* (Middletown, Conn.: Wesleyan University Press, 1987).

75. Most prominently Jon Butler in "Enthusiasm Described and Decried: The Great Awakening as Interpretive Fiction," *Journal of American History* 69, no. 2 (Sept. 1982): 305-25.

76. Lilley Eaton, *Genealogical History of the Town of Reading, Mass. . . .* (Boston, 1874), 14.

77. Erik R. Seeman, *Pious Persuasions: Laity and Clergy in Eighteenth-Century New England* (Baltimore: Johns Hopkins, 1999); and Seeman, "'Justise Must Take Plase': Three African Americans Speak of Religion in Eighteenth-Century New England," *William and Mary Quarterly* 56 (Apr. 1999): 393-414.

78. Quoted in Bliss, *Wakefield Congregational Church*, 30.

79. Quotes from John L. Sibley, *Biographical Sketches of Graduates of Harvard University*, vol. I, 1642-1658 (Cambridge, 1873), 128-29.

80. Sibley, *Biographical Sketches of Graduates of Harvard University*, vol. III, 1679-1689 (Cambridge, 1885), 349-51.

81. Sibley, *Biographical Sketches of Those Who Attended Harvard College*, vol. IV, 1690-1700 (Cambridge, 1933), 336-41; quotes on pp. 338, 339.

82. Quoted in Bliss, *Wakefield Congregational Church*, 38; on Hobby's life, see Sibley, *Biographical Sketches of Those Who Attended Harvard College*, vol. VII (Cambridge, 1945), 530-37.

83. J.C., *A twig of birch for Billy's breech: A letter to the Reverend Mr. William Hobby, a pastor of a church at Reading. Being a gentle and necessary correction of him, for his folly and wickedness lately published to the world, in a piece entitled, A defence of the itineracy and the conduct of the Reverend Mr. Whitefield* (Boston, 1745). See also Nathaniel Henchman (pastor of the Lynn church), *A letter to the Reverend Mr. William Hobby: occasioned by sundry passages in his printed letter, in vindication of Mr. Whitefield's itinerancy and conduct* (Boston, 1745).

84. Hobby, *A vindication of the protest against the result of the Northampton-council: In answer to a letter published by the Reverend Messieurs Robert Breck, Joseph Ashly, Timothy Woodbridge, Chester Williams; intitled, An account of the conduct of the council which dismiss'd the Reverend Mr. Edwards from the pastoral care of the First Church at Northampton; with reflections on the protestation accompanying the printed result of that council, and the letter published relating to that affair: In a letter to a gentleman* (Boston, 1751).

85. *Mr. Hobby's advice to his people from the grave* (Boston? 1765).

86. Benjamin Shurtleff, *The History of the Town of Revere* (Boston, 1937), 27.

87. Thomas Lechford, *Plain dealing, or, Newes from New-England* (London, 1642), 15.

88. Mather, *Diary*, I:180.

89. *The Diary of Samuel Sewall, 1674-1729*, ed. M. Halsey Thomas (2 vols., New York: Farrar, Straus Giroux, 1973), II:639.

90. Biographical information on Cheever is drawn from Mellen Chamberlain, *A Documentary History of Chelsea, Including the Boston Precincts of Winnisimmet, Rumney Marsh, and Pullen Point, 1624-1824* (Boston, 1908), 192-96.

91. Sibley, *Biographical Sketches of Graduates of Harvard University*, vol. II, 1659-1677 (Cambridge, 1881), 501-6.

The Reading Church Records

1648-1769

The Names of ye Brethren & Sisters of ye Church at Reading [4]^1

From ~~its first Gathering 1648~~ the 29 Sept. 1648. &c.

Leift: Marshall & 's wife: dismissd frõ Lyn

Francis Smith . Mrs Green

Tho Marshall Carpenter.

Willm Cowdry & his wife

Eliz: Hooper

John Pearson & his wife

Lidia Lakin

Bro. Dunton

Eliz: Wily

Tho Kendall & his wife

Eliz: Hart

Tho Parker & his wife

Zech Fitch & his wife
    dismissed frõ Lyn

George Davis

Will Eaton & his wife
    dismissed frõ Watertown

William Hooper

John Batchel^r & his wife
    dismissed frõ Dedham

Mary Swaine

Joan Marshall

Will Martin

Tho: Hartshorn & his wife

Jonas Eaton & his wife

~~Lidia~~

Edward Taylo^r & his wife

Tho Bancroft

Sister Martin

Judith Pool

——— ——— ———

Abigail Damon

In May 1648 Mr Henry

Leift: Smith & his wife before
some of y^e former

Green first Pasto^r of this

Church dyed. after whom

they Called to Supply his

roome. Samuel Haugh

who came hither Novemb 3

1648. & was Ordeyn'd

Pasto^r here March 26: 1650.

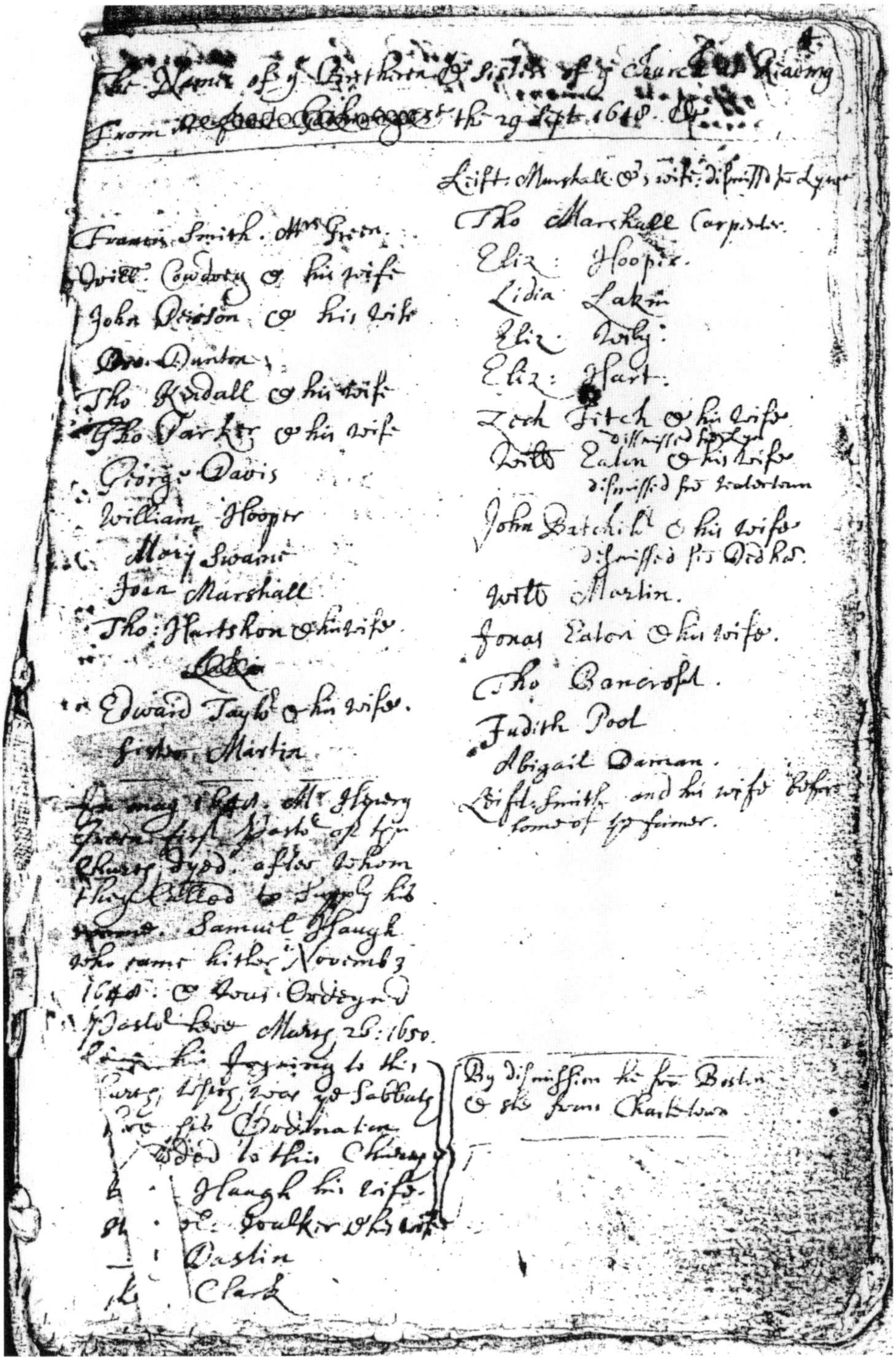
The Names of ye Brethren & Sisters of ye Church at Reading
From ... the 29 Sept. 1648

Francis Smith. Mrs Green.
Will Cowdrey & his wife
John Dixson & his wife
... Dunton
Tho Kendall & his wife
Tho Parker & his wife
George Davis
William Hooper
Mary Swain
Joan Marshall
Tho: Hartshorn & his wife
Edward Taylor & his wife
... Martin
... may 1648. Mr Henry Green first Pastor of the Church dyed after whom they called to supply his ... Samuel Haugh who came hither Novemb 1648 & was Ordayned Pastor here March 26: 1650 ...
... Haugh his wife
... Walker & his wife
... Bastin
... Clark

Lieft Marshall & wife dismissed to Lynn
Tho Marshall Carpenter
Eliz: Hooper
Lidia Lakin
Eliz: Wiley
Eliz: Hart
Zach Fitch & his wife
Will Eaton & his wife dismissed to Watertown
John Batchelder & his wife dismissed to Dedham
Will Martin
Jonas Eaton & his wife
Tho Bancroft
Judith Pool
Abigail Damon
Lieft Smith and his wife ...
By dismission he fro Boston & she from Charlstown

Since his joyning to this
Church which was yᵉ Sabbath
before his Ordination
was added to this Church   }{   By dismission he frō Boston
Sarah Haugh his wife.   & she from Charlestown

Samuel: Walker & his wife.

Lydia Dastin

Alice Clark

John Brocke called by yᵉ Church [to]²   [5]

officiate amongst them after mʳ Sam: Ha[ugh]

decease at Boston, & dismissed to them fr[õ]

Dedham church, was Joyned to them the

Lords day before yᵉ Ordination, & Nov. 13 : [6]2

hee was Ordained, & yᵉ day after he was

married to Mʳˢ Sarah Haugh a widdow indeed.

The Names of yᵉ Brethrin & Sisters
    yᵗ were joyned since his office work.

25 (10) 62 Jonathan Poole	16 (4) 66	Sister Cowdry
Goodman Wellman		dismissed from Lyn.
& his wife		Elizabeth Parker
Nath. Cowdry		Sister Bancroft
& his wife	22 (9) 69	dismissed from Dedham
Nath. Coutler		Brother Damon
		dismissed from Dedham
Hanna Lilly		Hanna Packer
John Eaton &		Mary Goodwin
his wife		Abraham Briant
Tho. Clarke		Mary Hodgman

Mary Eaton

Mary Parker

6 (2) 63   Sister Hartshorne

by letters from Ipswich.

Nich. Browne

& his wife

24 (4) 63   dismissed from Lyn:

Hanna Cowdry

Mary Swaine Junio^re

Goodwife Cutler

John Batcheller Junr

& his wife

Mary Briant

Martha Parker

Elizabeth Brown

Mary Burnap.

Sister Nichols

dismissed from Ipsw[ich][3]

Ester Dix

vide p. 20[4]

Saml Walker being Under some offence for high & ill Language [6]

given to ye Pasto^r: about ye year 1652 gave satisfaction

to ye church privately met at ye Pasto^rs house by acknowledging

his Evill therin.

Eliz. Hart being under offence in ye year 1653 for Inner

sinfullnesse in not Late harbouring travelers that were in

danger of y^r Lives y^rby at lest some of y^m: for Diverse

offensive words spoken to y^m concerning Some of ye Church &

town. for some Grosse suspicions of falshood: was before

the church brought to Give satisfaction; who Extended much

charity toward hir in taking y^t for Satisfaction w^ch

came frõ hir though far short of what they Judged

needfull.

George Davis publickly to ye church only acknowledged some offensive speech spoken by him to Tho Clark.

Feb: 1655

Eliz. Hart was Again brought before ye church first

in private for Sundry offences as namely (1) for Contempt

of Authority (2) for Evill surmising & falsely accusing

some of the bretheren. (3) for Boasting sinfully of y^t w^h

is Evill: y^t all ye wit ye church had could not keep hir

out nor beigin [to] cast hir out. [(4)] that she never had

ye worst of it befor^e Minister or church with many

other things wch were then testified ag^t her: as Saying

y^t she burnt ye warrant to teach old fooles more wit.

To these things at first she began to Answer with

shew of much hotienesse & Generally confessing her

proud high spirit, & much Hypocrisye, &c but

running to particulars she y^n So Excused &

teased as that gave no Satisfaction at all: So

she was referred to A more publick hearing y^t

in Case she came not of more freely she should

then be Admonished.

being so called forth in publick ye next L^{ds} day save one   [7]

(for ye next was Sacram^t Day from wch she was Suspended)

upon hope of better Satisfaction: She did give very small

signs of true repentance so as that upon propounding y^t

to ye church for their app^{r}hensions one or two Exp^{r}ssed

themselves Content to Sit down but others thought y^{m}selves

unsatisfied & some desired to deferre till another

time: & y^t being very late we concluded with
Prayer &c without fully Understanding y^e churches mind
But next L^ds day she was again called forth &
shewing Little signs of Repentance she was Admoni
shed : After wch she being again called forth on
Another Sabbath about three weeks after: she gave
Such Satisfaction as y^e church Sat down upon.

_____   _____

Feb 6: 1658. George Davis being brought before
y^e Church for an Offensive libell by him made
and published by Singing it in Verse did very
freely & plainly acknowledge his great Sin
therin & Lam^ted much y^t he had y^rin dishono^rd
God given offence to his bretheren and opened y^e
mouths of any ill affected : W^ch gave very good
Satisfaction to ye church. ^5

~~The~~ Octob. 26: 1659 At A Publick Church   [8]
meeting appoynted ye L^ds day before (though we
were constrayned to meet at my house bec: of
work being done at ye meeting house) George
Davis was Convened before the church and y^r
was Layd to his chardge

1) that having unto ye Pasto^r threatened that (y^t
he would not Call Sister Clark & Kendall
to answer Some offences he had to chardge y^m
With: wch ye Pasto^r Conceived was not yet ripe
for his Cognizance by X^ts rules) he then would

present y^m both for Liars & have y^m Recorded

So in Court: and then Bring the Courts Records

ag^r y^m in Church: Having thus Sayd to y^e

Pasto^r and his Wife, he afterward being questi

oned why he would So Say or doe by divers

he denied it Saying he intended no Such thing

& it never came into his heart or thought: &

this he then denyed to Tho. Clark and his wife

Willm Cowdrey & his wife. Tho. Kendall. Jonas

Eaton Zech Fitch. To this Lye thus punctually

proved: he owned what he had Sayd to ye Pas

to^r & his Wife but Sayd he could not Remem

ber y^t he Sayd So to Bro: Cowdrey and his Wife

in way of doing all of it. and So of ye rest profes

sing his Conscience did not accuse him of an intended

Lye in it.

2) That being dealt with by Tho. Kendall Jonas

Eaton & Zech Fitch for departing from y^e

Sacram^t bec: of offence he had taken at Sister

Kendall

and yet did not endeavour to remove the offence   [9]

before ye Sacram^t: He replyed No It was not

for any thing that he was offended ag^t Sister

Kendall but Some trouble upon his own Spirit

that he went from ye Sacram^t. So as y^t he

left them as Satisfyed with his answer: but af

terward it came to be known that he went

away in bitternesse ag^t hir: wch was plain

from Some bitter words Spoken ag^t hir unto

ye Pasto^r and his wife by George Davis w^{ch}

ye Pasto^r bringing Bro. Cowdrey wth him did deal

more privately wth Georg Davis for. this was

charged on him as A Second Lye: to wch also

he answered y^t he did not intend So to Leave

y^m in ye dark he thought they could not

but understand that y^r was offence taken

by him at Sister Kendall: but wthall his intent

was to hint to them that it was chiefly the

distemp. of his own Spirit upon y^t offence taken y^t

made him look at himself as unfit and therefore

did dep^t.   But it too plainly appears

that it was rather his disdeigning to speake with

hir, than Some of his own unfitnesse that made

him to dep^t.

3) that he was heard to Sing Some p^t of A

filthy song : and to scoff at those y^t took

offence at it . to wch he answered y^t it might

be possible he did Sing Some of it. but Sayd before

that he never could Sing one verse of it. wch being

now alledged ag^t him. Viz: how could y^t be

true y^t he never could Sing one verse of it and

yet y^t now he confesseth to have Sung Some of it

He answered he knew not how much a Verse was

Except it was so much as made ye Tune once.

[10]

but he Judged himself for this confessing ye Evill

of it.   W^ch Confession did in y^t Satisfie

many of ye church for this last offence: but

wth respect to ye former two Especially con

sidering he had been taken in two untruths

formerly he was wth consent of ye church

Layd under A formall admonition; & y^r

by pro tempore Suspended from ye L^ds

Table &c.

―――― ―――― ――――

Geo: Davis Feb 9 : 1659 Appeared before ye church assem

bled at ye Pasto^rs house and by his acknowledgem^t p^tly

in words & p^tly in writing he So far Judged himself

for what was Layd to his charge as y^t ye church accepted

of Satisfaction & tooke of ye Censure &c.

―――― ―――――― ―――――― ――――――――――――

January 14. 1661. Lidia Dastin Appeared before ye church

at A publique church meeting (appointed ye L^ds day before)

though at ye Pasto^rs house not for privacie, but for

conveniencie in regard of ye weather. And being there

required to owne the Confession wch She had formerly

made concerning hir offence and wch was then tendred

in writing, She did own ye Same, and although not

with y^t freedom and willingnesse as was to be desired

yet So as ye church p^t by Expression & ye rest by Si

lence manifested their acceptance of hir Satisfaction

tendred.

Now ye offences chardged upon hir was (I) that she

Reported concerning J. P. M. C. J. D. B. G. y^t

on ye L^{ds} day after their coming out of ye meeting

house they laughed and jeered at ye minister y^t

then had been dispencing ye word to them.

whereas afterward upon Examination it could not appear   [11]

that they did laugh at ye Minister but as they Sayd at

A Senseless Jest put forth by S G : concerning one who

at ye meeting broke wind:[6] (. . . . .

. . . . beagles opened)   now she seeing

& hearing them laugh, and another telling hir y^t

they laughed at ye Minister (as she then p^{t}y affirmeth she

hearing those words Spoken by them in or about ye time of

y^r laughing (So much for that or this) wch being the words

ye Minister concluded wthall as she Sayth was ye occasion of

hir Jealousy and report.   The ~~Second~~ (2) thing layd

to hir was that when she was dealt with by y^e

young men for blemishing y^r names, she denyed y^t

she had particularly named any of them: at least any

but one. whereas the testimonyes Say she did name

diverse of them. to this hir answer was that she

doth not yet rember y^t she named any in particular

her self: but y^t they were named she remembers but

whether by hir self or no she remembers not. w^{ch}

occasioned her denyall yet nevertheless she condem

ned hir self for hir Sinfull rashnesse therein &c.[7]

Mathew Edwards desiring his Condition   [12]

to be propounded to y^e Church, whiles
hee stood propounded, testimony Came in
against him to charge him with y^e guilt
22 (II) 62. of a Scandal, hee being desired to humble
himselfe & regaine Gods honour &c hee
went to y^e parties & made a Confessiõ
to their Satisfaction, which being testi=
fyed to the church hee was admitted
(& committed to God) according to y^e Judgm^t
of Charity.

George Davis having been some time in
y^e guilt of wanton words & carriage to
Mary Morrell, which being made knowne
to B^r Cowdrey Senr & B^r Kendall, they
came to y^e Elder & inquired darkly of such
a case   George Davis came & seconded them
he desired to acknowledge his fault in
publick, the Elder having heard the accusation
& his defense but not without some Confession
gave way to his desire: after his Confession
y^e Brethren dissatisfyed a day of humiliation
appointed for y^e church & his sinne more
applied to him   but his satisfaction offered
was Judged to be too short, & an Ad=
monition was aggreed on to be sollemnly
applied & bee left with God to humble
him for his Sinne and so waiting a time

upon God in y^e use of y^e Censure, the
Lord did helpe him to repent of it &
bewayled his greate hardnes of heart, &
lying under the guilt of it 18 months,
hee justifyed God in afflicting him for it,
& aggravated his sinne, & justifyed the
Censure & offering to Satisfy the church
they accepted of it, & his Censure tooke off
with a Signall testimony of forgiveness,
but not before hee gave Satisfaction
to Jeremy Swaine for words specifyed as

8 (6) 63. appeareth ye 8th (6) 63.

Nicholas Browne having given ye Towne
offense y^t is ye Selectmen, by inserting three
or four words into a grant of a piece of
meadow without their privity, for the explaining
of it, & having dealt with him for it, his honest

12 (3) 63 Confession was sent to y^e Church of Lyn
whereof hee was a member. they waighing
it, sent that hee should publikly acknowledge
his error &c: which being attended, the con=
gregation tooke satisfaction, & upon Letters
of dismission afterwards hee & his wife
were admitted (with their children) into y^e Church.

Joan Marshall having spoken some offensive
words against Sister Bancroft, & they dealing

[13]

with her to give them satisfaction, she stay=
ing at yᵉ Lords Supper, two of yᵉ Brethrin
riseing upp, & attested that she had not attended
to give Satisfaction, she was required to forbear
Comunion with us at that time, she gave some
offensive words before she went out; but God
helped her afterwards to Come upp to yᵉ rule
& to make her acknowledgement before
the Church, & was againe received into our hearts.

John Bachellor Junʳ having lien some
time in yᵉ guilt of yᵉ Sinne of wantonesse
making an attempt upon Mary Hodgman but
she resisted him; hee afterwards Joyned
to yᵉ church & held Comunion with us
but God left him to offer some dalliance wᵗ
one maid Servant of his after another,
which being blazd abroad, he confest his
guilt of Mary Hodgmans accusations for yᵉ
substance of it, hee confessed yᵉ guilt of
Sarah Hoopers accusation for yᵉ Substance
of it, but hee denied yᵉ substance of
G. Duttons daughters accusation of him;
The Church seriously Considering of the
Case of our Brother Bachellor, they
they thought it might be good to lay   [14]
him under an Admonition, which was
20 (4) 69 with their Consent attended; & the Sinne

with ye aggravations of it was publikly
charged on his Conscience, & not long, ere
hee came, & confest somthing of the
accusation, y^t hee formerly denyed to
be true, & saw his Snare to deny the
whole, because hee could owne but a part,
but after a time, God Sett home his
great Sinne to his heart, & hee Carried
the burden of it, & after several ad=
dresses on his part, Justifying God & the
church, presenting Certaine papers of
his humiliation for so great a sinne,
& flying to Christ for his great mercy,
the Church were by little & little
enclined to take off his Censure, and
renew their charity to him, as one y^t
obtained mercy of the Lord.

Vide p. 22

Ester Dix an Adult member of
ye Church of Christ in Ipswich   she
owning the Covenant, had her
Children Baptised, her habitation being
removed to us, by letters of dismissiõ
shee & her children were recom̄ended
to our Church. 30 (8) 1665. & were
accordingly owned of us, as ours in y^e Lord
& her Child thereupon was Baptised.

The minds of the Brethrin being fixed   [15]

as to y^e practice of childrens duty

to owne y^e Covenant in order to

their Childrens Baptisme themselves

not in full Communion.

(1) It was propounded in a Church meeting

WHITHER Confederate visible be=

lievers in particular Churches and

their Infant seed whose next parents

one or both are in Covenant are

acknowledged according to Scripture to

be y^e approved members of y^e visible

Church of Christ?

(2) WHITHER the Infant seed of y^e Church

(being members of the same church

with their parents) when they are

Adult or growne upp, they are per=

sonally under the watch discipline

& goverment of that Church?

(3) WHITHER Adult members of the

Church who were admitted in their

minority, although they are not

therfore to be admitted to full com=

munion, because they are & Continue

members, without such further qua=

lifications as the word of God re=

quireth thereunto; yet nevertheless

they understanding the doctrine of
Faith & publikly professing their
assent thereunto: not scandalous
in life & solemnely Owning the
Covenant before y^e Church wherein
they give up themselves & their
Children to y^e Lord, & Subject them   [16]
selves to y^e Goverment of Christ in
the Church, their Children are to be
Baptised?
The propositions were voted, & passed
        on ye Affirmative part
The Brethrin consented thereto —
        — by their Silence —
        & afterwards by their usual signe
        nemine Contradicente.
wherefore the Names of their
Adult children were desired and
given that according to their
number a place of Meeting for
their Awakening might be Appoynted.

The Meeting attended the most of
ye Adult children of ye Church
were instructed referring to the
duty of Owning ye Covenant, &
Exhorted, comforted & charged as
the case of any of y^m required

& told them y^t after such a time

for their serious Consideration

they had liberty to come to y^e

Elder to be Examined & giving

him Encouragement there were

severall of them propounded to

y^e Church & then to y^e Congrega=

tion   & nothing scandalous objected

within a fourtnight were

owned, in order to y^r Childrens Baptism.

The Names of y^e Children of   [17]

y^e Church y^t were Owned at

severall publike meetings   as

13 (11) 1670.

John Browne	Eliz. Haugh
David Bachelor	Sarai Haugh
Thomas Bancroft	Marie Pierson
Hananiah Parker	Martha Parker
John Pierson	Sarai Eaton

3 (12) 70.

Benjamin Fitts	Rebecca Bowtall
John Parker	Eliz. Bancroft
Josias Browne	Sarai Kendall
Cornelius Browne	Eliz. Wellman
Edward Browne	

Nath. Parker

Abraham Wellman

Isaac Wellman

Joseph Browne

24 (12) 70.

Joseph Davis	Mary Briant
Samuell ffitts	Abigail Damon
John Eaton Junr	Mary Hooper
John Hartshorne	
	vid: p. 19

(2) It was propounded in a Church   [18]

meeting upon occasion.

WHITHER Such Church members

who either by Death or some

other Extraordinary providence

have been inevitably hindred

from publik acting as others,

yet have given the Church

cause in the Judgment of

charity to looke at them

as so qualifyed, & such as had

they been called thereunto

would have so acted, their

children are to be baptised.

The proposition voted & passt

on ye Affirmative p^t.

Tho. Parker Junr. who seemes
to be inevitably hindred by
the afflicting hande of God
upon him from publick owne
ing of ye Covenant his ac
quayntance with God in Christ
& desires after him not
withstanding being testifyd
by ye Elder Brother Jonas
Eaton & Brother Damon
was owned & his children Baptised.

14 (2) 71

[19]

Jeremy Swayne	Mary Swayne
Tho. Hartshorne	Hanna Bowtall
John Wiley	

9 (6) 72

Daniel Eaton	Mary Eaton
Jonas Eaton	Lydia Wiley
Joseph Eaton	

21 (1) 73

Joseph Fitts	Benjamin Smith
Samuell Lamson	John Nichols
Mary Haugh	Elizabeth Davis
Sarai Poole	Abigael Kendal
Mary Nichols	Sarai Dixe
Susan Wiley	Mary Dixe

Mary Lamson   Mary Haugh

14 (5) 76

Ruth Hooper   Sarah Wiley

18 (6) 76

Timothy Wiley

Susan Kendal   Elizabeth Clarke

Susan Davis

20 (8) 76

Mary Everite   Tabatha Kendal

9 (1) 77

Jonathan Parker   John Bancroft

         vide p. 23.

Hanna Davis Joyned & Baptized   [20]

John Townsend   Abigael Gold

Samuel Lamson   Mary Harndell

 vide. p. 21 &c

George Tomson   Rebecca Bowtall

Thomas Parker Jun[r]   Elizabeth Haugh

~~Henry Merrow~~   Sarah Haugh

John Eaton Jun[r]   Deborah Parker

Thomas Bancroft   Sarah Bancroft

         Abigael Rogers

Sarah Thomson   Mary Swayne

Seabred Taylor   Dorcas Eaton

Joseph Laurance   Sarah Dunton

John Browne   Mary Browne

Benjamin Fitts

Hananiah Parker

Nathaniel Goodin

John Pierson

Abigael Nichols

Elizabeth Wiley

Susan Goodwin

Hanna Boyton
alias Burnap
though she liveth
at Newbury yet
her earnest desires
were granted & she
was Joyned to this
Church and had com=
munion in ye Seals
of the covenant ∧ &
∧ yᵉ 12 (10) 1680.
carried Letters of
dismission to Rowly
Church.

Rebecca Eaton

Hanna Eaton   vid p. 21

George Tomson being in dying case

desired that hee might have favour

to Joyne yᵉ Church tho hee having

small hopes to come himselfe to Gods

Ordinances yet hoping & desireing Gods

Covenant grace for his posterity

his earnest desires were taken notice

of by the pastor with some Bʳⁱⁿ

for a testimony & his case was

propounded & hee admitted to Church

fellowshipp (tho absent in body) &

his Children were Baptized.

[21]

　　31 (1) 82.

James Bowtall　　　Elizabeth Fittch.

　　9 (5) 82.

Mʳ John Wenborne joyned with us

in Ch. fellowshipp & yet at his request by

Letters Recom̄ended to y^e care of y^e Church
of Christ in Yorke=Eastward, or otherwise.

14 (4) 83

Tabitha pierson   Mary Taylor

Mary Lamson   Mary Burnap

Sarah Hartshorne   Sarah Townsend

Joseph Browne   Eliz. Arnold   Sarai Wesson

John Parker   Jo: Bancroft   Mary Dam̄on

11 (9) 83 Capt. Swaine   Bethiah Parker   mary Nichols

          Tho. Nichols   mary polly   Joanna Gowing

                                                vide p. 26

Brother Briant having spoken   [22]

passionately in a Towne meeting

some B^rin offended notwithstanding

some acknowledgment made they

cast it into the church disorderly

& unseasonably but after a debate

about it consent was given that

hee must be helped by writeing

his acknowledgment being read

before the Townsmen on a Lectur

day satisfaction was given & taken.

Brother Nat. Cutler having greived

some brethrin in prosecuting a

Complaint y^t hee made against B^r

Pike a member of Charlstowne
Church that hee might be bound
to ye peace for breaking his head
they being both in a quarrilling passion
about a few cocks of hay, the said
brethrin laying hold of the case as
within their reach & giving serious
warnings they perswaded to be first
reconciled in private. Brother pike
being first in acknowledgment they
professed & endeavoured reconciliation
but after a time B^r pike according
to advice made an Essay 3 times by word
& writeing to satisfy the Congregation.
B^r Cutler (ye day y^t hee had a dead Corps
at home) with others were putt to Silence.

20 (2) 77

[23]

Benjamin Hartshorn   Thomas Nichols
John Dixe

5 (7) 77

Joseph Hartshorne   Mary Colson

17 (11) 77

Joanne Nichols   Mary Poole

05 (2) 78

Francis Smith   Elizabeth Winborne

21 (4) 78

Rebecca Hooper   Elizabeth Eaton

25 (12) 79/80

Joshua Eaton   Jonathan Eaton

6 (4) 80

Mary Davis alias widdow Grover
after Just Satisfaction given, was owned
of the Church & her children Baptized
Joseph Eaton after Just Satisfaction
given was ye 19 (7) 80 owned of ye Church
& carried letters of Dismission to the
Church in Beverlie.

24 (10) 80

Rebecca Eaton   Mary Thomson

11 (1) 81

Elizabeth Browne   Hanna Browne

14 (6) 81

Raham Bancroft Sam. Dixe   Timothy Hartshorne

vid. p. 25

The Church having had Some time of perusing   [24]
the Booke Called the platforme of Discipline, & it
being distinctly read in their hearing, & they
approved of it for the substance of it to be
according to the word of God, their vote being

called for, it passed on the Affirmative 9 (11) 79 &
no man Contradicted, thanks be to the Lord.

The Church being asked whither they owned that
Silent vote they made formerly Concerning the weake
that say they can't speake their Experience of grace
before many (according to ye platforme) at one meeting
two Brethrin at another seaven Brethrin owned it
25 (2) 80. The rest (at least) would have some Brethrin
Joyned with y^e Elders to heare & Judge & represent the
Brotherhood; whither the season Calls for it, or y^e person
must Speake before sufficient witnesses for y^e Churches
safety & the persons admonition to learne y^e feare of God.

Mary Davis having broken the seaventh Com=
mand of God before her marriage had a true
sense of her Sinne & the dishonour y^t Comes
to the gospell thereby & did bewayle it before
the Church, so as they did at length accept of
her repentance, & it being published to the
Congregation, & she desired to own the
Covenant, after she stood a time propounded
she was freely acknowledged the 6 (4) 80
member
to stand as an approved of the Church
Capable of ye previledges to her belonging.

~~Henry Merrow being~~ overtaken with
drinke abroad, God made him sensible of
the evill of his Sinne, & after having given

Just satisfaction to the Church, hee
bewayld it in ye publick, & gave others
warning of the Sinne ye 23 (3) 80. & was
received into ye hearts of good people

13 (11) 81

[25]

James Nicholes	Nathaniel Cowdry
Thomas Dammon	Joseph Dammon

3 (1) 82

Samuel Cowdry	Joseph Burnap
John Wesson	John Woodward

The Church consented that Jo. Wesson
though a member of the Church in Salem
yet hee might take the Covenant heere.

The Church were willing that John
Woodward (being under Brother Jo. Brownes
education, (& his parents pious in O: England
should take hold of the Covenant heere.

7 (2) 82

William Hooper	Hanna Hooper
	Elizabeth Hooper

23 (2) 82

Sarah Tomson alias Upton

19 (6) 83

Susannah Deverix —

— alias Hartshorne

7 (8) 83

Nathaniel Cutler

Hanna Pike   Sarai Cutler

3 (6) 84

Lydia Burnap   Sarai Bancroft

Mary Briant   Martha Eaton

7 (7) 84

John Parker   Thomas Burnap

Jeremy Swayne   James Bowtal

Hanna Sternes Accepted into love 3I (6) 84

vid p. 29

Ralph Dix   Elizabeth Eaton   [26]

James pike Sen[r] dismissed from Charlstowne

Josiah Browne   Cornelius Browne

Thomas Taylor Jun[r]

Mary Mackentir accepted & Baptized

Deliverance Belflower Baptised accepted

Sarah Bates

vide p. 22

22 (8) I684

This Church, in Conscience of

the Lords Exceeding care over

us that wee might bring forth

fruits meet for amendment

of Life. Considering how much
wee are Concerned in the holy
warnings given us referring to
ye Platforme of Discipline,
with ye Confession of Faith; &
the Childrens Interest in y^e
Covenant, the Lawes for a
Reformation, & the Lawes for
Sanctification of ye Sabbath
the Synods urging us by some
discovery of the provoaking Evills
with Certaine Expedients to
further a Reformation, & y^t a
Sollemne renewing of the
Covenant to be, (in Cases like
to ours) not displeasing to God

Wee, being conscious of our   [27]
breaking of the tables of y^e
Covenant by multiplied Moral
transgressions, with frequent
slighting of the new Testam^t
of our Lord and Saviour, with
the most sacred seales of it:
wee do in the feare of God
with selfe condemnings, upon
this day of publick humiliation, wee do, (from ye least

to ye greatest) attend to the

Reading of ye Covenant

& testify our Avouching of

the Lord to be ours &

our childrens forever;

trusting to ye merrits of

Christ, & ye exceeding

riches of Gods grace that

he will Remember his

Covenant made with us

& establish it, & give us all

hearts to feare him & keep

all his Commands allways

for our Everlasting good

for Evermore   Amen.

This done, in Conscience of Gods   [28]

good will Commended both by the

man of God Moses, Deut. Chap. 26 & 20

Exod. 19 & 20 & Nehemiah Chap. 9 & 10th

for our direction incouragement

& Admonition & ye Rebukes of our Lord.

Abraham Wellman	Sarah Wellman
Isaac Wellman	Hanna Wellman

3 (11) 1684

A Church-Order voted, con-

cerning ye Communicants pay

for ye Lords table Annually, y^e

yeare beginneth March 1st 1684/5.

That every one y^t have not com-

municated at that time or quarter

hee or she shall pay nothing, &

such as have Communicated a-

bove halfe a yeare they shall

pay but for ye halfe yeare,

y^t is ye proportion of Eighteene

pence in silver for a yeare, to

be privately paid to the Deacon,

within the season thereof.

John Bowtall	Rebeccah Nichols
Daniell Eaton	Mary Eaton
	John Wesson Junior

vid. p. 30

22 (12) 84   [29]

John Lilly	Samuell Lilly
William Eaton	John Eaton
Cornelius Browne	John Browne
Elizabeth Parker	Mary Burnap

19 (21) 85

David Hartshorne	John Bachellor
Ebenezer Bancroft	Matthew Edwards

12 (7) 86

Thomas Bowtall   Joseph Davis

17 (11) 86

Mary Poole   Mary Bancroft

Mary Parker   Elizabeth Browne

Sarai Browne   Sarai Bachellor

Lydia Cutler   Mary Cowdry

Brigett Fitch   Judith Mason

20 (12) 86

John Parker   Samuell Poole

Henrie Bachellor   William Eaton

Samuell Parker   George Tomson

Dugliss Tomson   Thomas Parker

William Cowdry   John Tomson

John Bowtall   Samuell Parker

Benjamin Swayne   Eliz. fflint.

7 (6) 87

Susan Lawrence   Martha Browne   Mary Eaton

                                     vide[8]

Francis Hutcherson   Joshua Eaton   [30]

Mary Burnap   Elizabeth Bancroft

Sarah Browne   Richard Harnden

John Nichols   Mary Wesson

          Dorcas Gould

Brother Seabred Taylor for some

misdemenour was privately instructed &

warned of the Church, but upon his
sense of God therein, was reconciled and
unanimously taken into favour againe.

Edward Marshall	Marie Smith
Abigael Briggs	Sarah Browne
Nathaniel Parker	James Nicholes
John Burnap	Samuel Damon
David Hartshorne	Jonas Eaton
Elizabeth Felch	Hanna pike
Jonathan Eaton	Timothy Hartshorne
Rebecca Hartshorne	Martha Hartshorne
Thomas Dammon	Lucian Dammon
Mary Taylor	Elizabeth Cowdry
Sarai Cutler	Sarah wesson
Jane lilly	Cornelius Browne
Henry Bellflour	William Arnold Bap: & accepted.
Susanna Hooper	Mary Cutler
Thomas Barnap	Jeremiah Swayne
John Browne	William Robins
William Eaton	Nathaniel Gowing
Margaret pike	Mary Burnap
Mary Burt Baptized & Confirmed	
Joseph Hartshorne	John Eaton Juni[r]
John Woodward	Sarah Woodward
John Parker Juni[r]	Nathaniel Cowdry Juni[r]
James Bowtall Juni[r]	Matthew Edwards
Samuell Smith	Rebeccah Dutton

[31]

Benjamin Hartshorn   Elizabeth Hartshorn

Marie Poole

[. . .]⁹

And Sett them in Joynt againe that have   [31a]

been through Infirmity overtaken in any

fault amongst us.

(4) Wee will not in yᵉ Congregation be

forward to shew our gifts or parts in

Speaking, nor be ready to disgrace our

Brethrin or discover their faylings, but

attend an orderly Call before wee putt

forth our selves, doing nothing to the

offense of yᵉ Church, but in all things

endeavouring our owne & our Brethrins

edification, & trust God.

(5) Wee further bind our selves in yᵉ strength

of christ to labour how wee may ad-

vance the Gospell, & how wee may

advance the Kingdome of Christ, & how

wee may winne & gayne those yᵗ

are without, & how we may settle

grace & peace among our selves, &

seeke as much as in us lieth the

peace of all the Churches, seeking

yᵉ helpe & Counsell & direction of

other Churches if neede be, not

putting any Stumbling block before
any, but labouring to abstayne from
all Appearance of evill.

(6) WEE do hereby promise to behave &
demeane our selves obediently in all
lawfull things to those that God
hath placed over us in ye Church or
Commonwealth. Knowing that its
our duty not to greive them, but to
Encourage them in their places & in
the Administration of their Charge
that God has committed to them.

(7) WEE resolve in ye same Strength   [31b]
to approve our selves in our particular
Callings, shuning Idlenes not sloathful
in business, knowing that Idlenes is
ye bane of any Society &c: neither
will we deale hardly or oppressingly
with any wherein wee are the Lords
Stewards, Promising to our best
abillities to Teach our Children
good Knowledge of the Lord that
they may also Learne to serve &
feare him with us, that it may
goe well with them & with us
for ever.

memorand. That those words in the tenth
Line, that is to say, WITH OUR SEEDE

18 (II) 1670 AFTER US IN THEIR GENERATIONS

were inserted with the consent

of yᵉ Brethren.

Daniel Gould[10]   [31c]

Daniel Gould Jun

Samuell Sprͣgue

Ebenezer Knight

Ebenezer Parker

Thomas Cutler

David Gould

Epherem ~~Lehelly~~ Larrbee

Abraham Gould

Jacob How

Edward bucknam

Joseph Bryant

Jonathan Griffin

Thomas Burnap[11]	Jeremiah Swaine	John Brown	[31d]
William Robins	William Eaton	Nathaniel Gowing	
Margaret Pike	Mary Burnap	Joseph Hartshorne	
John Eaton Junʳ	John Woodward	Sarah Woodward	
John Parker Junʳ	Nathaniel Cowdry Junʳ	James Boutel Junʳ	
Mathew Edwards	Samuel Smith	Rebecca Dutton	
Benjamin Hartshorn Senʳ	Elizabeth Hartshorn	Mary Pool	
Mary Burt Baptized & Confirmed			

2ᵈ. 11ᵐ. 1687

Voted in the Affirmative that a blame less

person, who by His personall Act professing
his, or Her assent publickly Unto the Christian
faith according to the word of God, Contained in
the Holy Scriptures, & His beleif in God ye father in
Jesus Christ His onely Son, and in His holy Spirit, to
bring him to God, & by renouncing sin, the world,
& Satan, & solemnly taking the Covenant, Accord
ing to the 5th proposition, in the Synod book 62[12]
as an Expedient for the Church seed to Receive
baptisme for their Children, the which in
Ecclesiasticall Charitable reputation may Evidence His Right & fittness to be baptised himself
& His Children.

8^d. 11^m. 1687
Richard Temple —baptised
Job Lane — baptised
Edward Polley —baptised & Confirmed
John Tonie —Baptised[13]

June 18. 1688. The Revd Mr John Brocke de
ceased.

[32]

July 1. 1688. J. Pierpont being Invited, preach
ed first at Reading.

Sept. 10. 1688. J. P. was invited to ~~preach~~ engadge in the
work of the ministry in Reading.

June 26. 1689. J. Pierpont was Ordained
Pastor of the Church of Reading.

—————

Persons received in
to ye Church. An. Dom.
1689.[14]

July. 7. 1689. Mercy Hutchenson owned ye Covenant

July 14. Hañah Stearns

and was Baptised.

Aug. 4. Mary Fish own'd ye Cov: & was Baptised.

Aug. 25. Mary &
Sarah } Burt own'd ye Cov: & w^r Baptised.

Dec. 10. John Boutel, Abiah Briant, & Jonathan
Tompson, Owned the Coven^t.

Febr. 9. Mary Swain, Eliz. Fitch, Eliz. Goodwin,
Eliz. Frothingham, Sar. Bennet, Sar: Townsend
Abig. Weston, Abig. Lilly, Jos. Fitch
Saml Weston, Tho. Rist, Reub. Lilly,
owned the Covenant.

And - Anna Fitch, Mary Hay, John Swain
Saml Swain, Josiah Hodgman, owned the
Coven^t & were Baptised.

— — — — — — —

1690. June 24. Isaac Southwick } owned ye Cov:
Tho. Stimson - - } & w^r Baptis'd.

July. Eliz. Cutler, Deliver: Hobs, Mary Jones; Baptisd.

Aug. 17. Hannah Boutel, Sarah Parker, ⎫ ownd
Liddea Kendal. Sarah Streeter, ⎬ the Cov.
Tho. Briant. Saml Dunton. ⎭

Nov. 23. John Swain. Tho. Pool. ⎫ owned y^e
Tho. Bancroft. John Goodwin. ⎬ Covenant.
Josh. Davis. - - - - - - - ⎭

NB: Febr. 15. Deacon Fitch ordained.

Mercy Hutchenson.

Aug. 11. Eliz. Coudrey
Hañah Duntlin.

Sept. 8. Shub^l Stearns
Mary Fish.

Oct. 27. Andr. Phillips
Saml Pool.
Sarah Davis.
John Torie, a black.

Dec. 29. Willm Eaton
Saml Lilly.

Feb. 23. Eliz. Waltham
Sarah Burnet.
Liddea Dix.

1690
March. Timothy Willy.
Job Lane.

Jun. 8. Jos. Dutton
Liddea Cutler.
Ruth. Dunton.

July 6. Steph. Fish.
Jos. Burnap.
David Fox.
Mary Burt. Junr

Oct. 5. Sarah Upton.
Benjamin Swain.
Eben: Bancroft.

Nov. 2. Thankf. Parker.
23. Liddea Burnap.

			Jan. II. Martha Gold.

1691

May 31. M. Colson publickly Admonish'd for Fornication.

Jun. 7.   Ab. Lilly publickly admonished for Fornication.

———

	Hannah Brown,	Eliz. Pool.	Mehit. Bancroft
	Rebec. Dunton.	Grace Eaton.	Susan Hartshorn
Sept.	Sarah Hartshorn.	Eben: Emerson.	Eben. Parker.
	Nathan Batchelder.	Nicol. Brown.	Saml Frothingham.
	Tho. Davis.	Nath. Warren.	Owned ye Covn^t.

1691.

July 27.   Jonath. Pool.

   Ruth Briant.

Febr. 7.   Phil. Makentire

Car. ov^r 33

brought ov^r 33^{15} [33]

———

1692.   Apr. Tab. Pond own'd ye Coven^t.

May.	Miriam Merry	Abig. Rogers
	Abig. Gold.	Adam Hart

} Own'd ye Covenant.

June.	John Dickerman.	John Upton
	Rebec. Hamlet.	John Cole
	July 21.Benjam. Larrabee, Baptised.	

} own'd ye Cov: and were Baptised.

Aug.	Mary Fitch.	Sarah Boutel.	Eliz. Arnold.
	Dorcas Burnap.	Hen: Frothingham.	Bethiah Burnap.
	Ana Davis.	Mary Tounsend.	Benj: Burnap.
	Nath. Goodwin.	Kendal Parker.	Joh. Nickols.
	Willm. Briant.	Willm Sawyer.	

} own'd the Co venant.

Persons received into
   the Church.
1692.

March 13. John Cole, Senr.

July 22.   Eliz. Newel.

   Sarah Dickermam

   John Dickerman.

   Tho. Boutel.

   John Boutel.

   Saml Batchelder.

   Abrah. Briant.

Aug. 14. Elizab. Pierpont.

Oct. 16.   John Pool.

   Mary Jones.

Jan. I.   Mary Eaton.

   Eliz. Boutel.

1693. Apr. Sarah &   Hartshorn, own'd ye Covenant.
              Ha̅nah

June.   Deb. Parker.   Mary Parker.   ⎱
        Mary Merrow. Deb: Merrow   ⎰ owned ye Coven^t.

May.   Jos. Damon manifesting Repentance of a Sin he had

        comited, was accepted.

        Eliz. Russel.   Francis Nurse.   ⎱
        Sarah Nurse.   Mary Broun.   ⎰ ownd ye Coven^t.

1694.

        Marg. Leeman.   Hephsib. Swain.   John Nickols.

        John Tounsend.   James Pierson.   Tho. Grover.

        Saml. Broun.   Jos. Carter.   Henery Wilson

        Ephraim Broun.   Owned the Covenant.

        Josiah Broun   Saml Lambson.   Stephen Johnson

        Mathew Grover,   Owned the Coven^t.

1695.   Mary Colson & Abig. Lilly manifesting

        Repentance of their Sins were accepted.

                   n
Apr.   Joana Jefferds ownd the Covenant.
                   ^

July 7. Steph. Johns. Admonished for Scandalous Sins

        afterwards manifesting Repentence was Loosed.

        Mary Bancroft.   Tabit. Pierson.   Mary Everit.

        Mary Streeter.   Rebec. Eaton.   Mary Lambson.

        Rebec. Pierse.   Owned the Covenant.

Feb. 16. Ha̅nah Endicut, Baptised.

1693.

March. 26.   Ruth Eaton.

Oct. 9.   Mary Swain

             Sarah Bancroft.

             Ana Briant.

             Eliz. Broun.

             Sarah Parker.

             Sarah Gowing.

             Ha̅nah Lilly.

1694

July 1.   John Goodwin.

             Thom. Bancroft.

July 15.   Mary Pool

             Ruth Smith.

Jan: Abig. Boutel.

             Marg: Leeman

1695.

Apr. 21.   Bridget Pool.

             Abig. Bancroft.

             Henery Loomis.

Jan. 21.   Francis ⎱ Smith
             Ruth   ⎰

1696.

        Mary Broun.   Tabitha Boutel.

        Eliz. Edwards,   owned the Covenant.

1696.

Mehit. Tounsend.

Carry ov^r 66

Brought ov^r 66.   [34]

1697.

Apr: M^r Jn. Perkins. Richard Nickols. John Willey.

           Nathan^l Parker. Kendal Briant.   Jonath Bancroft.

           Saml Damon.   Jonath. Parker.   Owned ye Coven^t

May.   Sarah Swain.   Susan͞a Goodwin. Rebec. Arnold.

           Eliz. Eaton.   Joanna Lambson. Owned ye Coven^t

William Sawyer & Abig. Lilly were admonished

publickly for Fornication.

Mary Merrow, & Ana Holden, owned ye Coven^t.

Sept. 5. Sarah Hayes, Sarah Grover, Eliz. Grover w^r Baptised.

Persons received
into the Church.
1697.

June 4.   Marg. Swain.

          Peter Hinkson

          Stephen Wesson.

Aug. 21. Eliz. Upham

          Sarah Bates.

Sept. 19. Eliz. Russel

          Han͞ah Eaton.

          Nov. 28. Anna Fitch.

Dec.   Sarah Hayes.

          Rebec. Bates.

Feb. 27. Willm. Russel.

1698.

March.   Tho. Grov. was admonished for Scandalous evils.

Jan. 22. Confessing his sins he was loosed and accepted.

June 26. Jonathan Parker. John Makentire.

         Edward Broun.Mary Boutel.

         Eliz. Boutel.Owned the Covenant.

Sept. 18. M. Salmon was publickly admonished

1698.

June 26. Tho. Briant.

Aug. 21. M^{rs} An: E͞merson.

Oct. 7. Sarah Prat.

          Rebecca Upton.

Jan. 1.   Joh. Boutel.

          Sarah Boutel.

for the Sin of Drunkenness.

Samuel Hart & Sarah Hart, owned the Coven.ᵗ

1699.

Apr. 30. Sarah Roberts, owned yᵉ Covenᵗ & was Baptisd.

July 2.   Deborah Hopkins was Baptised.

Febr. 5. Tho. Nickols, & John Bancroft, own'd yᵉ Covenᵗ.

Febr.   Rebec. Nickols. Hannah Elsely, Barbara Elsely,

and Hañah Streeter,   owned the covenᵗ.

1700. March. 31. Wᵐ. Sawyʳ. manifesting Repentance, was ac-
    cepted.

July 28. Hannah Cañady owned the Covenᵗ and was baptised, with her Children. David Cannady also owned

the Covenᵗ and was baptised.

Aug. 18. John Ingersol, owned the Covent & was baptised.

Sept. Mary Rich ownd yᵉ Covenᵗ. // Abig. Boutel, owned yᵉ Cove

nant, and was baptised.   Novemb. Han. Bates own'd the Covenant.

Decemb. 1. Mary Salmon was cast out of the Church for

continuing in the Sin of Drunkeness, after publick admo

Feb. 26. John Dix.

1699.

March. 12. Mary Giggles.

        Tho. Pool.

Apr. 2.   John Going.

        Ellenor Larrabe.

——— 9. John Prat.

Oct. 15. Mʳˢ Reb. Brown.

        Deborah Hopkins.

Dec. 24. Mary Briant.

        Mary Batchelder.

        Rebec. Davis.

Feb. 4.   Tabitha Goodwin.

        Grace Boutel.

        Abig. Upham.

        Eliz. Hastings.

1700.

March.   John Parker.

        Elizab. Parker.

May 12. 8 sp. Feltch.[16]

        Hannah Green.

June 9.   Dorcas Walden.

July 7.   Rebec. Parker.

Sept. 1.   Mary Bancroft.

        Mehitab: Parker.

Octob.   Hañah Cañady.

nition.

Nov: 3. Deliver: Parker.

Decemb. 22. Eliz. Burnap.

Carry over 109.

Brought over 109.   [35]

1701.

April. 13. Mary Roberts, Ann Roberts, Eliz. Roberts,

Owned the Covenant, and were Baptised.

May 18. Mary Damon,   Abigail Parker,   Han: Eaton,

Sarah Eaton,   Bethiah Parker,   Mary Nickols,

Tabitha Briant,   Thomas Nickols, Kendal Boutel.

—— 25. Raham Bancroft, James Nickols, Willm Arnold.

Joseph Eaton, Owned the Covenant.

June 22. John Pierson,   Joshua Eaton,   John Foster,

Joseph Underwood, Owned ye Covenant.

—— David Hartshorn, and Rebecka his wife were dis-

missed to the Church in Norwich.

Sarah Ebbons, Lucy Daman, Dorcas Gold, owned ye Covenant.

Received into the Church,

1701.

May 11.   Tabitha Boutel.

Nicol: Brown.

July 13.   Susanna Roberts.

Aug. 10.   Rebec. Pool.

—— 17.   Priscilla Smith.

Nov. 2.   Mrs Flint.

Rebec. Brown.

Jan. 11.   Samuel Damon, Junr

John Bancroft, Junr

1702.

Eliz Swain, Mary Harvard, and Mehet. Gold,

Owned the Covenant.

[———————————————]^17

Samuel Merrow having been guilty of frau-

dulent dealing and lyeing, the Church sent to

him to Come to them on May 3. but he came not.

May 17. The Church sent for him again, but

he came not.   It was then voted by the Church

1702.

March. 1. Nathaniel Parker,

Jonathan Parker.

May 31.   Eliz. Boutel.

June, 7.   Mr Peter Emerson

June 28. Hephs. Pierson.

Tabitha Burnap.

Sarah Swain.

Mary Parker.

y[t] he should be admonished for his sins. July 26.

He was sent for, came, and was admonished.

May 31　Judith Bancroft, & Eliz. Eaton, owned y[e] Coven[t].

July.　　Eliz. Parker, Martha Emmons. Kendal Goodwin.

　　　　Timothy Willey,　　Owned the Covenant.

Sept. 13. Rebec Pierson,　⎫
　　　　　　　　　　　　　⎬ Owned the Covenant.
—— 20 Abig. Wellman　⎭

Oct. 11. Hannah Brown, —- Nov. 8. Sarah Welman, Own'd Cov[t].

Nov. 15. Abig. Ebbons Own'd the Coven[t] & was baptised.

Nov.　　Sam[l] Walton, John Smith　⎫
　　　　　　　　　　　　　　　　　⎬ Own'd y[e] Covenant.
　　　　Isaac Smith. Nath. Evens　⎭

　　　　The last of these was Baptised.

Dec.　　Annis Gowing owned the Covenant.

Febr. 7.　Jonath. Barret, Abig. Barret, Daniel Gold,

　　　　own'd y[e] Covenant. The first of these was Baptis'd.

1703

Apr. 25.　M[rs] Jenkinson, owned the Covenant.

May. 9.　Mary Jefferds own'd the Covenant.

Aug. 1.　John Wesson, Tho. Eaton, Ebenezar Daman,

　　　　Jonath. Eaton, Eben: Taylor, Own'd y[e] Coven[t].

Octob. 3. Marg. Bates, owned the Covenant.

Nov. 14.　Ruth Taylor owned the Covenant.

Jan. 2.　Bethyah Williams, own'd Coven[t] and

　　　　was Baptized.

　　—— Susanna Parker, Abigail Daman,

　　　　Sarah Boutell, Susana Boutel,

　　　　Dorcas Burnap, & Hanah Merry, own'd Coven[t].

Febr. 6. Hannah White, own'd the Coven[t].

　　　　　　　　Hannah Sterns.

Aug. 30.　Sarah Broun.

　　　　Joseph Hastings.

　　　　Oct. 4. Mary Feltch.

Nov. 1.　　Sarah Tounsend.

Febr. 28.　John Pierson, Jun[r]

1703.

Apr. 18.　Sarah Pike.

　　　　James Pierson.

　　　　Daniel Snow.

　　　　John Tounsend.

May. 30.　Sarah Bancroft.

　　　　Deborah Temple.

　　　　Thomas Wesson.

Aug. 1.　Eliz. Cutler.

Oct. 24.　Eliz. Wellman.

Febr. 20.　Mary Broun.

———- 20. Rebecca Hinkson, own'd Coven.t, and was baptis'd

Carry ov.r 142.

Brought ov.r 142.　　　[36]

1704.

Apr. 30. Cather. Smith, & Mary Walton, Own'd y.e Coven.t

May 7. Naomi Grover, was baptised

——— 28. Anna Foster, & Sarah Foster, were baptised.

July 16. Mary Cann, ~~owned the~~ Publickly manifested Repentance of a Sin she had formerly comited, and owned the Covenant.

July 30. Abig. Eaton own'd the Covenant.

Aug. 1. Mary Green, (formerly Parker) Dismissed to the Church in Woburn.　　And

Mary Polly, Dismissed to the Church at Colchester, in Connect:

Aug. 20. Mary Batchelder, Mary Arnold, Mary Fish, Sarah Fish, & Sarah Daniels, own'd the Covenant.

1705.　　Joseph Hartshorn, & Sarah his wife were Dismissed to the Church in Dedham.

Aug. 12. Judith Nichols, Sarah Lampson & Phineas Upham, jun.r Owned the Covenant.

Sept. 2. Benjamin Willey, Joseph Daman, Timothy Goodwin, & Ebenezer Nickols, Owned the Covenant.

Octob. 7. Kendal Pierson, & John Bates, owned

Persons received into the Church.
An. Dom. 1704.

March 19. Anne Roberts.

Apr. 9.　　Dorcas Sawyer.

　　　　Sarah Foster.

May 7.　　Jonath. Bennet.

　　　　Abigail Bennet.

June 4.　　Tho. Upham.

——— 25.　　Anne Holdin.

July 30.　　Martha Parker.

Sept. 3.　　M.rs Jenkinson.

　　　　Tabitha Brooks.

Oct. 15.　　Ruth Tayler.

Dec. 17.　　Richard Bolcher.

March. 11.

Abigail Garey.

Apr. 15.　　Eliz: Batcheldor,

　　　　John Walker.

Aug. 19.　　Sarah Gold.

Sept. 16.　　Eliz. Briant.

　　　　Eliz. Makentire.

Oct. 26.　　Rebec: Pierson

the Covenant.

Nov. 4. Eben: Daman, Abraham Wesson, Benjam:

Johnson, & James Nickols, own'd the Covenant.

Nov. 25. Tim. Hartshorn, Junr Own'd the Covenant.

— Miriam Ashfield, was baptised.

Jan. 13. Susanna Pierson, Mary Boutel, Dorcas Eaton,

and Phebe Eaton, Owned the Covenant.

Mary Nickols.

Dec: 2. Tabitha Briant.

Abig: Eaton.

Joaña Lambson.

Decr. 9. Judith Bancroft.

Eliz. Eaton.

Febr. 10. John Smith,

Eliz. Smith,

Abig: Hawkins.

John Nickols, jun^r.

1706.   March 31. Eliz: Bacheldor, Eliz: Bancroft,

Hephsibah Brown, & Eliz: Jefferds, own'd ye Covenant.

Apr. 28. Sarah Lewis, entred into Covenant & was Baptised.

June 16. Mary Pierson, Eliz: Willey, Esther Daman,

and Tabitha Burnap, Own'd the Covenant.

July 14. Hannah Wellman,   Own'd ye Coven^t.

——— 28. Mary Jenkins & Martha Chadwick, entred into Co-

venant and were baptised.

March. 10. Barbara Elseley.

Mary Batcheldor.

Apr. 14. William Briant.

May 5. Bethiah Parker.

Eliz. Grover.

Sarah Eaton.

June 2: Eliz. Lambson.

Aug. 30. Mary Brown, (wid.)

Mary Nickols.

Rebec: Briant.

Jos: Underwood.

Sept. 22. Susaña Parker.

Oct. 20. Batcheldor.[18]

Sarah Batcheldor.

Hannah Batcheldor.

Eliz: Cutler.

Carry over 187.

Brought ov[r] 187   [37]

<u>Receiv'd into ye Church.</u>

Oct. 20.   Phebe Brown.

            Hañah White.

            Jonathan Eaton.

Dec. 15.   Nathan: Goodwin

            Ebenezer Emerson.

Jan. 26.   Kendal Goodwin.

1707.

May. 23. John Layton, own'd the Covanant.

June, 8.   Mary Gold, own'd the Covenant.

—— 22.   Eliz: Dix, owned the Covenant.

July. 6.   Joseph Parker, Eben: Parker, &

         Timothy Manning,   Own'd y[e] Covenant.

Oct. 26. Sam[l]. Lewis, Entred into Covenant, &

         was Baptised.

Jan. 4.   Jane Belcher, & Mary Grover,

            own'd the Covenant.

NB. Dec. 31. Tho: Boutel, was chosen Dea-

con

Apr: 4.   Phebe Rise.

May. 25. Kendal Parker.

July. 20.   Tho: Taylor.

Aug. 24.   Mary Taylor.

Sept. 21. M[rs]. Sarah Hart.

Nov. 23.   Martha Makentire.

Dec. 7.   Susanna Broun

———   Hannah Garey.

<u>1708</u>   May 23: Eliz. Harndel, was Baptised.

June. 12. Mary Eaton own'd the Covenant.

Sept. 5.   John Lambson, Thomas Burnap,

         Mercy Daman, & Sarah Burnap,

         own'd the Covenant.

NB. Sept. 12. Thomas Boutel was

ordained a Deacon of y[e] Church.

March. 21. Sam[l]. Holdin.

            Thomas Nickols, jun[r].

June 27.   Joseph Daman.

July 25.   Ruth Parker.

            Samuel Parker, (Lyn)

Aug. 8.   Susana Pierson.

            Judith Nickols.

Oct. 3.   Tho. Eaton, (Lyn) own'd the Covenant.

Nov. 7.   Rachel Atwol, Baptised.

Dec. 26. Mary Stimson, entred into Cove-

nant and was Baptised.

Sept. 12. Abigail Nickols.

Oct. 18. Sarah Wellman.

_____

1709.

Apr. 3.   Mary Knight, own'd the Covenant.

—— 17. Rebekah Miller, own'd the Covenant.

May.   Eliz. Boutel and Susaña Pond, own'd

the Covenant.

The Reverend M^r. Jonathan

Pierpont Departed this Life

on y^e 2 June 1709. — — — —[19]

Apr. 17. Mary Jenkins.

Total facit. 210

_____

1711   Apr. 22nd R: Brown upon invitation given, first

preached at Reading.

& accepted y^e call y^r given him to y^e pastoral office in

y^t Church about y^e 12th of Septemb^r, & w^s admited in

to y^s Chh y^e Sabbath before his ordination.

R: Brown w^s ordained pastor of y^s Church June 25th 1712.

[38]

John Burnap and his wife both admited memb^rs of y^s Church

1712 July 6th upon y^r Request to y^s Church, w^r orderly dismist

& recomended to ye Church of Christ at Windham.

Persons y^t have owned ye Covenant		Persons Received into Church fellowship since I w^s ordained — viz:
1712	Augt 10th. John Merrow Junr.	1712 July 20 Shubael Stearns.
	Augt 24 Samuell Stearns (Lyn)	~~Augt 24th Sam^ll Ste~~
Sep^t: 28	Elizabeth Boutel.	Augt 24th Mary wife of Jo: Eaton
Novr 16	Joshua Felt.	Sept: 28 Kendal Pearson & Lydia his wife (Lyn)

Deacon Thomas Bancroft Stone, Wakefield, Mass. Cemetery. Courtesy First Church of Wakefield, Mass.

Rev. Jonathan Pierpont Stone, Wakefield, Mass. Cemetery. Courtesy First Church of Wakefield, Mass.

Nov^r: 23^d John Slaughter.

Dec^r: 28th Sarah Jeffords. &

Mary Eaton (Lyn)

Jany 4th. Mary Libbey (Lyn)

Feby 15th John Roby

Jonathan Gowing.

————

1713

March 8th Caleb Taylor

Thomas Parker

Thomas Wesson

Joseph Arnold.

A record of Such as have own'd

ye Covenant. —— —— ——

1713 Elizabeth Cowdrey &

May 24 Elizabeth Damon.

June 14 Thomas Green (Maldon)

Augt 2. Mary Eburn (Lyn)

Sep^t 13 Abigail daught^r of Ens: Parker.

Sarah daught^r of Abra: Bri: Junr

Hannah Daman

Abigail Wright.

Octo: 11. Benjamin Damon

Obediah Parker

John Lilley.

Octob^r 24 John fish &

Dorcas ~~Gold~~ Brown

Nath: Stone

Elizabeth Bancroft &

Mary Briant.

Nov^r: 23. Timothy Hartshorn jun^r

Joshua Felt.

Elisabeth Nickols.

& Sarah Felt.

Dec^r: 28 Joseph Eaton

Esther Gowing

Jany 24th Matthew Grover &

Mercy Damon.

Hannah Bates.

17^20

A record of Such as [40]

are received in ye Church.

1712

Feb: 8th. Samuell Dix.

Timothy Goodwin

James Smith

———— Mary wife of Sam^ll Brown.

Eliz: wife of Tim: Goodwin.

1713

March 8th Nathaniel Batchelder.

Abiel Goodwin.

May 24th Lamuel Lewis and

Sarah Lewis his wife, &

Lucy ye wife of K: Boutel.

Mary ye wife of Jno Fish.

Feb 7th   Tabitha Goodwin

═══════════

[1714]

May 9th   Susanna Cowdrey

July 25   Issabell Hays &

       Joannah Phillips   } Charls:

Jan^ry 16.   Abigail Hodgman.

─────────

1715

April 24th   Thomas Hutchinson &

       Elizabeth his wife

       Mary Slaughter

       Sarah Slaughter. (Lyn)

May 8.   John Dickerman.

A Record of Such as have own'd

ye Covenant.

May 31   Caleb Taylor.

July 12.   Wm Batchelder.

Augt 16   Thomas Green (Mauldon)

Augt 30th   Eliza: wife of Nath:

       Parker Junr.

Sep^t 13th   Ephraim Chandler.

Octob^r 11th   Hannah Eaton.

Nov: 8th   Samuell Leman &

       Thomas Parker.

Novr 15   Hepsibah Brown.

1714   ─────────────

April 4th   John Batchelder.

June 27th   Jonathan Nickols.

Augt 15th   John Stearns.

       Naomi Grover

       Mary Boutell.

A Record of Such as are   [42]

recieved into ye Church

1715 June 15 Martha Williams

July 31   Jonathan Hibbard

       Ruth Fish &

       Sarah Grover (of Charl:T:)

Augt 14   Abigail Hadly wife

       of Anthony Hadley. &

       Mary Holden.

Sept: 11th Hannah daught^r of Henry

       Green of Charlestown ~~&~~

       ~~Tho: Cutler jun^r of Charlest: End~~

       own'd ye Covenant.

Sep^t 12th   Anna Brown

Sep^t 26   Ens: Jonathan Parker.

Jan^r 19th   Eliz: wife to Jonath: Nikols

─────

Ap: 17th

1715.   Susannah Harndel.

May. I.   Samuel Bancroft.

May 22.   Martha (wife of Nath: Gowing)

Jun: 5th   Mary Eaton.

June 15th   Timothy Baldwin sen^r

       Sarah Bancroft ye wife of S: B:

June 28   D: Nath Larenie (dismist from y^e

May 6th: Sam^{ll} Foster ownd y^e

    Cove: & w^s baptized.

May 27th Martha Hartshorn ownd ye Coven^t.

~~1718 Augt 24th~~

    ~~Anna ye wife of Eben:~~

    ~~Knight of Charlstown End~~

    ~~ownd ye Covenant.~~

	chh of Groton) w^s rec^d to o^r Com̄)
July 17th	Mary wife of Zac: Howard
	Eliz: Harndell
Augt 17th	Ebenezar Parker
	Jonathan Gawing
	Joanna Goold.
Sep^t 18th	Joseph Parker.
Novr 13th	Sam^{ll} Hart.

1716

April 29th	Benjamin Burnap.
	Benjamin Bigsby &
	Martha Bigsby his wife.
	Timothy Maning & his wife
	Susanna Maning.
	Ruth Upham of Charlst: End.
May 13th	Kendal Boutell.
	John Wiley.
	Samuell Lambson
	Benjamin Daman
	Thomas Upham Junr
	Dorkas ye wife of John Wiley
	Mercy ye wife of Benj: Daman

                                   29

Those y^t have ownd ye Cove^t:

A Record of y^{os} who are   [44]

    received into ye Church.

1716

May 27	Isaac Smith. & his wife
	Mary ~~Smith his~~

1716.

June 10ᵗʰ Elizabeth yᵉ wife of Eben:
            Daman Senʳ.
            Susanna Daman.

July 8ᵗʰ.   Mercy Fish
            Abigail Roberts
            Elizabeth Taylor.

July 15ᵗʰ Hannah daughtʳ of Jnº Eaton
            Sarah Furbush

Octobʳ 28ᵗʰ Sarah Goold of C:T: End.

1717   June 16ᵗʰ
            Tabitha Brown.

Feb: 2ⁿᵈ. Thomas Cutler (Charlstown)
            & Hannah Green of Malden.

Feb: 9ᵗʰ   Mehetable Daman

            Ann Nickols.
            Abigail Taylor.
            Elizabeth Upham.

June 10ᵗʰ   Kendal Briant.
            Raham Bancroft of Reading

June 24ᵗʰ   John Layton.

July 15ᵗʰ   John Bates
            Mary Cole wife of Jnº Cole
            Sarah yᵉ wife of Step: Wesson Junʳ.
            Mary yᵉ wife of Nath: Goodwin.

Septᵗ 2ⁿᵈ: Elizabeth Taylor
            Sarah Furbush.

Octobʳ: 7ᵗʰ   Abigail Aburn

Novʳ 11ᵗʰ   Mary Wesson.

Feb. 10ᵗʰ   Esther Pool.
            Dorkas Burnap.

1717

March 23ᵈ Ebenezer Nicols

July 21   Mʳ Jonathan Pierpont
            Hannah Wesson

Augᵗ 18ᵗʰ   Thomas Nicols Junʳ
            Sarah Briant.

Novʳ 3ᵈ   Sarah Hawks (Lynn)

Janʳʸ 5ᵗʰ   Joannah Phillips.

Feb: 9ᵗʰ   Mary Phillips (Charlest=End.)
            & Lydia Bancroft dismist from[21] New
            bury West Chh: to us.

<u>26</u>

Carry ov^r 96

Those y^t have owned y^e Cove:

A record of Such as are   [46]

rec^d into full Communion.

1718

March 2nd   Judeth wife of Jno Goold

jun^r of Charlstown End.

~~Sep^t 14th~~   ~~John Brown 3^d~~

Augt 24.   Anna ye wife

of Ebenezer Knight ownd

ye Covenant.

1718

March 30th   Jonathan Pool Junr

May 11th   Joel Jenkins.

June   29   M^r. Nathaniel Henchman

Edward Brown

Benjamin Pool

Sarah wife of Dan^{ll} Goold Senr.

July   6.   Sarah, wife to Edwd Brown

July   20   Hannah Hay.

Sarah Nicols.

Elizabeth Parker.

July   27   Hannah Walton

Sep^t   14   Mary Fish.

Ruth Fish.

October   12   Lydia Eaton &

Anna Knight (Charlst:)

Nov^r   9   Daniell Goold Senr.

Nov^r   30   Ebenezer Knight

Daniel Goold jun^r.

1719

April   26   Elizabeth Baldwin

May   24   Tho: Burt sen^r aged 79 y^{rs}.

31   William flint &

Abigail his wife

June	7	Naomi Holding.
July	26	Mary Eaton aged 77
		Sarah Prat.
Aug^t	2	Mary wife of Jn° Fish.
	9	Ann ye wife of Ensign
		Jonathan Parker.
		Mary Flint.
		28.

brout ov^r persons rec^d to Com^n: 124   [48]

Those y^t have
ownd ye Covenant.

A record of y^os y^t are rec^d: into
full Communion

1719

Augt 9th Rebecca Prat.

Sep^t 20th		Bethiah wife to Benj: Pool
Novr 8		Mary ye wife of Tho: Rich:

1720		
May	22	Judeth Goold of Charls:T. End
June	12	Phoebe Nichols.
Aug^t	14	Mehetable Briant.
Sep^t	11	Ann Merrow.
	18	Elizabeth Pool
		Ruth Boutel.
		Mary Burnap
		Rebecca Burnap.
Octob^r	~~19~~	Anna Emerson
	16	Elizabeth Cowdry .
		Susanna Cowdry.
	30	John Merrow Junr.

	Tabitha Goodwin
	Mary Boutell
	Mary Goodwin
	Judeth Pool
	Tabitha Boutell.
Novr 27th	Susanna Tounsend
	Abigail Roberts.
Jan^{ry} I.	William Hay & Abigail
	his wife added to y^s Chh.
	by y^r dismission from y^e
	first chh: in Marblehead
	to us, Signify'd by Letter
	to us Signd by y^r Pastor,
	& by ye unanimous vote
	of y^s Chh: receiving y^m
	under o^r watch & care, & to
	o^r Com̄union.

147

[49]

first
The Covenant of ye Chh in Reading, being in a loose
⌃

pap^r, w^c is liable to be Shatterd & lost, & I thinking

it might be a Service to ye Chh to have it inserted

in y^s book for its bett^r Security, did Jan^{ry} I. 1720

ask y^e Chh leave to record it here, w^c

they agreed unto by a silential vote. And

accordingly I have faithfully recorded it on

y^e following leaf. ——————— R^d Brown.

[50]

A coppy of y^e covenant made at y^e Gathering of y^e first
in
chh: in Reading, New England, about y^e y^r 1644.
⌃

=====

We whose names are und^r written, do Covenant wth y^e L^d &
one with an other, & do Solemnly bind o^{rs} before y^e L^d and
his people, y^t we will, thrû y^e help of Christ strengthening of
us, walk aft^r y^e L^d in all his ways, according as he has
traced them out to us in his word of grace & truth. &

1. We Avouch ye L^d to be o^r God, & give our selves (wth
   our seed aft^r us in their Generations) to be his people,
   in ye truth & Sincerity of o^r hearts.

2. We give up our-selves to ye Ld Jesus Christ, to be ruled
   & guided by him in ye matt^{rs} of his worship, & in our whole
   conversation, Acknowledging him not only o^r alone Sa
   -viour, but also o^r King to reign & rule ov^r us, & our
   Prophet and Teacher by his <u>word</u> & <u>Spirit</u>, forsakeing
   all oth^r Teachers & doctrines w^c he has not Com̄anded : &
   we wholly disclaim o^r own Righ: in pont of Justifica
   tion, & look at it as a menstruous Cloath; & do cleave
   unto him for Righteousness & life, grace, & glory.

3. We do farther promise by ye help of Christ to walk
   with our brethren & Sisters of ye Congregation, in
   ye Spirit of brotherly love, watching over them &
   careing for them; Avoiding all Jelousies, Suspitious
   backbiteings, censurings, quarrelings, & Secret riseings
   of heart against them; forgiving & forbareing, &
   yet Seasonably admonishing & restoreing them by
   a Spirit of meekness; And Sett them in Joynt again

that have been thrû infirmity overtaken in any
fault among us.

4. We will not in ye Congregation be forward to Shew our
gifts or parts in Speaking, nor be ready to disgrace our
brethren or discover y^r failings, but attend an orderly call be
-fore we put forth our selves, doing nothing to ye the
offence of ye Church, but in all things ende   [51]
-avouring our own & our brethrens edification
& trust in God.

5. We farther bind our selves in the Strength of Christ
to labour how we may advance the gospel, and how
we may advance the Kingdome of Christ, & how we
may winn & gain them y^t are without, and how
we may Settle grace and peace among our selves,
and Seek as much as in us lieth the peace of all
the Churches; Seeking the help, & counsel & direction
of other Churches if need be, not puting any Stumbling
-block before any, but labouring to abstain from
all appearance of evill.

6. We do hereby promise to behave and demean our-
selves obediently in all lawfull things to those y^t
God hath placed over us in ye Church and Comon
-wealth: Knowing y^t its our duty not to grieve
them, but to incourage them in their places, and in
ye administration of y^r Charge y^t God hath
committed to them.

7. We resolve in ye Same Strength to approve ourselves

in our particular callings, Shuning idleness, not Sloth
-full in buisness, knowing y^t idleness is ye bane of
any Society &c: Neither will we deal hardly or
oppressingly with any w^{r}in we are the Lords
Stewards: Promising to our best abillities to
teach our Children the good knowledge of the
Lord, y^t they may also learn to Serve & fear
him with us, y^t it may go well with them &
with us forever.

———

A List of The Names of ye brethren & Sist^{rs} Now belonging
to ye first Chh: in Reading, taken this 3^d day of
January Anno 1720/21. here followeth.

A Chatelogue of ye brethren & Sisters, in full Comūnion   [52]
in y^e ~~Ch~~ first Chh of Reading, here unde^r followeth.[22]

I S. Richard Brown pastor,   Mary ye wife of Jno Fish.
& Martha his wife.   Joseph Eaton &

2 D. Thomas Boutell &   Mary his wife.
Abigail his wife.   Samuell Lilley &

3 D. Thomas Nichols &   Hannah his wife.
Rebecca his wife.   Jeremiah Sweayn &
Joel Jenkins   Sarah his wife
John Tounsend. &   John Merrow Junr.
Sarah   his wife.   Deliverance wife of Jno merrow sen^r.
Thomas Bancroft &   Ann ye wife of Jno merrow Junr.
Mary his wife.   Nathaniell Park^r: Junr
Lydia Bancroft.   Eliz: his wife.
Sarah Bancroft, Widdow.   Widdow Sarah Briant

Samuell Bancroft &

Sarah his wife.

Raham Bancroft &

Abigail his wife.

Stephen Wesson &

Sarah his wife.

Phebe Rice.

Joseph Daman &

Mary his wife.

Kendal Goodwin &

Mary his wife.

Hannah Wesson.

Mary Feltch.

Mary Wesson Widdow.

Joanna Wesson.

John Parker &

Eliz: his wife.

Widdow Parker

Deborah Temple

John Boutel &

Sarah his wife.

Sarah Foster.

Abigail Nichols.

Joseph Parker &

Eliz: his wife.

Nathaniell Stow.

Sarah Briant.

Mehetabell Briant

James Nichols

Sarah Nichols

Joseph Burnap.

& his wife.

Thomas Pool &

Rebecca his wife.

Nathaniel Parker sen[r].

and his wife.

Samuell Daman &

his wife.

Widow Grace Boutell.

Tabitha Boutell.

Samuel Lambson &

Eliz: his wife.

Jonathan Parker &

Barbary his wife.

Joanna Nichols.

Jonathan Nichols &

Phebe his wife.

Nathaniell Batchelder

& Hannah his wife.

Timothy Hartshorn sen[r]

and his wife.

Timothy Hartshorn Jun[r]

Eben: Emerson.

& Mary his wife.

40

42.

Eliz: ye wife of Steph: Parker.

Goodwife Roberts.

Dorkas Brown.

Abigail Roberts.

Sarah Pool.

John Woodward

and his wife.

Pet^r Emerson &

Anna his wife &

Anna y^r daught^r.

Mary Burt.

John Prat.

& his wife. &

Sarah Prat y^r daught^r.

Widdow Brown

John Batchelder:

and his wife.

widdow Batchelder.

Ebenezer Nichols

and his wife.

John Dix

& his wife.

Lt Sweayn

and his wife.

Ruth Boutell.

Lt Hananiah Parker

& his wife.

Ebenezer Parker

Thomas Wesson.   [53]

Benjamin Pool.

Widdow Jeagles.

Thomas Nichols.

& Mary his wife.

Capt Jonathan Pool

& Bridget his wife.

Timothy Wiley Senr

& his wife.

John Wiley

& his wife.

Mary Wiley.

John Smith

& his wife.

James Smith & Abigail his wife

Dea: Francis Smith.

Isaac Smith

& his wife

Timothy Goodwin

& his wife.

Mrs Pierpont

Mr Jonathan Pierpont.

Wm Briant &

Rebecca his wife.

Benja: Burnap

& Eliza: his wife

Mary Hodgman

Kendal Boutell

& his wife.

Susanna Touns End

Susanna Brown

Anna Brown

Edward Brown

and his wife.

John Brown.

& his wife.

Mary wife to Sam[ll] Brown

Serg[t] Tho: Burnap.

& his wife.

Mary Burnap &

Rebecca Burnap.

Jonathan Pool

& Esther his wife.

43.

Thomas Damon

& his wife.

Mary Eaton.

Lydia Eaton.

Jonathan Eaton

& his wife.

L[t] Kendal Parker

& his wife.

Widdow Taylor

Widow Brown

Widow Cowdry.

Tabitha Cowdry

& Lucy his wife.

Mary Boutell

Dea: Jn[o] Goodwin

& his wife.

Tabitha Goodwin

Mary Goodwin

W[m] Hay &

Abigail his wife.

Rebecca Davis widdow.

John Nichols Sen[r]

& his wife.

John Nichols Jun[r]

Dorkas Briant, widdow

Kendal Briant

& his wife.

Tabitha Briant

43.

Joshua Felt   [54]

~~Jos~~ & his moth[r].

Sarah Hawks.

20.

memb[rs] of o[r] Chh: in o[r]

Mauldon Neighbourhood. viz

Thomas Upham

& his wife.

Eliz: Upham

y[e] wife of Rich[rd] Upham

Thomas Green &

Susanna Cowdry

Elisabeth Cowdry.

Mary Fish

Ruth Fish

16

40
42
43
43

184

All y^es belong to Reading

Memb^rs of y^s Chh: belonging

to Lyn: End not yet dismist from[23]

us are y^es following viz:

Lt Jno Pool &

Mary his wife.

Judeth Pool.

Sarah Bates.

Kendall Pierson

& Lydia his wife

Rebecca Williams.

Sam^ll Hart.

Sarah Hart.

Shubael Stearns

Hannah Walton.

William Russel of S: Village

& Elizabeth his wife.

William Batchelder.

his wife.

ye wife of James Taylor

7

Memb^rs of y^s Chh: in o^r Charlstown

neighbourhood. viz.

Widdow Goold.

Daniel Goold Senr.

& his wife

Dan^ll Goold Junr

and his wife.

Mary Phillips.

ye wife of James Hay.

D: Laurance & his wife.

Ebenezer Knight

& his wife

John Houlden

and his wife

Naomi Holden.

Thomas Gary's wife.

Widow Belcher.

Joanna Lawrance

Mercy Parker.

Judeth Goold.

y^e wife of Jno Goold Junr

Timothy Bauldwin

& his wife.

Mrs Hay.

Goody Welman.

Isaac Welman & ~~his~~

his wife.

In all yᵉ Total is.
persons yᵗ ownd yᵉ Covenant

Hannah Hay

Mʳˢ Abigail Gary

goody Cutler.

$$
\begin{array}{rl}
25 & 184 \\
 & 020 \\
 & 007 \\
 & 25 \\
\hline
 & 236^{24}
\end{array}
$$

pʳsons received to full Comu̅:   [56]

nion since I came.   147

1722.

Dec: 15 Sarah Hull ownd yᵉ

      Cove: & ws baptized.

1720

Feb: 12   Abraham Smith &

         Elizabeth Smith, his wife.

1721

March 26. Susannah Hartshorn.

Ap: 3ᵈ   Elizabeth Gary

May 14   Nath: Cowdry & his wife.

         Mehetabel Cowdry.

June 4   Elizabeth Nichols &

         ~~Anna Emerson~~

         Elizabeth Emerson.

    13   Margaret Allin.

July 16   Ivory Upham

         Hannah Burnap:

    30   Rebecca Bucknam (charlest:)

Octo: 29   Rebecca Prat &

         Rebecca Batchelder.

Decʳ: 10   Abigail Briant.

Janʳʸ 21   John Sweayn

    Tho: Cutler Junʳ

John Touns End Junr

1722	March 4th
	Ebenezer Daman &
	Dorcas Daman his wife.
Ap: I	Heph=zibah Woodward.
Jun: 3	Sarah Boutell.
July 8th	Mary Goodwin &
	Eliz: Parker.
Octo: 2I	Stephen Wesson 3^d
	Sarah Welman.
Jan^{ry} I9	Tabitha Brown

1723	March I0th
	Ruth Boutel wife of T: Boutel
22nd	Richrd Nicols.
June I6	Joannah ~~Wal Prat~~ Prat.

Those y^t have ownd y^e Covenant	Those y^t are received to full Comunion.	[58]

Dec^m: 3I: I724		brout ov^r — 177
Eliza: Gary wife to John Gary of Charlst: End.	Augt. 4th	Elizabeth Prat. & Susannah Upham.
	25th	Mary Sweayn.
Augt. 7th. I726.	Octob: I	Joseph Wesson.
Mary ye wife of J^o Walton ownd ye Covenant & w^s baptizd.	Novr I7	Joannah Wesson.
	Dec^m. I.	Isaac Welman Mary Welman
	Feb.I6.	Ephraim Wesson

Dea^c: Brown Emerson

1724

Mar: 1.   Thomas Eaton

   15   James Wesson

        Elias Smith

Ap^{ll} 5th   John Parker Junr. &

        Sarah Parker his wife

May 17th   Stephen Wesson Junr

June 7th   Thomas Wiley.

July 5th   Sarah Evins.

Augt. 23^d   Joseph Bancroft

Sep^t. 19th   Benjamin Brown

Nov^r: 8th.   Ruth Bancroft.

1725

Mar: 7.   Timothy Pratt.

Ap: 11   Elizabeth Gary wife

        to J^o Gary.

Ap: 18.   Abigail ye wife of

        Samuell Nichols dis

        mist from[25] Wenham &

        recievd to o^r watch & Com

        munion.

                  199.

P^rsons received   [60]

into full Comunion

1725   brought ov^r   199.

June 6:	Elizabeth Goold wife
	of Benj. Goold. Charls:
Feb: 27th	Ruth Lambson. She
N. B.	makes up. 201.

1726.

Mar: 13th	Benjamin Parker
	Jonathan Woodward
D^o. 27th.	John Daman.
	James Townsend.
May. 1.	Nathaniell Emerson
	Hepsibah Emerson.
	Ebenezer Wesson
~~D^o 22nd~~	
D^o. 22nd	Benjamin Smith
	Elizabeth Smith his W.
	Sarah Wesson.
Augt. 7th	Timothy Wesson &
	Abigail his wife
Sep^t: 18th	John Walton &
	Mary his wife &
	Abigail Smith.
25th.	Mrs Deborah Brintnall
Octob: 9th	Benjamin Wesson
	Unice Wesson.
23^d	Hannah Nichols, w: to T: Nich.
Dec^m. 18th	Lidia ye wife of Nath: Eaton.
Jan: 15th	Eben: Nichols jun^r &
	Susanna his wife.

Feb: 26. Nathaniell Eaton.

————————

Carry ov^r 224

Those y^t ownd ye Covenant.		P^rsons rec^d. to full Comūnion. [62]

1727.

Mar: 26th. Elizabeth Merrow.

Dec^m: 10th Timothy Pool & his wife
      Elizabeth Pool.

17th.   James Brown.

24.   Benjamin Southerick.

    Samuel Salter.

    Josiah Walton.

    John Pratt:

    Mary Nichols.

1727.   Brought ov^r   224.

May 7th   Isaac Wesson

Dec^m: 10th.   Sarah Sawyer.

Eliza: Stimpson

Eliza: Batchelder

Hannah Batchelder

17th   R^d Upham dismist from Mauldon & rec^d. here.

D^o. 28th.   Thomas Burnap & Sarah Burnap.

at a chh meet^g y^es 27 rec^d

Joseph Bryant & Sarah Bryant

Anna Pierpoint

Lucy Emerson

Jane Emerson

Eliza: Batchelder

Rebec: Boutell

Dorkas Boutell.

Josiah Brown

Samuell Pratt.

Phineas Parker

Eliza. Towns End.

Mary Parker

Hannah Boutell

Bethiah Burnap.

Abraham Goold. &

Mary Goold.

William Cowdry

Mary Cowdry.

Jonathan Temple

———

Carry over 252

persons y^t ownd ye Cove: Persons reciev'd into ye Church   [64]

1727.   1727   Brought over   252.

Dec^m: 31. David Green.		Dec^m: 28. John Temple
John Nichols.		Tabitha Townsend
Sarah Parker		Elizabeth Wesson
Tabitha Cowdry		Elizabeth Lambson
Mary Cowdry		Kendall Bryant.
Dorkas Damon	Jan: 18th.	John Poole.
Anna Bryant.		John Eaton
Jan: 7th. Mary Parker	@ a chh meeting y^es 16 w^r rec^d ye Chh mett @ ye Past^rs house because of ye Extre^m cold.	Thomas Bancroft jun^r
Rebecca Parker		Nathaniell Goodwin.
Sarah Wesson		John Batt.
Rebecca Cowdry		Abigail Nichols
Susanna Brown		Sarah Bates.
Symon Stow.		Hannah Walton
14th. Ruth Joy.		Joannah Jeffords
James Nichols 3^d.		Rebecca Davise
Joanna Nichols		David Green.
Anna Burnap		Edward Bucknam

William Batt.

21. Abigail Gowing

Mary Lambson

Isaac Burnap

Sarah Parker

Ruth Smith

Susanna Jeffords

Ebenezer Foster

Mary Hawks

Mary Brown

Katherine } negros
& Susanna }

James Nichols jun^r.

Elizabeth Hartshorn

Rebecca Mellandi.

Phebe Temple

Carry over 273

1727. Persons y^t ownd ye Cove:

1728 Persons admit: to Com: [66]

Brought over 273.

Jan: 28. Mary Hawks

Jonathan Lilley

John Burnap

Sarah Pool.

Mary Smith

Sarah Smith

Rebecca Bryant

Elizabeth Goodwin

Feb: 11th: John Bryant

Martha Burnap

Elizab: Smith

Abigail Goold.

Mary Adams.

25th Eliz: wife of Dav^d. Goold

Mar: 14. Mary Holden.

Sarah Parker.

Martha Townsend

Mary Stimpson

Dorkas Brown

Samuell Batchelder

~~Ebenezer Parson~~

Jonathan Griffin

Sarah Griffin

Elizabeth Burnap

Mary Lilley.

Thomas Sweayn

David Goold.

Elizab: Goold.

Priscilla a negro of
Justice B: Pools

Elizabeth Merrow

Daniell Nichols.

1728.

Susanna Brown

Mar: 3ᵈ. Mary Bancroft

Ann Taylor

Jabez Temple

Joanna Nichols

Nath: Parker 3ᵈ.

Eben. Parker of R:

Thomas Rice.

Hannah Parker.

Joseph Daman.

31. William Bryant

31. Samuell Brown

Thomas Nichols.

Samuell Bancroft.

Ap: 21 Benj: Swain &

Elizabeth Brown

Sarah Swin his wife.

Susannah Goold

Sarah Wesson.

Abigail Damon.

28. Benjamin Wiley

James Nichols 3ᵈ.

_____

Carry over — 301

1728. Persons yᵗ owned
the Covenant.

1728. persons recieved
to full Comunion.

Brout over   301

June 2ⁿᵈ. Wᵐ Johnson ownd yᵉ
Cove: & wˢ Baptized.

May 19 Timothy Nickols.

June 2ⁿᵈ Hannah Cutler

Sepᵗ: I. Sarah May.

Rebecca Boutel

Phebe Gary.

July 7ᵗʰ Mary Williams.

Hannah Charnock

John Burnap.

Mary Gary

28ᵗʰ Hannah wife of Tho. Cutler

Priscillah Griffin.

Mary wife to Tho: Green

Hannah Tompson of Woburn

Novʳ. 17 Hannah Grover:

Sarah Parker &

	Mary Nickols
Octo: 27th	Mehetable Nichols
Nov[r]: 17	Sam[ll]. Lambson jun[r].
Jan: 5.	Abigail Brown ⎫ of Lyn
	Joannah Crocker ⎭
	Eliz: Richardson. of Woburn

Mar: 2nd.   Unice Green.

Ap[l]: 20th.   Abigail y[e] wife of

              Tho: Gary Jun[r] of Stonh:

May 11th.   Phebe y[e] wife of Noah

              Eaton.

Aug[t]. 10th.   Annah Swain &

              Hepzibah Swain.

1729.	
Mar: 2	Thomas Gary
	Jonathan Dix
June 8th	Eben: Felch
	Lydia Felch
29th	Ephraim Brown
Aug[t]. 24	Elizabeth Smith
	Ruth Smith
Octo: 26th	Abigail Parker.
	Elizabeth Pool.
	Mary Lambson
Feb: 1:	Simon Stow
	Samuell Salter

Carry over —— 328

1729	Persons y[t] have	1729	Brought over Persons [70]
	ownd y[e] Covenant.		rec[d]. to Comunion. 328.

Feb: 8th.	Elizabeth Green.	Feb: 22nd	Martha Brown
1730			Sarah Parker
July 5th	Elizabeth Lambert		
Jan[rt]. 24th.	Mary Wiley.	1730	

___ ___ ___ ___ ___

The[26] Reverend M[r]
Richard Brown Depart=
=ed this Life on y[e] 20
October ~~1732~~ __ __ __ ___

      1732

Mar: 8th.	Benj[e] Hartshorn
29th	Jabez Temple
	Mary Adams
	Joanna Cowdry
May 3[d].	Unice Pool.
Aug[t] 29.	Elizabeth Hinkson
	James Brown

———   ———

1731

Mar: 25.	Benjamin Chaplin
May 16.	Rebecca Pool. rec[d]
	by dismiss: from[27] L. End.
June 13.	Joseph Eaton Jun[r].
Aug[t] 29.	Elizab: his wife
	by dismission from[28] Lynn.
Feb: 6.	Hannah Swain.
	Dorothy Merrow

_____

1732	Margarett All
	W[m] Glenne
	Mary Glenne
Aug[r]. 13th	James Parker

_____

    19
  328
  ——
  347

    1732 [71]

William Hobby was Invited to preach at Reading Dec[r] 17: 1732
to y[e] Pastoral Office May 1st: 1733

Which Invitation he Accepted on y[e] Latter

End of June next following & was Ordaind

Pastor of y[e] first Church in Reading Sep[r] 5th: 1733

The Churches whose Assistance was Asked were y[e] following Ten

The O North to w[ch] he belonged, y[e] New North, y[e] N Brick these in

Boston, y[e] Church of Cambridge, y[e] Church of Malden, y[e] Church of

Lynn, y[e] Church of Lynn End y[e] Church of Woburn y[e] Church

of Stoneham y[e] Second Church in Reading —— ——

The Service of y[e] Day was Carryed on in y[e] following Manner

M[r] Emerson of Malden began wth Prayer, M[r] Appleton of

Cambridge preach'd from those words in 2[d] Tim[o] 2[d] Ch 21[v] – After

which M[r] Wellstead of Boston prayed M[r] Webb of Boston

Gave the Charge, and M[r] Putnam of Reading y[e] right hand

of Fellowship – the Psalm propos'd & a Blessing given by

y[e] Ordained, —— May he Obtain Mercy from y[e] L[d] & be found faithfull.

Persons who have Own'd y[e] Covenant   Persons rec[d] to full Communion   [72]

    Since the Ordination of M[r] W[m] Hobby.

1733

Oct[o] 21st:	Mary Wiley
Dec[r] 9th:	Ruth Upham
—— 29th	Phoeby Eaton
Jan[y]: 13th:	Mary Mansfeild
	Mary Walton
Feb[y]: 10th:	Sam[ll] Wesson
	W[m] Bancroft
17th:	Noah Eaton
March 24	Anna Parker

<u>1734</u>

May 5th:	John Smith Deacn:
Sepr 22d	John Wesson
	Thomas Temple
Novr 17th:	Samll Bancroft Junr
Decr: 8th:	Isaac Burnap
22d	Robt Thompson
	Abigail his wife.
Jany: 5th	Susannah Foster
	Sarah Emerson
	Elisabeth Wesson
Feby: 23d	Abigail Bacheller
<u>1735</u>	
March 23d	Hannah Parker
Apll 20th.	Ruth Bryant
May 4th:	Daniel Emerson
	Jonas Eaton
	Mary Cowdry
	Lydia Parker

26

1735. Persons yt have Own'd ye Covenant.	Persons Recd: to full Communion	[74]
	1735 Brôt over 26	
	June 1st: Martha Upham	
	Ruth Upham	
	June 29th Joseph Dammon Junr	
	July 27th Mary Eaton	
	Augt 3d James Townsend & Eliza: his	
	wife dismist from Wilmington.	
Octo: 19th: Chester Negro Servt: of	Octo: 19t Joseph Underwood	
Deacon Boutell ownd ye Covt:	Robt: Laith	

and was baptis'd.	Novr 2^d:	Jeremiah Sweyn Junr
	—- 16th:	Henry Merrow
		Abigail his wife
		Jon^a Parker Junr
	<u>1736</u>	
March 14th Primus Negro	March 28	James Goodwin
Servt: of Mr Joseph Dammon		Jon^a: Nicoll
Ownd ye Cov^t & was baptizd.		Josh: Parker
	Ap^l: 4th:	Eliz^a: Dammon
	May 2^d	Ruth Nicolls
		Mary Nicolls
		David Bancroft
		Thos: Burnap
May 30th Ruth Bancroft wife to	June 13th	Ruth Bancroft wife [of] Raham
M^r: Raham Bancroft Own'd y^e	July 4th	Martha Parker
Cov^t: and was Baptis'd	Augt 1st:	John Boutell Junr
		Anna Parker
	Sepr 19th	Ann Hutchinson
		Mary Nicolls
	Oct^o: 10th:	Tim^o: Burnap
		Dorcas Gold
	Decr 5th:	Nath: Brown
	26th:	Jon^a: Eaton
		Sarah Parker

55

1737. Persons y^t have Own'd ye Covenant.		Rec^d: to full Communion	[76]
brôt forward	3	bro't forward	55
Feb^y: 13th Timothy Bryant and	Jan^y: 16th:	Jeremy Bryant	
Susanna his wife then Own'd ye Cov^t:	Feb^y: 13th	Tim^o: Wiley	

		John Nicolls Jun[r]
	<u>1737</u>	
	March 6th:	W[m] Johnson
		Jon[a]: Forster
		Isaac Smith
		Mehitebel Parker
	— 20th:	Edmund Bancroft
	Ap[l]: 3[d]:	Rich[d]: Temple
		Joseph Boutell
		Eliz[a]: Johnson
		Eliz[a]: Bisco
		Abigail Walton
		Anna Smith.
May 15: Reuben Horton Ownd y[e] Cov[r]: & was baptis'd.	May 1st:	Rebecca Barrett
	— 29th	Eliz[a]: Smith
		Katherine Smith
		Primus, Negro man.
	June 26	Nath[ll] Bancroft
	July 3[d]:	Jonathan Boutell &
		Eliz[a]: his Wife
	Aug[t]: 7th:	Ruth Burnap
	—— 21st:	Jeremy Brown
		Anna his wife
		Nath[ll]: Bacheller
		Mary Sweetser
	Sep[r] 11th:	John Woodward Jun[r].
		Lydia Mansfield
	Oct[o]: 9th:	Mary Vinten
Feb[y]: 26 W[m]: Green & Eliz[a]: his wife	——16th:	Mary Bryant

Ownd ye Cov^t: & were Baptis'd

1738

March 19th Rose a Negro Servt of Benj^a:

Brown Ownd ye Cov^t: & was Baptisd.

Decr 11th:	Joshua Bancroft
Jan^y: 29	Eason Dix
1738	Sam^ll. Nicols
March 19	Sarah Pool
Ap^l 2^d	John Walton Junr.
May 7th:	Jotham Walton
	Eliz^a: Green Junr
	98

1738	Persons y^t have Own'd ye Cov^t:	Receiv'd to full Communion [78]
	bro't forward 9	bro't forward 98

June 11th:	James Negro Servt: of Tim^o: Nicolls	May 21st:	William Green

Ownd y^e   Cov^t: & was baptisd.

Eliz^a: his wife

June 19th:	Eben^r Merrow Own'd ye Cov^t	June 27th:	Sarah Goodwin
	& was baptis'd.	July 23^d	Eben^r Merrow
Aug^t: 6th:	Sarah ye wife of Sam^ll. Evans	Aug^t: 6th:	Eunice Parke
	Own'd ye Cov^t. & was baptisd.	Sepr 3^d:	Eliz^a: Nicolls
Oct^o: 29	Meriah Negro Servt: to	Oct^o: 8:	Jacob Walton
	M^rs: Stow Ownd ye Covt		Susannah Green
	& Was baptisd.		————

1739		1739	
March 4th:	Thos: Richardson	Ap^l: 15	Sarah Bancroft
	Own'd ye Cov^t: & was Baptisd.		Anna Nicolls
May 13	George Negro Servt: of	———— 29	Susannah Burnap
	Mr Peter Emerson Own'd	May 30th:	Chester Negro Servt:
	ye Cov^t: & was baptisd	———— 27	Lois Green
		June 10th:	Samuel Felch
			Jacob Smith
		July 1st:	James Abbott
		Aug^t: 5th:	Hannah Dammon

—— 20th:	Hephzibah Brown
Sepr: 9th:	Rebecca Temple
Octo: 14	Mary Walton dismist
	from Newbury.
Feby: 10th:	Joseph Coggins &
	Mary his Wife
	Abigail Prat from Woburn
—— 24th	Samll: Pool

1740

March 16	Jacob Barrett
Apl: 13	Phebe Smith
—— 20th:	Mary Goodwin
	by Dismissn from[29] Lyn End.
—— 27	Edwd: Dammon
John Nicolls	
May 25	Edward Merrow
June 29th	Richard Upham

June 8th: Andrew Beard Own'd ye
Covt: & was Baptisd.

Augt: 3d:	Sarah Emerson dismist
	from[30] 1st: Chh: in Salisbury.
Sepr 7th:	Martha Richardson
—— 14th:	Natha: Appleton
Novr 2	John Goodwin Tertius
	Eunice Walton
Decr. 14th:	John Sweyn
Jany: 4th	Eliza: Upham
—— 18th	Abigail Bryant
1741 Apl 26	Phebe Wardwell

132

1741	Persons y^t have Own'd ye Cov^t.			Rec^d: to full Communion [80]
May	brot forward 16			brot forward 132
			May 24th	Braviter Grey
				James Bryant
				Susannah Bryant
				Katharine Emerson
				Abigail Hay
			June 21st:	David Green
				Joseph Parker
				Hephizibah Bryant
			Aug^t: 9th	Sarah Gold
			—— 16	Peter Wait
				Phebe Nicolls
Oct^o: 25th:	London Negro Servt: to		Sep^r: 13th:	Mahitabel Dammon
	Capt Eaton Own'd ye Cov^t & was		Oct^o: 25:	Ebenez^r Hopkinson
	baptisd		Novr 1st.	Pompey Negro Servt: to
				Mrs David Green
			6th:	Mary Boutell Dismist
				from Lyn End.
			8th:	Amos Upham ~~of Maldon~~
				Dorcas Prat
			15th:	Richd Nicolls &
				Mary his Wife
Nov^r: 22^d:	Titus Negro Servt: to Thos:			Jacob Bancroft
	Green Own'd ye Cov^t: & was bap^d:		22^d	Tabitha Cowdry
			Decr 20	Nehemiah Williams
			Jan^y: 17th:	James Emerson
				Sarah Smith
				Eliz^a Parker

<u>1742</u>

March 7th	James Wesson &	
	Esther his wife	
14	Mary Farrow	
—— 15	Moses Bancroft	
—— 21.	Abigail Smith.	
May 9th	Hephzibah Nicolls	
	George Negro Servt. to Mr Emerson	
23^d	Abigail Nicolls.	
June 6th:	Zachary Nicolls	
	Mary Richardson	
—— 20th	David Bacheller	
July 4th:	Rebecca Nicolls	
	London Ser: [to] Capt. Eaton	
	Titus Servt. [to] Th^o Green	
Augt 22^d	Jabez Dammon	
	Hephzibah Smith	

1742   Persons y^t have Own'd Cov^t

          brot forward   18

Brot forward	173 [82

Sep^t. 12th: Sam^{ll}: Evans apprehended to be drawing [to]

his End Desir'd to dy in Cov^t. wth: G^d: ~~accordingly~~

                                                    to

Accordingly having given notice of it ye Chh.

I administr'd ye Cov^t. & Bapt: ye Seal of it

to him.

Dec^r.	Abigail Evans
Jan^y: 16 [1743]	Abigail Hartshorn
Ap^l: 3^d	Peter Neg: Ser^t. to Capt Pool Lyn En
May 15.	Lydia Evans.

1743

May 15th Hannah Evans Own'd ye Cov^t.

          & was baptis'd

July 17th:	Joseph Wait.
	Jeremiah Smith
Sep^r: 18	Mary Wiley
Oct^o: 9th	Susannah Dammon
23	Joseph Upham &
	Eliz^a. his Wife

Priscilla Negro Servt: to

Mrs Gary

Jan^y: Sarah Wife to Jon^a: Temple

Dismiss^d — Wilmington

1744

May 20   Joanna Prat

June 3^d: Eliz^a. Newell

Sepr 2^d: Sarah Wesson

Oct^o 14   Joseph Swain

Benj^a. Forster

Jeremiah Bancroft

Hephzibah Nicolls

Decr. 16   Sam^ll Wessen Junr

Sarah his Wife

Jan^y: 20th: James Woodward

1745

June 2^d   Mary Hartshorn

— 30th   Abigail Holden

1745

March 17th: Meriah Negro Servt to Deacon

Parker Ownd ye Cov^t & was baptisd,

w^th: her Children.

Margaret Farrow

Sep^r: 15th: Hannah Gold

Feb^y: 2^d   Abigail Smith

1747

Sep^r: 20th: M^r. Nath^ll. Evans

Oct^o 11th   Lydia Nicols by dismiss^n

from Stoneham

Jan^y: 3^d: Eliz^a Prat

Thos: Parker

1748

May 1st: Priscilla Smith

Oct⁰ 6ᵗʰ	Jacob Upham
	Rebeccah Upham

	Persons Recᵈ into full Communⁿ	[84]
	brot forward 207	
1749	Zerviah Upton Dismist	
	from Windham	
	Jonᵃ. Pierson dismist	
	from Lyn End	
Janʸ: 14	Lydia Gold	
Febʸ: 11ᵗʰ:	Mary Wife of Mos. Bancroft	
— 25	Samˡˡ. Smith	
1750		
Novʳ: 18ᵗʰ:	Rebecca Pool	
	James an Adult Negro	
Decʳ. 23	Jacob Parker	
	Abigˡ: his Wife	
	John Vinton	
	Josiah Walton	
	dismist from Lynn End	
1 Decʳ: 1751	Joshua Nicolls	
Decr. 15	John Sparhawk	
Janʸ: 12	Mary Wife to Eb: Smith	
1752	Mary Wife of Nath. Wiley	
	dismist from Andover	
July 19:	Hephziba Wife to Joshua	
	Nicolls dismist 2ᵈ: Ch Reading	
Augʳ: 9ᵗʰ:	Susannah Hartshorn	
	Lydia Sweyn	
Sepʳ: 17	Jonᵃ: Parker	

	Ruth his Wife
Oct° 8:	Bethiah Boutell
15	Ruth Temple
Nov[r] 19	Lydia Boutell
1753 Feb[y] 18	Mary Wife Tim°: Smith
March 18	James Wiley
	Hannah Wife to
	Benj[a] Brown Sen[r]

233

Persons Rec[d]: to full Comunion   [86]

bro't forward   233

March 25	Meriah Neg. Serv[t]. to
	Deacon Parker
Ap[l]. 1.	John Prat
—— 8	James Bancroft
	Phebe Emerson
— 22	Eliz[a]: Wait
May 13	Lydia Williams
Aug[r]: 19th	John Mead
Sep[r] 9	Eliz[a] Forster dismist
	from[31] 2[d] Chh in[32] Woburn
Dec[r]. 2:	Lydia Hawks Lyn End
Feb[y]: 3.	Joseph Gold Dan[l].[33]
1754	
March 17	Joseph Gold Son Ab[m]
June 23	M[r]. Will[m] Gold
Aug[r]: 11	Eliz[a] Larrabee
Sep[r] 15	Eunice Eaton Lynn End
Feb[y] 23	Hannah Bancroft

	1755		
	June 29	Mary Wesson	
	Aug[r] 24	Mary Hervey	
	Nov[r] 16	Widow Esther Coy	
		Sarah Townsend	
	Dec[r] 21	Abigail Forster	
		Anna Prat	
1756	Jan[y] 11	Lucy Dammon	
~~1756~~	Ap[r]: 25	Eph[m]. Parker	
		Jacob Townsend	
		Sarah Bryant	
		Mary Parker	
		Rec[d]. to full Comunion 259	[88]
		Hepzibah Wife of W[m] Melendy	
		Tabitha Wife [of] James Hartshorn	
	Aug[t]. 15	Martha Wife [of] Maonn[34] Smith	
	29	Mary Richardson	
	Oct[o] 17	Eliz[a] Eaton	
	1758		
	Ap[l] 23	Sarah Dammon	
	May 21	Hannah Wife to W[m] Pool	
	—— 28	Rebecca Parker	
	July 2[d]	Sarah Wife to Caleb Bancroft.	
	—— 16	Eunice Boutell	
	—— 30	Joseph Bancroft &	
		Elliz[a] his Wife.	
	Dec[r]. 31	Martha Melandy.	
	1759		
	July 22	Eliz[a] Wife [of] Sam[ll]. Pool	

Aug[t]: 5	Eliz[a] Wiley Dismist from y[e]
	I[st] Chh in Malden
1761	
March	Sarah Bancroft
June 21	Jacob Emerson
July 12	Margaret Negro
—— 19	Martha Willson
Aug[t]. 2	Joseph Brown
Sep[t] 13	Eben: Gold
Oct[o] 11	Jemy Bancroft
Nov[r] 1	Sarah Nicolls
— 15	Caleb Bancroft
	Eliz[a] Emerson Wife [of] James
1762	Peter Emerson
May 1.	Margaret Walton
July 4	Mary Emerson
Aug[t] 22	Lois Wife to James Eaton
Sep[t] 19	Timo Prat Jun[r]
	Tabitha his wife.

290

	Persons Rec[d]: to full Commun[n]	[90]
	brot forward	290
Oct[o] 17	Hannah Simons	
Nov[r] 28	Abigail Hartshorn	
	Hephzibah Parker	
	Anne Merrow	
1763.		
March 20	Abig[l]: Nicolls	
	Hannah Emerson	

	Martha Emerson
	Mary Nicolls
May 1:	Bethiah Wife J^n Nicolls
	Mehitabel Nicolls
—— 22	Eliz^a Wife Wm Green Junr
	Hannah Wife [of] J^n Temple Senr.
Augt 28	John Rogers
1764.	Hannah Parker
	Mehitabel Nicolls
Oct. 14:	Eliz^a Eaton
	Ruth Boutell

307[35]

Timothy Nichols and his wife Dismised to the Chh in

amherst

Persons Rec^d Into full Communion after ye Decease

of our Revd Pastor Mr William Hobby

October 13: 1765	Daniel Gould
	Hannah Swain wife [of] Jacob Swain
	Abigal Roggers
	the wife of John Roggers
August 10 1766	Hannah ye wife of Joshua
	Bancroft & ~~Elizabeth~~
	Abigal Eaton

Persons Receved Into full Communion   [91]

october the 12th 1766	Charity Eaton
November 2	John Bacheller Junr
	Nathanel Cowdry
	his wife Sarah Cowdry

December 14 1766:   Sarah Woolley ye wife

           of Nathan Wolley

                      Eaton

May 31 1767   Sarah Eaton Wife of Lille

                         ^

           Elisabeth Townsend   wife of

           Jacob Townsend

August 16th 1767   Hannah ye Wife of Thomas

           Symonds Junr

Sep^t 27 1767: Lydia Boutttel ye wife of Thomas

Bouttel Junr Dismised from this chh: to ye chh: of

Christ in Amherst.

Decem^r 7 1767: Joseph cogin and

wife Dismist to the Church of Christ

in willmington.

august 17: 1768 John Roggers & wife Dismised to

the 3^d chh: in Ipswich & Recommended

August 18: 1769 Amos Upham and Lois his wife

Dismised And Recommended to the first Church

of Christ in Maldon

                                                  [92]

                  Nathen Person

march: 19: 1769 Kaziah ye wife of Calab: Parker

                 Junr

Sepr 24: 1769: John Emerson & Catharine his wife

                 ^

October 1 1769: John Meeds Dismised: to Hisbrough

                Sutervat[36]   18

The Rev^nd Mr Hobby died in the Year

of Christ 1765 on ye 18th of June

Aged 58.[37]

                  ✿✿✿✿✿✿✿✿✿✿✿✿✿✿✿✿✿✿✿✿

Church Meetings and y[r] acts.

At a Legal Meeting of y[e] Church in Reading

Novem[r] 13th 1712:

L[t] John Pearson (Lynn) & Cap[t] Thomas Nichols were

chosen to y[e] office of Deacons in this church.

Jan[r] 18 1712 The Church being stayd aft[r] ~~aftr~~ y[e] publick

worship w[s] Ended did, at y[e] Request of Anna Barret

now of ~~Mauldon~~ Charlestown, formerly Bryant of Reading & a

member of y[s] Church, by vote, readily dismiss y[e] s[d]

Anna Barret To y[e] watch, fellowship & comunion

of y[e] Church in Mauldon.

Feb: 16th John Roby & hannah his wife ~~ha~~ w[o] in time past

w[r] guilty of y[e] Sin of fornication, did now humble

them selves and confessing y[r] Sin, takeing Shame

and blame to y[m]: selves, w[r] accepted into favour in

y[s] church.

1713.

Nov[r]   Sam[ll] Brown now of Boxford @ his desire w[s]

dismist from y[e] watch of y[s] to y[t] of y[e] Church at Bradford.

1714.

April 4th   Then John Walker and his wife formerly

Inhabitants of y[s] Town & admited memb[rs] of y[s]

church, now being by God's[38] providence, w[c] bounds

out all o[r] habitations , removed to West town

and for[39] more y[r] conveniency desireing to be

dismist to y[e] Church y[r], accordingly w[r] dismist

by vote of y[s] Church from[40] us to y[e] watch & fellowship

of y[e] Church y[r].

Church Meetings and y^r acts. · 98 ·

At a Legal Meeting of ye Church in Reading
Novemb^r 13th 1712:
Lt John Pearson (?) & Capt. Thomas Nickols were
chosen to ye office of Deacons in this church.

Jan^e 18th 1712 The Church being stayd after ye publick
worship w^s ended, did, at ye Request of Anna Barret
now of Charlstowne, formerly Bryant of Reading & a
member of y^s Church. by vote, readily dismiss ye s^d
Anna Barret To ye watch, fellowship & comunion
of ye Church in Mauldon.

Feb: 15 John Roby & Hannah his wife t^e w^e in time past
w^r guilty of s^t fornication, did now humbly
home ſeluet and ... ſ^g y^r sin taking shame
and blame to y^{selue}, w^r accepted into favour in
y^s church.

1713
Nov^r   Sam^{ll} Brown now of Boxford at his desire w^s
dismist from ye watch of y^s to y^t of ye Church at Bradford

1714
April 4th Then John Walker and his wife formerly
Inhabitants of y^s Town & admited memb^{rs} of y^s
church, now being by ye providence w^r bound
out all o^r habitation, removed to West-town
and y^r more conveniency desireing to be
dismist to ye Church y^r accordingly w^r dismist
by vote of ye Church in w^s to ye watch & fellowship
of ye Church y^r.

Reading Church Records Book, MS p. [A1] of "Church Meetings and y^r Acts."
Courtesy First Church of Wakefield, Mass.

June 12 1714. The Church being Stayed after yᵉ pub: worship   [A2]

          was Ended.

          Then Sarah yᵉ wife of James Pike, and

          Elizabeth yᵉ wife [of] John Lampson upon yʳ

          request wʳ dismist from[41] us to yᵉ watch and

          fellowship of yᵉ Church of Weston.

  also Then Hannah Bates (yᵗ wˢ) wˢ @ her request

          dismist ~~to yᵉ~~ from us to yᵉ watch and fellow-

          ship of yᵉ Church at Mansfield.

Novʳ 14 1714 The Church being Stayed aftʳ yᵉ Publick worship

          wˢ Ended, Then Mary Jones, (now Streetʳ) wᵒ had been

          formerly admonished for[42] ye Sin of fornication, manifesting re

          -pentance and desireing forgivness, wˢ recieved and released.

          She also desireing a dismission to yᵉ Church @ Attleburrah wˢ

          accordingly dismissed.

itᵐ   Mʳˢ Hannah yᵉ wife of Mʳ John Bancroft ~~of~~ (Lyn) being

          at her request dismist from yᵉ Church at Maldon to this

          church, wˢ by a vote of yˢ church recieved to our comu:

          nion.

          ———

          At a Legal Meeting of yᵉ Church, April 12ᵗʰ: 1715

          It was voted that for yᵉ year next ensuing every comuni=

          cant Should pay 2ˢ for yᵉ Support of yᵉ ordinance of yᵉ

          Lords Supper.

          ———

~~June~~
May 22   Elizabeth Jeffords alias Hinckson wˢ publickly

          admonished for yᵉ Sin of fornication, and manifesting

          repentance wˢ forgiven and recieved again into charity.

June 28ᵗʰ 1715 Decⁿ Lawrence being @ his desire dismist

orderly from ye Church of Groton was by a vote

of y^s Church rec^d into our Comunion.

Sep^t 16   1716 ye Church being Stayed.   [A3]

Judith Parker & Thomas Parker and Hepsibah his wife

being removed from^43 us to Marblehead & desireing a dismission

from us to ye first church y^r, w^r accordingly dismist by a

vote of y^s chh: to ye watch, fellowship and comunion of ye s^d

chh: y^r.

Novr 11th   John Dickerman & his wife being removed to
1716
Milton & desireing a Dismission from^44 y^s Chh to ye chh y^r

y^s chh's mind being asked, did readily comply to y^r

desire and by a vote dismiss y^m to ye watch and comunion

of ye Chh of Milton.

Octob^r 20th   Aft^r ye Publick worship w^s Ended. The Chh
1717
w^s Stayed, And ye Desires of Josoph Hastings

& Elizabeth his wife to be dismist to ye Chh

@ Weston; as also ye desires of Benjamin

Bigsby & Martha his wife for dismission from^45 us

to ye Chh @ Killinsley^46 w^r Signifyd to this Chh

w^o did readily Comply to y^r respective desires &

by y^r Vote dismist y^m aft^r y^r desires, to ye watch

& comunion of y^os chh^s respectively.

Octob^r 27th   The Church being Stayd aft^r ye publick
1717
worship w^s Ended.

Samuell Smith y^t is Removed to Mansfield

desireing y^s Chh to Dismiss him to ye Chh y^r

y^s Church did accordingly by y^r vote dismiss

him.

Octob^r 19th   The Church being Stayed, Aft^r publick

1718

worship w^s ended, ~~The~~ Priscilla ye wife

of ye s^d Sam^{ll} Smith desireing to be dis-

mist from us to ye chh of Mansfield, ye chh did

accordingly by y^r vote dismiss her.

Aug^r 16 1719 Then Sarah How manifesting repentanc   [A4]

of her Sin w^s rec^d: to favour.

Dec^m: 13th 1719 Then Thomas Cutler and his wife manifesting

repentance for^{47} ye Sin of fornication, w^r rec^d to o^r

charity & watch again.

~~March~~

~~March 27th 1720 ye Desires of Jno Pearson,~~

~~John Tounsend,~~ ^{48}

March 27 1720 The Chh: being Stayed aft^r ye publick   [A5]

worship w^s over. The Desires of Some of o^r Lyn

Neighbours (y^t belonged to y^s chh) for a dismission or[der]

to y^r being a chh by y^{ms} y^r, w^s Signifyd to y^s Chh, and A

vote asked and y^r desires w^r granted, but by a Slend^r
 in ye affirmative, & not one in ye negative.
vote. y^r names w^r <u>Jno Pearson</u>, <u>John Tounsend,</u>
        ^

<u>Samuell Parker</u>, <u>William Eaton</u>, <u>James Pearson,</u>

<u>John Going</u>, <u>John Bancroft</u>, <u>Nath: Going</u>, <u>Jno Bancroft Junr</u>,

<u>Jonathan Going</u>. ten in all.

April 5th 1720 I rec^d: a lett^r from o^r Lyn Neigh=

bours, directed to o^r Chh, requesting o^r help to

ordain Mr Sparhawk y^r on y^e 13th instant, &

April 10th. I Stayed y^e Chh aft^r y^e public worship w^s

ended, and read y^e s^d Lett^r to y^m. and Signifyd

my unwillingness to go, with y^e reasons for it.

upon w^c Lt Parker Stood up & s^d he thout it not

best to Send, & so s^d Capt Burnap, and no word w^s

s^d by any one for sending, upon w^c I proposed

to ye Chh y^t if y^y w^r not for Sending now I would

take y^r Silence for consent, & no man s^d a word.

Haveing receiv^d a petition dated May 24th 1720   [A6]

Signed by Thomas Briant, John Eaton, Thomas Taylor

Jonathan Parker, Sam^{ll}. Dix, Sam^{ll}. Lewis, Caleb Taylor,

Thomas Nickols Wm Flint, Benjamin Damon Sam^{ll}. Leman

& Thomas Burt. all memb^{rs} in full Comunion wth

this Chh; for a Dismission from^{49} us ~~to~~ in ord^r to y^r being

embodyed into a Chh: state y^r in o^r North precinct

This y^r desire w^s Layd before this 5th day of June   ye Church

and ye Church did by a Clear vote dismiss y^m ac

-cording to y^r request.

Sep^t 4th 1720 Timothy Maning desiring y^e

Chh to dismiss him in ord^r to his Embodying with

the Chh y^t is to be Gatherd at Sutton, ye Chh

did at his request by y^r vote dismiss him.

Jan^{ry} I. 1720 Elizabeth ~~Sybley alias~~ Boutel alias

Sybley & Susanna Maning @ y^r Request by

Timothy Maning preferd to me, R: B: w^o carryd

y^s y^r request to o^r Chh w^r dismist by a vote of y^s

Chh: to ye watch & comunion of ye Chh of X in Sutton.

Feb: Mary Eaton dismist from^{50} us to Medford.

A Coppy of ye Covenant w^c ye brethren of ye first   [A7]

Chh: in Reading en^{t}red into upon ye gathering of y^e

s^d Chh: about ye year 1645.

We whose names are und^r written

At a Legal meeting of ye Church May 25. 1721
The chh Cove: w^s read. &
Capt Pool, Capt Burnap, Lt Pool, D: Nath: Lawrance,

Mr Smith, Ens: Goodwin & Ens: Bancroft w^r chosen

to look ov^r ye DD^s acc^ts of ye Contributions made

for ye poor in Several y^rs past & make re-

port to ye Chh:

           clear
They reported y^t ye acc^ts w^r & y^t w^t mony had

been laid out w^s done done prudently & noth: but w^t

w^s needf: & y^t Should they declare how, they

believed all w^d be Satisfyd. wth w^c answ^r ye chh

app^rd well pleasd.

Voted y^t each memb^r pay 2^s p^r head toward y^e

Support of ye ordinance of ye L^ds Supp^r for y^s

y^r ensuing - w^c begins July next. ~~But ev^r aft^r~~
~~of formerly on ye first of March annually~~
Voted, y^t ye Chh accept ~~y^e~~ all ye Deacons

acc^ts & are Satisfyd with y^r faithfulness, and

acquit y^m from[51] all w^rin they have been concernd

in provideing for ye Lords Table before y^s day
    & for all ye oth^r mannagement of contributions.

June 4th 1721. Matthew Grov^r being removed from us to

Coventree,[52] & Desireing a dismission for himselfe &

wife from[53] us to y^m. The Chh: voted y^r dismission acc^d:

to y^r req^t, & to recom̄end y^m as Such w^m w^c cand give

Testimony for.

August 2nd Recieving a Lett^r from Several   [A8]

persons in Woster in ye name of ye rest of
y^m y^t are agrieved at ye Settlement of
Mr Andrew Gardener y^r, w^rin they request
ye presence & help of o^r Chh by its Elder &
messeng^rs or messeng^r, togeth^r with y^os of
diverse oth^r Chhs sent too, ~~on ye occasion~~
w^o are all desird to Conveen in Counsel ~~att~~
on y^t occasion, on ye 16th currant.
Accordingly, Augt 6th I Stayd ye Chh,
aft^r ye publick worship w^s done, read
y^r Lett^rs, & proposd y^r request, & y^t if y^s Chh
would Send, & w^r free y^t ~~Chap C~~ Capt Burnap
Should go with me, they Should manifest it
by holding up y^r hands, w^c many, did nemi-
-ne Contradicente.

————

Sep^t: 17th: 1721. This day John Brown Junr (w^o has
been guilty of ye Sin of fornication) acknow
-ledging his Sin & manifesting Repentance
w^s received to favour again.

Feb: 19th. 1721/2 Thomas Nichols w^s ordaind Deacon
of the first church in Reading.

I haveing received a Lett^r from ye agrieved [A9]
party @ Woster Dated April 18. 1722. ~~I Comu~~
to be Comunicated to o^r Chh, w^rin p^rsuant to y^e
advice of ye Counsel y^t last mett y^r, y^y request
o^r presence & advice, accordingly May 13, 1722
I read y^r Lett^r to y^s Chh & desird y^m to Signify y^r minds
Capt Pool, Deacon Boutell, Lt Wm Briant & L^t

Parker Spake to oppose o^r Sending, Capt Pool

urged ye length of ye way, Lt Briant affirmd, y^e

Counsel y^t w^s last y^r unanimously agreed, y^t

Mr Gardener's call & Settlem^t to & in Woster w^s

right, & y^{r}upon advised ye dissenting party to

fall in, & y^n Lt Kendal Parker objected y^t

but one party sent & y^{r}fore he thout it w^s

not best for[54] us to send, bec: both did not Joyn

w^r upon I calld for y^e vote of y^e Chh, & but

few hands w^r held up for[55] it, & y^{r}f I desird y^e

negative, & it seemd to me y^t upon w^t L^t

Parker s^d more voted against it y^n for it

w^{r}f: I ~~refuse to~~ goe not.

_____

At a Legal meeting of y^e first Chh: in Reading

May 28. 1722. | y^e End to Chuse a deacon.

Deacon Nichols, James Nicols & Lt Sweayn

being necessarily absent Sent y^r votes Some

discourse y^r w^s about allowing y^m. it w^s put

to vote & voted in y^e affirmative by all y^e

brethren present, except m^r Wily, L. Bryant

& L^t ~~Parker~~ Kendal Parker.

_____

NB. Brother Francis Smith & Brother John Goodwin

w^r chosen to y^e office of Deacons in y^s Chh.

ANNO 1722

There haveing been Sad confusions w^c I often   [A10]

observed for Several years past, (& did often in

mention wth trouble

y^e publick ~~Observe~~ & pray might be reform'd) in o^r

Singing, Some w[r] above oth[rs] Some before oth[rs] &

and all y[s], as I apprehended for want of going more

together w[c] I urged to no purpose: & und[rs] y[t] y[r] w[s] a

Rule I Lookt on it, & concieveing y[e] Knowl: & keeping

to y[et] rule would prevent y[s] Confusion in y[t] p[t] of y[e]

publick worship; I promoted learning to Sing to y[t] End,

Several publick Lect[rs] w[r] had to promote it, y[e]

I preacht by my Selfe, y[e] 2nd by m[r] Symes, y[e] 3[d]

by m[r] Fisk[56] w[r] much w[s] s[d] to incourage it, & in

each of w[c] y[y] Sang 4 time Exact by y[e] rule,

no man opposing a School w[s] set up, mãy both

men & women Learnt. Some indeed w[r] not so

clear in it, (as by mistake) concieving it popery,

incouraged
but at lenght having been ~~urged~~ by Several

as by all y[e] Deacons, Cap[t] Pool & Cap[t] Burnap,

Ensign Bancroft, Serg[t] Thomas Pool, & Lt Bryant

(w[o] mett wth y[m] @ ye School) y[t] learnt, y[e] first night y[y]

began Sang wth y[m], wisht y[m] success, 4 of his family attend

ed y[e] Schools, he Learnt hims: Sang by rule in his

family, diverse months togeth[r], & as I observed

often Sang by rule in the ~~family~~ publick, & [(] as

I hear, Set y[e] tune by rule 3 times in y[e]

publick one day, w[n] I was sick.) L[t] Kendal Parker,

& urged by some to bring it into y[e] assembly & Espe

cially by D: Boutel y[e] Eldest Deacon, diverse

times. ------- Nov[r] 8th being Thanksgiving day aft[r]

church &
y[e] publick worship w[s] ov[r] I proposd it to y[e] Congre

gation to Sing by rule, & by w[t] I had heard not ex-

pecting any opposition, I s[d] That if they w[r] all

willing I would take y^r Silence for Consent, &

No man answerd one word, but all w^r Silent &   [A11]

went away.

―――――――――

Whereas Several persons of this Parish did some y^{rs} past

Subscribe to give Something annually, for five years tow^d ye Sup
-port of y^e
Rev^d m^r Daniel Putnum calld to be minist^r in o^r North
        ^
precinct, & Some of y^{os} men are dead, & oth^{rs} of y^m removed

out of Town, w^{r}by considerable y^t w^s subscribed is be

-hind, & s^d m^r Putnum at present (as is s^d) is in great

Strats; Some considerable men of the parish Signifying

this to me, desird I would move to y^s congregation for

a contribution to make up w^t w^s wanting of y^e

Subscription by reason of ye defunct & removed

as afores^d ; Accordingly Dec^m: 2. 1722. Aft^r ye publick
                                 a
worship w^s Ended, I signify'd y^r desire to ye Congregtion
                                                                        ^
& y^t if y^y w^r free to Contribute for^{57} ye End afores^d y^y

would Speedily let me know y^r minds herein, y^t I might

appoint ye time for s^d Contribution; And accordingly

ye Select men, Deacons & Diverse oth^{rs} came & told

me it w^s a good thing w^c they desird might proceed;

y^{r}fore Dec^m: 9th I appointed ye next Sabbath

for y^t contribution to be on; And Dec^m: 16th: 1722

This parish contributed to ye End afores^d, & y^e

contribution amounts to 5^{ll}——17^s——0.

Joseph Underwood & his wife being removed   [A12]

from us to Chelmsford, he Speaking to me to Sig

-nify to y^s Chh y^r desire of dismission from us

to ye Chh y^r; Accordingly

Feb: 24th 1722 aft^r ye publick worship w^s
ov^r, I proposd y^r desire to y^s Chh: and calld for a vote
by w^c y^r desire of dismission to ye watch and
fellowship of ye Chh @ Chelmsford w^s complyed
unto.

Octob^r 27th 1723 This Day Susannah Harndell
ye new wife of Joseph Kendal of Woburn
haveing been gilty of ye Sin of fornication,
acknowledging her Sin, w^s rec^d to charity.

———

1723.

Susannah ye wife of Thomas Hartshorn
w^s at her repeated request, dismist
fom us to ye Chh in ye North precinct

1724. Wm Russel & his wife now of Salem
village haveing Signified to me
y^r desire of dismission from[58] y^s first
Chh in Reading to ye Chh in Salem
village, accordingly y^r desire w^s proposd
Novr 29th. 1724 to this chh, and by
vote consented unto.

1724. Jan: 10th. O^r Congregation contributed
£9 − 3 − 0 towards redeeing Blanchard
Children.[59]

Jan: 14. I deliverd s^d Contribution to s^d
Blanchard for ye End aboves^d &
took his receipt.   R. B.

Jan: 17th. This day I Enformd ye Chh of   [A13]

Ephraim Chandlers fall into ye Sin

of fornication, & he making confes

-sion ~~of his s~~ ye Chh. manifested

y^r acceptance, & by y^r vote reciev^d

him again to y^r Charity.

ite^m This Day Brother John Leighton &

his wife desired a dismission ~~from~~

to ye Chh of Lexinton & y^s Chh

granted it by y^r vote.

Jan: 31.   Samuell Damon w^s (@ his) request

dismist from us to ye watch & Com̄union

of ye Chh at woburn.

1725.   Dec^m: 12th: ye Chh being Stayed. Thomas Nichols

& Eliz: his wife y^t had been dismist from^{60} us

to ye Chh in ye North precinct, being

returnd to live with us & @ y^r desire rec^d

lett^{rs} of Dismission from^{61} y^m to us, y^s Day I

read ye lett^r to o^r Chh, w^o y^{r}upon by y^r

vote rec^d. y^m to o^r fellowship & watch

again.

1726.   April 24th. ----------- This day ------------

Brother Francis Smith & John Goodwin w^r

both ordaind Deacons of ye first Chh in

Reading by ye consent & vote of ye Chh

------------------ p^r me R^d. Brown Pastor.

to God   [A14]

July 13th. 1726. This day w^s observed by y^s Chh &
                                    ^
Congregation, as a Day of Solemn fasting &

pray^r, for y^s Chh, & ye Riseing generation, & y^s

Chh y^s day solemnly recognized & renued y^r

Covenant wth God, both for y^ms & y^r Seed.

———————

Sep^t 18th. Susanna Cowdry alias Burrell

~~des~~ being removed from us to Boston

& desiring to be dismist from[62] us to ye New

north Chh, y^r, y^s,Chh by y^r vote complyd

to her request.   R. B.

———————

Octob^r 9th. Thomas Upham desireing a dismissi

-on, from us to ye Chh in Weston (w^r he

is removed) y^s Chh voted his dismission

acc^d: to his request, this day.

                    R. B.

———————

Dec^m: 18th. John Stearnes being removed to Toland

in ye Province of Conneticut, & desireing

a dismission from us to ye Chh y^r, his desire

w^s this day Signifyd to y^s Chh, w^c voted his

dismission & recomendation according to his

request.   R. B.

1727. Sep^t. 24th. Sarah Nichols ye now wife

of Joseph Barnap Junr, w^s at her request

dismist to ye Chh in ye North Precinct.

1727. Dec: 28. At a church meeting for takeing in 27 p^rsons   [A15]

y^t Stood propounded for full Communion.[63]

I proposed to ye Chh Ephraim Chandlers desire of being

Dismist from us & by us recommended to ye watch

& fellowship of ye 2nd Chh in Chelmsford. & it w^s

readily voted by ye Chh, nemine Contradicente.

Jan: 7th. ye Chh being Stayd @ Evening ~~here~~ I Signifyd to
ye chh y^t p^rcieving Some of o^r peop: w^r uneasie @
~~B y~~ Benj: Chaplin, Tho: Gowing, & Benj: Gowing;
Abigail Brown, & Joanna ~~Crockers~~ Joyning to o^r
chh to w^c y^y have been pr^po^ounded bec: y^y are
in difference @ Lyn End, not yet healed & y^t D: P:
has been with me, & Signifyd So much, & so Lt Pearson
& D: Bancroft; & y^t if y^y had made up y^r Differ: w^th
m^r Sparhawk & w^r @ peace y^r, y^y w^r free y^y
Should Joyn here. and farth^r y^t I had bec: of
w^t opposition w^s laid in ye way (as above s^d)
desird y^m ^to desist @ present till w^e had more
light in y^t matt^r. —— Farther I told ye Chh y^t
Martha Townsend of Lyn-End ~~and Abigail Gowing &~~
~~M~~ desird admission into full com̄union here, & y^t
Abigail Gowing desird Baptisme here, & mary
ye Daughter of John Hawks desird Baptisme —
& y^t I could not und^rs by y^m, (y^t is) ye 2 former y^t y^y
w^r any way Engaged in y^r quarrels, but desird
to come here now bec: y^r w^s So much difference
y^r, & I desird again and again y^t if any one
of ye Chh w^r not free to comply wth y^r desires
y^y would Speak & declare it; & Some s^d they
thout ye matt^r clear, & y^t needed no more to be
s^d & B: Jo: Parker Speaking @ my request, s^d, he
thout it ye Churches duty ^to allow y^r requests. & no
man contradicting it, I dismist ye Chh.

1727. Jan: 14th. After ye publick worship ws Ended.   [A16]

I Signifyd to ye Chh yt Severall persons Stood propound
ed for64 ye full Comunion, and bec: ye days wr Short & yrfore it
could not well bee done on a Sab: Even: I desired yt ye Chh
would meet for ~~ordr to proceed~~ yr admission into church fellow
-ship on thursday next at I a Clock & if yt day proved Stormy
yn ye next day @ one of ye Clock in ye aftr noon.

1727. Jan. 18. It proved clear but a very Cold day, I waited
till past one ~~and~~ a Clock and no prson apprd at ye meeting
house, @ 3/4 past one I got ready to go yr, and going into
ye Kitching (with my cloake on) in ordr to go to ye meeting
house, about 12 of ye brethren wr yr in ye Kitchen,
& prayd ye meeting might be ~~@~~ here @ my house
bec: of ye Sharpness of ye present cold. I told ym yt prhaps
ye Chh wd expect us @ ye meeting house, & I ws going yr.
yy pleaded ye Cold ws Such yt yy could not well bare it &
desird it might be here; If it wd not be a trouble to
me; I told ym, If ye Chh wr Easy It wd be no trouble to me:
they sd yy bel: ye Chh wd be glad of it. I told ym yt Some
prhaps wd depend on ye Chhs meeting yr. & wd not
know of yr meeting here, however @ yr Earnest re
quest, I desird Ens: Nichols & Jo Merrow to go to ye
meeting house & desire yos yt wr yr, to come here
 bec: of ye present cold, & so yy did. & ye Chh here
mett proceeded to Recieve ye Relations of & to
admitt yos to full communion yt Stood propounded
for it. Except 3 yt did not appr & one of ym had not
given me in her relation. ys is write ye more fully
bec: I heare Some that came @ about 3 a Clock

w^r unreasonably troubled or angry @ ye Chhs meeting

here. & Sam^{ll} Lambson w^s ye man y^t Showd most uneasi

-ness, & denyd ye Legallity of ye meeting. however 16

p^rsons w^r yⁿ & here rec^d without any objection.

1727/8. Feb: 18th. haveing rec^d a lett^r directed to o^r Chh   [A17]

from Sundry aggrieved of ye Congre[g]ational Chh in Ports

-mouth Rode Iland, requesting o^r help & advice in

& und^r y^r difficulties. I this day read it to y^e Chh w^o

voted to Send. & Tho: Nichols Junr wth me.

ite^m   We went acc^d: Ap: 1. 1727.

1728.   Ap^l. 19th. I rec^d a lett^r directed to o^r chh from Some

of y^e agrieved in Lynn=End, in y^e name of y^e rest, acc^d.

Ap: 21.   Aft^r y^e publick worship w^s Ended. I read it to y^e Chh

Jo. Eaton Sam: Lambson, & J^o Merrow Junr opposed it

& Deacon Smith old Ens: Parker, James Nichols Senr

Capt Burnap & Tho: Nichols 3^d w^r for it. a vote w^s

calld for,⁶⁵ and it w^s voted for Sending by a g^t Majori

ty. & Capt Parker Lt Bancroft & Sam^{ll} Lilly w^r

as w^s requested

voted to go with me y^r by a Silential vote.

Augt. 11th. Ivory Upham w^s dismist from o^r Chh to y^t of

Killinsly by an hand vote of y^s Chh.⁶⁶

1729.   June 20. ~~I ree^d petition written request~~   [A19]

haveing recieved a petition Dated June 18. 1729

Signed by Daniel Goold, Daniell Goold Junr,

Ebenezer Knight, David Goold, Ebenezer Parker,

Abraham Goold, Edward Bucknam, Tho: Cutler,

Joseph Bryant & Jonathan Griffin (10 in all)

all of Stonham, but members in full Com͞union

wth y^s Chh, for a dismission from[67] us in order to

y^r Embodying wth Some oth^{rs} into a Chh State y^r

in Stonham, as Soon as conveniently y^y may

This y^r desire w^s laid before y^s Chh, & I desir'd

y^t if any one had any thing to object against it

he w^d do So; but no one did, y^rfore I desired

y^t if ye brethren of y^s Chh did comply to y^r re

quest, and dismiss y^m. & y^t y^y be dismist from[68] o^r

care & watch as Soon as y^y w^r Embodied into

a chh y^r in Stonham, y^t y^y w^d Shew it by

y^r usual Sign w^c y^y did nemine contradicente.

June 29. 1729.

—————

1729. Jan: 4th. The Chh being Stayed. ye desire of y^{es}

Eleven member of y^s chh viz: Anna Holden

Naomi Holden, Eliza: Gary, wife of Benj. Gary

Eliz^a: wife of J^o Gary, Hannah Gary, Abigaill

Taylor, Mary Souter, Hannah Hay, Judeth Goold

Sarah Goold, & Eliz^a: Goold, for a dismission

from us to ye chh in Stonham, was gran

-ted, and accordingly y^y w^r now dismist acc^d:

to y^r request.

May 14th. 1732. This day Ephraim Wesson & his   [A20]

wife, and John Batt & his wife confessed

y^r Sin of fornication to ye Chh & obtained

forgivness & w^r recieved to Charity again.

Ite^m this day Samuell Lilly & his wife @ y^r

request w^r dismist from us to ye Chh in

Sutton.

Item, Abigail Nickols w^s @ her desire dismist from
from us to ye Second Chh in Marblehead w^rof
Mr Holyoke[69] is pastor.[70]

June 7th 1730.   [A21]

Jonathan Brown & his wife haveing been guilty
of fornication, in haveing a child to[o] Soon, They both
ownd y^r Sins to ye Chh before ye congregation, gave
glory to god, begd forgivness of him & ye Church, thô
he w^r only a child of ye Chh by his baptism, but She
had ownd ye Covenant & ye Chh takeing Satisfaction
from y^r humble confession restored y^m to y^r Charity
and allowed y^m baptism for y^r child, w^c w^s on y^s day
baptized th[e]y being to move to Billerica on next
Tuesday.

————————

July 5th. 1730 Margaret Swain alias Ordoway
w^s At her request, by ye vote of y^s Chh dis-
-mist to ye watch and Communion of y^t Chh
in Newbury w^rof m^r Lowell[71] is pastor.

————————

Augt 23. 1730. ye Chh being Stayed after y^e
publick worship w^s Ended; Mrs Martha Brown
now ~~alias~~ Wigglesworth, w^s at her request, by y^e
vote of y^s Chh dismist to ye watch & Com̄union
of ye 3^d Chh in Ipswich.

————————

Sep^t 27th. 1730. Danniell Nickols & Elizabeth his
now wife, being found guilty of fornication by
haveing a child born to y^m in 6 months & two days

they this day aft^r Sermon in ye Sabbath Evening

confest y^r Sin & guilt to ye Chh before ye Congre

-gation, and begd forgivness of God[72] & this chh, & y^e

chh ~~y by f~~ y^{r}upon forgave y^m & restored y^m to

y^r Charity & Comunion again & to ye priviledge

of Special ordinances, y^y being both memb^{rs} of y^s

chh.[73]

The Complaint of Broth^r Isaac Smith against Broth^r W^m [A23]

Bryant Senr. brought to me to be laid bef: y^s Chh: is as followeth: viz

To ye Rev^d. M^r. Brown pastor of ye first Chh in Reading,

Revd. S^r.[74]

1733

Octo^r 21. ye Service of ye Sabbath being Over I stayed ye Church to

Signify to them ye Desires of Stephen Wesson and James

Townsend wth y^r wives, all Members in full Communion

wth ye Ist Chh in Reading, to be dismisst from y^r Relation

to us in Order to y^r Embodying into a Chh at Wilmington

W^{ch}: Desire was Complyed wth Nemine Contradic^e: A Sabbath

or two before this Time were Dismist Capt. Kendal Pierson wth

his wife to ye Same Church in Wilmington, & Mr Ephraim Good

win to ye Church of Sutton of wch Mr Hall[75] is Pastor

Decr 23^d. After Service, were Dismissed Jonathan Barrett & Rebeccah his

wife to ye Church of Christ in Malden.

1734

March 31st: After Service was Dismissed Mary Brooks (rec^d into ye Chh

under ye name of Mary Boutell) to ye Chh of Christ in

Medford.

July 8th

At a Church Meeting assembled at ye Desire of John Wesson & Eliz^a.
his wife who Demanded Baptism for y^r Child she haveing Own'd
ye Covenant in y^s Church; a Number of Circumstances Concurring
to prove y^r Innocence Nothwithstanding y^t Child was born in Six
Months & nine days; it was then voted (ye Persons Concern'd then
Appearing to Assert y^r Innocence in a Most Solemn Manner)
y^t Baptism be Allowed to the Infant.

at ye Same Time voted that there be an Addition of one Shilling
to ye two Shillings formerly ~~Voted in Order to make~~ Imposed on
Each particular Member in Order to ye making a proper
provision of Elements for ye L^{ds} Table.

Feb. 23^d

ye Service of ye Sabbath being finishd, I Stayed ye Chh
who Dismist Mrs Mary Fish, at her Request, to ye Chh of
Christ in Mendam, of wch. ye Revd Mr Dorr is Minister[76]

[A24]

Augt 3^d

1735

The Service of ye Sabbath being Over I Stayed ye Chh who Rec^d into y^r Communion
James Townsend & Eliz^a his wife upon ye Recommendation from ye Chh of
Wilmington, to wch. Chh: they had Sometime before been dismist and
Recommended.

Nov 2

The Service of Sabbath being over I Signifyd to Chh: ye Desires [of] M^r
Sam^{ll} Bacheller to be dismist to ~~Chh Christ~~ Third Church of
Christ in Haverhill who Voted his Dismission; I also Signify'd y^e
Desires of S^d church in Haverhill, y^t we woud by our Elder &
Messengers, Assist in ye Ordination of Mr Sam^{ll} Bacheller to y^e
Pastoral Office in that Church, w^{ch}:Desires were Opposd; I then Nominated
Deacon Goodwin Capt Parker Capt Nicolls Capt Bryant Mr Underwood
Mr Nathan^{ll} Bacheller as ye Delegates or Messengers, wch ye Chh agreed to.

Novr 30th

The Service of ye Sabbath being over, I Stayed ye Chh & Signifyd
to y^m ye Desires of Judith Procter (formerly Rec^d into ye Chh under y^e
Name of Judith Nicolls) to be dismist from her Relation to us, & Recommended

to ye Second Chh of Christ in Woburn, wch was readily granted

<u>1736</u>

Ap^l: 4th ye Service of ye Sabbath being over I proposd to ye Chh y^e

Desires of Eliz^a Welch to be dismist from us & Recommended to

Dr Colmans Chh @ Boston,[77] wch desires were Readily Complyd w^th.

——— A Sabbath or two before y^s was Benja: Chaplin at his Request

Second

dismist & Recommended to ye Chh of Christ in Windham of w^ch

Mr Sam^ll: Mosely is Pastor.[78]

June 24th Upon a Complaint bro't before me by a Number of ye Brethren

of ye Chh against Brother Eben: Dammon & Kendal Bryant Junr: ye One

of Whom viz Brother Dammon Charging Brother Bryant w^th: Drunkeness,

ye Other, Brother Bryant Accusing Brother Dammon of Slander; I Desird

ye Chh to meet on y^s: day to Consider of these points of Difference. Accordingly

y^y did so When Brother Dammon persisted in Charging his Brother Bryant

wth Drunkeness. Brother Bryant tho he disown'd ye Charge of Habitual

Drunkeness yet Seem'd disposd to Acknowledge that he had been Overtaken

wth ye Sin of Drunkeness: provided it might be tho't an Unchristian procedure

in any, to Call him a Drunkard upon Such Acknowledgm^t: Wherupon the

Church passed a Vote y^t: it Shoud be look'd upon as Something Unchristian   [A25]

& Unjustifiable, to Call Brother Bryant a Drunkard upon his Acknowledgment

Upon w^ch: Vote, Brother Bryant Acknowledged y^t: whereas he had been gui

:lty of ye Sin of Drunkeness by w^ch: he had Offended ye Chh; he was heartily

Sorry for his Sin & beggd forgiveness of G^d: & his Church. this Acknowledgm^t

ye Church lookd upon as Satisfaction, & thereupon Rec^d: him to y^r Charity.

July 4th: Daniel Dodge & his wife together w^th: Mary Adams this day

Confessd ye Sin of Fornication, & were again Received to Charity.

——— 18th: Phebe ye wife of Joseph Rist was y^s day dismist from her Relation

to us & Recommended to ye Chh: of Christ at Uxbridge, Nathan Webb Past:

Nov 21.   Isaac Burnap & Wife this day confessd ye Sin of Fornicat^n their Child being born in a little more than six Months after Marriage, and so were again Received to ye Charity of ye Church.

Decr 5th: This Day upon y^r Desire Tim^o: Goodwin & Wife were dismist & Recommended to ye Chh of Christ in Willington in Connecticut of w^ch: ye Rev^d: M^r: Fuller is Pastor.[79]

—- On y^s Also was Read a Letter Sign'd Benj^a: Lynde, Benj^a Lynde Junr In ye name of ye Brethren Worshipping in ye Antient place of worship in Salem; Signifying y^r Desires y^t: we woud by our Elder & Messengers Assist in ye Ordinat^n of M^r <u>John Sparhawk</u> to ye Pastoral Care over y^m; After this was Read a Letter Signd Sam^ll Fisk Pastor, Nath Osgood, Tim^o Pickering &c in ye name of ye First Chh in Salem; protesting ag^n our Assistance in Afores^d: Ordinat^n: After a very short Debate ye Chh unanimously Voted Assistance by ye Elder, Deacon Goodwin, Peter Emerson, & Capt Parker.

1736/7

Jan 9th   W^m: Williams, Tim^o: Bryant & Wife this day Acknowledg'd ye Sin of Fornication, & were ag^n: Receiv'd to Charity

1737

March 6   The Church being Stayed John Wesson & Wife were at y^r Request dismist & Recom̄ended to ye Chh of X at Willington in Connecticut

——-13th: Nath^ll: Cowdry and Mehitabel his wife at their Request were Dismist their Relation to us, and Recommended to ye Chh of Christ in East Haddam[80]

June 12.   Eliz^a: Boutell formerly Eliz^a Bacheller was at her request dismist from us   [A26] & Recom̄ended to ye Chh of Christ in Sutton

—— 26 Isaac Wellman & Mary his wife were at their Request dismist from us & Recom̄ended to y^e: Chh of Christ at Norton at ye Same time Dorcas Dodge were dismist to ye Chh at Dudley

Oct^o: 2^d: Stephen Wessen & Hannah his wife, Tim^o: Wessen

and Abigail his wife were at their Desire dismist and
Recommended to ye Chh of Christ in Concord

Oct^o 4th   This Day at a Meeting of ye Chh M^r: Raham Bancroft
and M^r: Nath^ll: Stow, were Chosen to ye Office of Deacons.
on y^s: day also Ebenezer Parker Junr: upon Complaint laid ag^st:
him for ye Sin of Drunkeness, and full proof of ye Charge,
was laid under a Solemn Admonition, & Suspension for y^e:
Space of Six Months.

Feb. 26   Joseph Eaton Junr & wife were at y^r Request dismist & Recomended
to ye Chh in Lyn End.

~~1738~~

~~March 2~~

Feb. 28   at a Chh Meeting then Voted y^t whereas in times past
ye Communion table had been Maintaind by a Rate, it should
the Coming Year be maintain'd by a free Contribution.
Voted Likewise at ye Same Time y^t ye Chh w^d Speedily proceed
to y^e: Choice of two more Deacons.   Accordingly

1738

May 1st: At a Church Meeting Capt: Kendal Parker & Capt: Thos:
Nicolls were Chosen to y^e: Office of Deacons ——— at ye Same time
Time Voted y^t: ye Suspension formerly Laid on Eben^r Parker Junr
shou'd be Continued for ye Space of three Months longer, he not
having Shewed that hearty Repentance ye Chh wou'd gladly See in him.

May 21st.   Joseph Dammon Junr. & Mary his wife were this Day at their Request
Dismist & Recommended to ye Chh of Christ in Uxbridge whereto y^y
had lately Removed.

Aug^t: 6th.   I Signfy'd to y^e: Church ye urgent Desires of Sarah y^e: wife of Sam^ll Evans
to be baptis'd in private, her bodily Circumstances Rendring her Uncapable
of Attending upon that Ordinance in Public — Drawing, as was Supposed Near

her End ; & at ye Same time Signify'd my Intention of Administring

y^e: Ordinance According to her Desires. Accordingly About an hour after y^e

public Service, I in y^e: presence of a Considerable Number of ye Chh. Administred

y^e: ordinance to her, She having in ye Ist place Own'd ye Cov^t — a few hours after wch. she Dyed

Oct^o. 29: Joseph Eaton was at his Request, dismist, & Recomended to y^e [A27]

  1739 Chh. of Christ in Lyn End.

~~Sep^r~~ Aug^t: 27th At a Chh Meeting; Voted upon ye Recomendation of y^e

Gen^e Court to ye Dissenting Chhes thro ye Province; y^t there be a

general Contribution ye Next Sabbath Sen'night, to Assist

ye Rev^d: M^r. Torrey Pastor of a Dissenting Chh at Narraganset[81]

in Defraying ye Charges of an Action bro't agst: him by y^e

Rev^d: D^r: McSparren, a Minister of ye Chh of England[82]

w^{ch}: much Affects ye Interest of ye Dissenting Churches

provided at ye Same time, y^t Such Money Contributed be found

Necessary, w^{ch}, if thro ye Contribution of Other Chhes it be not

Tis then Voted y^t: it be Applyed to ye fund for ye propagat^n: of y^e

Gospel Among ye Dissenters; The Use or Advantage of w^{ch}

Money to be Dispos'd of by ye Convention of Dissenting Ministers

at Boston[83]

--------   At ye Same Time Voted upon ye Request of ye Rev^d

M^r. Osborn, Pastor of a Chh at Eastham, & Some of y^e

Brethren of ye Chh his Adherents; to Joyn wth: a Number of

Other Chhes, Call'd to Sit in Councill upon some Difficultys y^t

have Arisen there:[84] y^t In Considerat^n. of ye Late long Absence of y^r

Pastor from them; & ye great Number of Chhes Sent to, Many of

Whom will in all probability Meet in Council; They Cannot

See ye Necessity of going

--------   At ye Same Time Voted, y^t: ye Suspension under W^{ch}:

Mr Eben^r Parker Junr has long laid be on Acct. of ye Sin of Drunkenness Continued two

Months longer

Sep.ʳ 9.ᵗʰ: Agreable to yᵉ Aboves.ᵈ Vote yᵉ Congregation Contributed

Sixteen Pounds twelve shillings & ten pence W.ᶜʰ: I Deliverd

to D.ʳ: Colman, for w.ᶜʰ: I took his Receipt

———— 30.ᵗʰ   Benj.ᵃ Wiley & Wife at their Request were Dismis't

from yᵉ Chh. in Order to their Embodying w.ᵗʰ: a Number

of Other Brethren in a Chh Society in yᵉ Western Part of Lynn

Oct.ᵒ: I4   At yᵉ Request of W.ᵐ: Taylor & others of yᵉ Western

Society at Lȳn y.ᵗ we w.ᵈ Joyn in Councill w.ᵗʰ other Chhes

In Embodying y.ᵐ: as a Distinct Chh, Voted a Compliance

w.ᵗʰ y.ᵗ Request Deacon Parker & Goodwin Serg.ᵗ Parker

& Cap.ᵗ Bancroft Messengers.

Nov.ʳ: At yᵉ Convening of yᵉ Councill, the Incorporat.ⁿ of yᵉ Chh. was Con:

cluded upon, but deferr'd to yᵉ Councill for Ordinat.ⁿ

Upon the Request of W.ᵐ: Taylor & Others, y.ᵗ yᵉ Chh. w.ᵈ

Joyn w.ᵗʰ: other Chhes in Incorporating a Chh in yᵉ Western   [A28]

Part of Lyn, & Separating M.ʳ Edw.ᵈ: Cheever to yᵉ Pastorall

Office in it ————- Voted to Send

Feb.ʸ: 26.ᵗʰ. ————   At a Chh Meeting Appointed to Consider

Some Matters of Difference Subsisting between Bro.ʳ

Tho.ˢ: Eaton & Bro.ʳ Eben.ʳ Merrow, & Some Articles

of Charge brot by yᵉ former ag.ˢᵗ: yᵉ Latter: The

Chh Voted y.ᵐSelves Dissatisfyd w.ᵗʰ: Bro.ʳ Merrow

on yᵉ Acc.ᵗ of Lying & Slander: Bro.ʳ Merrow

Acknowledged his Offences or y.ᵗ he had great Reason

to believe himself guilty: but not Seeing those

Marks of hearty Grief & Sincere Rep.ᵉ: y.ʸ: Voted

his Suspension for Six Weeks, & left a W.ᵈ of

Admonition w.ᵗʰ: him.

1740

Ap^l 18 At a Chh: Meeting Appointed to consider farther of ye Affair
of Bro^r Eben^r Merrow as Above; The Time of his Suspension
being Expired: & he Solemnly protesting his forgetfullness of
y^e ~~Sins~~ Crimes laid to his charge: the Chh herupon Rec^d: him
to y^r Charity, upon ye following Confess^n:———— Wheras in
ye long Controversy Subsisting between Bro^r Eaton &
my Self, I Believe, (upon ye Evidence of Others) I have been
guilty of ye Sin of Lying, & Slander to ye Dishonour of
G^d: & his pple, I am heartily Sorry for it, I beg Pardon
of God & his Chh: hoping my future Conduct & Conversat^n
will be more Agreable to ye Gospell of Christ.

Augt 3^d: The Chh being Stayed Rebecca Boutell wife of John Boutell
was at her Request Dismist to ye first Chh in Woburn.
at ye Same Time Sarah Emerson Wife to Mr Brown Emerson
was Rec^d: into full Communion w^th: us, upon ye Recommendat: of
~~ye Chh~~ Rev^d: Caleb Cushing Pastor of ye I^st: Chh: in Salisbury
to w^ch: she belong'd
Ebenezer Phillips a Member of ye Anabaptist Chh
in Boston, presenting a Request to us y^t: he might Joyn wth us
at ye Table of ye Lord ————; ye Chh Considerd his Request &
Unanimously Complyd w^th: it

Jan^y: 7th: Upon a Complaint brot before me by Severall
of ye Members of ye Chh in Stoneham; as Also
by Bro^r Thos: Eaton; Ag^st. Bro^r. Nath Eaton
a Member of ye Chh In wch Complaint S^d Nath^ll is Chargd
with ye Sin of Lying ———— I herupon Calld ye Chh together, who after   [A29]
Prayer to G^d: for Direction, and a Long Debate upon ye Matters of Contro:
:versy at Length Came into ye Following Votes.   First

That it Appears to ye Chh y^t: Bro^r Thos. & Nath^ll: Eaton After Some

Difference between y^m Came to a Cov^t: or Agreement in wch all Matters of

Difference were to be laid Aside: and a New Amity or friendship was to

begin. ———— Sec^dly: y^t it Appears to y^e: Chh y^t Bro^r Nath^ll: has Denyd

& persists in Denying y^t Ever any Such Contract or Agreement was Made.

———— Sec^dly: In Relation to ye Matter of Complaint bro't by ye Stoneham

Brethren: it Appears to ye Chh y^t: Bro^r Nath^ll Eatons Conversat^n: has

been Utterly Inconsistent w^th: y^e: Truth Sincerity & Undisguisd Behaviour

of a Christian ———— Herupon ye Meeting was Adjournd to y^e

Tuesday preceeding ye Next Sacrement ———— at One o'Clock ——

Sabbath preceeding S^d Tuesday I for Special Reasons Adjournd ye Meeting

till Friday ——— On Friday y^e: Chh Met When Bro^r Nath^ll

Eaton presented His Acknowledgm^t to ye Chh W^ch: being Read once

& Again ye Chh Voted y^m Selves Satisfyd.

Feb^y: 11th: There having been Matters of a Scandalous Nature blaz'd about in

Relation to ye Conduct of Mr Joseph Underwood, who was Reported to

have been found Stealing Corn from Brother Noah Eaton; I herupon

Calld ye Chh together to Enquire into y^e: Matter; And After prayer to g^d for

Direction & Sufficient Debate upon ye premises, I put ye Matter to Vote

"Whether this Chh were Satisfyd or Dissatisfyd wth Bro:^r Jos: Underwoods

"Conduct in Relation to a Complaint bro't ag^st. him as bearing hard upon

the Eig^th Comm^t: ———— who Voted Dissatisfyed.

1742

March 2^d   I Calld ye Chh together to Consider ye Affair of Mr Underwood

with Whom ye Chh had Voted y^mselves Dissatisfyd; When Mr Underwood

presented an humble Acknowledgment to ye Chh wth wch. ye Chh declared y^r

Satisfaction & Restored him to y^r Charity

Ap^l: 9th: It being Commonly Reported y^t Eben^r Merrow a Member

of y^s Chh. had been Convicted of Stealing before Thos: Hubbard

Esqr. & by him Committed to Goal; I wrote to S^d. Hubbard for

Information in ye Affair, I having Receiv'd an Answer from [him] I laid

before ye Chh who upon partic. Examinat^n of ye Affair Voted y^mSelves

Dissatisfyd w^th: S^d: Merrow, & then Suspended him from y^r Communion

till they Should See in him a Conversation more becoming ye Gospell of X^t.

May 2^d: Jonathan Nicolls Junr & Wife having been Guilty of Fornication

presented y^r Acknowledgment & Confess^n: to ye Chh of y^r own free will

That they had had Carnal Knoledge of One Another before   [A30]

Marriage, & having humbled y^mSelves before G^d: & his People

The Chh Voted to Accept y^r Acknowledgm^t & So y^r Charity to y^m

Sepr 5th: Nath^ll. Cowdry & Mehitabel his wife Dismist to ye Chh

at Sunderland —— Jabez Temple & Wife Dismist to ye Chh

at Wilmington as also ye Wife of Nath^ll Townsend

— 19th   Rebecca Walton Dismist to ye Chh at South hegen.[85]

Oct^o: 17th. Joseph Boutell Dismist to ye Chh at South-hegen.

1743

May 8   This Day Mary Pool formerly Leeman having obtaind

Letters of Dismiss^n from ye Chh. of York[86] was Rec^d: at her

Request to Our Watch & holy fellowship, as also

Sam^ll Nicolls & Hannah his Wife from a Chh. of Christ

In Willington

June 5th: The Chh being Stayed Braviter Gray was at his Request

dismist & Recomended to ye Chh of X in Billerica

Oct^o. 23^d   The Chh being Stayd I Read to em two Letters w^ch

I had Rec^d: to be Communicated y^e: one from a Number of

Aggrieved Breth: at ye Chh of Worcester ye other from a

Number of Aggrieved Breth: In ye Chh at Newbury under

ye Pastoral Care of ye Rev^d. M^r. Tappan; Each Desiring our

Assistance in Councill wth. other Chhes, under y^r Distressed

Circumstances. y^e: Counsills being Calld to Convene at ye Same

Time we were Unable to Joyn in both; & therefore Voted

y^t. we w^d: send to Worcester where our Assistance was

first Asked.

~~Dec^r:~~ Jan^y: 1st: M^r. Eben^r. Parker Senr: haveing Some time past

been grossly guilty of ye Sin of Drunkeness, did

very Early, Offer his Repent: to y^e: Chh w^ch: had ye Appearance

of great Sincerity: However Esteeming ye fruits of Rep^e:

ye best Evidence of its Sincerity, We deferr'd y^e: Acceptance

of his Confess^n: for a Considerable Time; In wch. Time having

behaved himself w^th: much Humility & Watchfulness We

this Day Receiv'd him to Our Charity again

1744

Apr 8th: The Chh being Stayed Judith Boutell Wife to

M^r. James Boutell was dismist & Recom̄ended to y^e

Chh at LeMinster ——————— Jno: Rogers Pastor

May 13th: The Chh being Stayed ~~Mary~~ Ruth Burt was Dismist

& Recom̄ended to ye Chh at Mendam ——— Joseph Dorr Pastor

May 17th: Zechary Nicols & Rebecca his Wife were then Dismist to ye Chh   [A31]

of X is Sherbourne ——————— Rev^d: M^r S: Porter Minister

(Forgot to rec^d in order) y^t: A Number of Breth: belonging to y^e. 1st Chh: in Newbury

Applying to us for Councill in Matters of Difference Subsisting

between ye Pastor & y^mSelves, I Read ye Letters to ye Chh who

thôt it adviseable to send in Councill & Accordingly Voted Benj. Brown

D^r: Hay Brown Emerson to be ye Chhes Messengers in Attendance

on y^r. Pastor. The Councill having Met at Time & place

The Rev^d. M^r. Tappan Pastor of ye Chh in Newbury Under

his Own Hand oblig'd himself to Joyn w^th: ye Aggrieved in

Calling a Mutual Councill, upon w^ch: ye Counc: Dissolv'd. but

M^r. Tappan afterw^d: being Unequal to his Engagements y^e

Aggriev'd Renewedly Made applica^n: to us to Joyn in Councill

w^th: Other Chhes in Regard of y^e. premises; Matters being laid

before ye Chh, y^y thôt it necessary to comply w^th: ye desire

of y^e: Aggrieved & Accordingly Voted to Send; & y^t ye former

Messengers go again w^th: ye Addition of Eben^r Nicolls Junr.

Sep^r.   I then Rec^d. Letters from ye Pastor & Chh in Grafton

Representing y^t. a number of Breth: there were & had for a long

time been Uneasy With y^t Part: Chh: but now Desirous y^t Matters

of Diff: might be Accomodated y^y: had Agreed wth. ye Chh to Ask

Councill: Every of ye Chhes of S^d Councill being Acceptab: to Each party
& agreed upon by
^

Accordingly I Read ye Letters to ye Chh who Voted to Send in Councill

& y^t Deacon Goodwin Deacon Bancroft be Messengers to

wch. Number I added a third p^rson. Capt. Bancroft.

NB: Every Person Came in to Receive Councill given. Glory to G^d. peace on Earth.

Novr. 25   James Dix & Wife together wth Kath^n: Hutchinson having

been found guilty of ye Sin of Fornicat^n. y^y. then Sensible of

y^t Sin made Humble Confess^n. of it before ye Congregation of G^ds: pple

& had ye Chhes Charity Voted to y^m.

1745

May   Jacob Barrett dismist to ye Sec^d: Chh in Lancaster

Sepr 22   Signify'd to Chh y^t. I had Rec^d. Letters from I^st: Chh

In Salem (as y^y. Style y^mSelves) wishing us to Joyn w^th

y^m. in y^e. Ordination Mr Dudley Leavitt to ye Pastorate

Charge in y^e. Room of M^r. Sam^ll. Fisk dismist on Acc^t

of Some Scandals he was Convicted of; ye Letters being

Read y^y. Voted to go by Capt. Parker Capt. Eaton &

Capt. Brown as y^r Delegates

1746

Ap^r 30   James Brown James Goodwin & Wife wth [A32]

David Bancroft were then at their Desire

dismist & Recom̄ended to ye Chh of X in Norwich

as also Katharine Conant to ye Chh in Hollis

(Ap^l. be'g Omitted)   A Considerable Number of ye Breth of ye Chh

in Framingham Signifying their Uneasiness at

ye Doctrines deliver'd by y^r Pastor[87] as bordering

upon ye Arminian Scheme, desird our Assistance

in Fellowship wth. Some Other Chhes by Advising y^m

in y^r. present Difficultys; but ye Circumstances of

my Family not Allowing Me to go; ye Chh Voted in ye Negat^e.

May 18th A Considerable Number of ye Town & Chh in

Framingham having Remonstrated agst: ye Preaching of

ye Pastor of S^d Town & Chh Earnestly & Repeatedly

Desird ye Assistance of Our Chh in Concurrence wth

Other Chhes to Advise y^m in y^r present Difficultys:

at ye same Time a great Number of ye Chh

of X in Hopkington being Offended at ye Conduct

of y^r Pastor & a Number of y^r Breth: desird

Our presence in Councill wth Other Chhes. ye Letters

Relating to w^{ch}: Difficultys I laid before ye Chh who

tho't it adviseable to Send Help & assistance & Accordingly

Eben^r Nicolls Junr John Walton & Thos Burnap

were Appointed Delegates.

Augt A Number of ye Breth of ye 2^d; Chh in Bradford

having Signifyd y^r Uneasiness wth ye Pastor[88] on

acc^t: of false Doct: deliver'd by him as also wth

y^e: Chh on Acc^t of Some Male Administrat^n. desird

ye Assist^c of ye Chh to Joyn in Councill wth Other

Chhes, w^ch: being Signifyd to Our Chh they Refusd

to grant ye Request of ye Complainants

As also y^y Refus'd to Assist a Number of Breth in Dor: [A33]

chester Uneasy at ye Conduct of ye Pastor of Chh there

—— ye Main Reason of Such Refusals —- Our being so

frequently Engag'd in ye Affairs of Other Chhes

Augt 26 — Lecture Day — The Chh being Stayed after

Lecture proceeded to ye Choice of two Deacons to

Supply y^e. places of Deacon Smith & Nicolls, dec^d

When Mr Brown Emerson & Jon^a. Temple were

Chosen by a Majority of Votes.

At ye Same Time, London, a Negro Man belonging

to Bro^r: Thos. Eaton Confess'd y^e Sin of Fornication

& was Suspended till he sh^d shew good Evidence of an

Evangelical Humiliat^n.

Oct^o 5th.   Edwd: Dammon & Eliz^a his Wife were then at

their Request dismist from their Relation to y^s Chh

in Order to their Embodying into a Chh at Ware=

=River.

Novr. 30   M^r. Brown Emerson having Signifyd to me his

Accept^e. of y^e Chhes Call to y^e Office of a Deacon

I manifested my Concurrence wth y^e Chh's Vote &

Invited him to his proper place in Deacons Seat

—— at y^e Same Time Hannah Daggett was Dismist

to Chh at Sutton & Jacob Smith to ye Chh in Hollis

Dec^r   The Chh of Stoneham having Sent Letters Desiring

Our Assistance at ye Ordination of Mr John Carney

Whom they had Chosen for their Pastor, I read the

Letters to ye Chh Who Readily Voted to gratify ye Request

& Sent wth ye Pastor Mr Emerson Deacon Goodwin

Capt Bryant & Deacon Parker

At ye Same Time I had Letters from ye Chh of   [A34]

Woburn Intreating us to Compassionate their

Melancholly Circumstances[89] by Assisting in Councill

wch y^y had calld to Sit & Judge upon them, ye Chh Voted

Assistance & Accordingly Sent wth their

Pastor Capt Bancroft & Capt Brown.

1747 July ye Sec^d: Chh in Malden having desir'd our presence

                   Installation

& Assistance in y^e ~~Ordination~~ of ye Rev^d M^r. Cleveland[90]

I read ye Letters to ye Chh Who Seem'd dispos'd to go till

I Informed y^m: y^t: I had no Acquaintance w^th: ye Gent^n

to be Installd & therefore dar'd not in Conscience to

Assist, on W^ch: we proceeded no farther.

Aug^t: The Third Chh in Lynn having desir'd Our presence

     & Assistance in some Difficult Matters Relating Chiefly to

     ye Pastor of S^d. Chh[91] who had been Charg'd wth Very Indecent

     Carriage towards his Maid, Mary Burrill, ye Chh

     Voted Assistance, & w^th: their Pastor Sent Deacon

     Parker & Deacon Bancroft.

May it Sh^d: have been Inserted above y^t ye Chh of Dorchester

     having a Number who had Separated from its Communion

     did w^th: their Separating Breth^n. desire ye Assistance of this

     Chh to Sit in Councill wth. Others & advise them in their

     Difficultys; ye Chh accordingly Voted to Send, Upon W^ch. Deacon

     Bancroft was Nominated & Voted to go wth ye Pastor

Oct^o: Lydia Nicolls was Rec^d: into ye Watch of this Chh by a

     Recomendat^n from Stonham.

       at ye Same Time I Read to Chh Letters Sent from Billerica

desiring Our Assistance in ye Ordinat^n of M^r. John Chandler

with w^{ch}: ye Chh Comply'd & Chose Capt Bancroft Deacon

Emerson & Mr Sam^{ll} Pool

Jany. Jon^n. Eaton ~~Junr~~ having Entred a Complaint agst

Wm Bryant Junr. wth. Respect to Some Slanderous

& Vilifying Expressions Used by S^d. Bryant, I

Appointed a Chh Meeting for ye Consideration of

this Affair ——— ye Chh having Met at Time Appointed & y^e [A35]

Defend^t: pleaded y^t: S^d: Eaton had not taken ye private

Steps prescribed by Our Sav^r: & therefore y^t ye Matter

was not Under ye Cognizance of ye Chh. this being debated

it Appear'd y^t. however M^r. Eatons Behaviour was Agreable

to ye Letter Yet it was by no Means to ye Charitable Design

& End of ye Gospell w^{ch}: is to Reclaim an Offender & therefore

Voted y^t: Mr. Eatons Conduct be look'd upon by y^s. Chh

as Defective in ye Essentials of it, on W^{ch}: it was flung

out & Recomended to 'em y^t ye Matter be privately Accomodated.

——— at ye Same Time it was Motion'd to ye Chh, y^t Inasmuch as

John Dammon a Member of y^e Chh had fallen into y^e Depths of

Enthusiasm thrô w^{ch}: he had Vented y^e Most Uncharitable Express^s

not only agst. y^e Pastors of y^s. Chhs but y^e Chh itself, nor only y^s Chh but

Indeed y^e whole Chh of X, as being Antichristian, & had Withdrawn

from y^e preached Word & y^e $\overset{\text{public}}{\wedge}$ Ordinances; ——— y^t. therefore Something be

done in Charity to y^e Offender in Order to Reclaim him — hereupon

Voted y^t Deacon Parker Deacon Bancroft Deacon Emerson

& Deacon Temple wth. Capt. Brown & Capt. Nicolls be a Committee

of Enquiry into y^e Conduct of Broth^r Dammon & y^e Reasons of it

& Make Report to y^e. Pastor of y^s. Chh.[92] ——— at ye Same

Time it was Motion'd to ye Chh y^t: Inasmuch as Brother Eben^r

Parker Junr: having been guilty of ye Sin of Drunkeness had

been long Suspended y^e: Commun^n of ye Chh, & no fruits of Repent^n

Appearing, nor he Manifesting a desire to Return to ye fellowship

of y^e: Chh; ⸺ ~~Whither~~ it be Consider'd W^t. was proper to be done

Hereupon Voted y^t. two of ye Deacons wth M^r. Thos Burnap, John

Sweyn, Benjn. Sweyn be a Committee to Inform Bro^r Parker

y^t: Unless a Reformation Appears in him the Chh will proceed to

Excommunicat^n in ye Space of three Months ⸺ In ye Mean

While S^d Committee are Desird particularly to watch over him.

1748 Ap^l 10   The Second Chh in Ipswich being Offended at y^e. Conduct of y^e.

First, & having, to no purpose Endeavour'd to compromise &

heal Matters y^y: proceeded to Administer Letters of Admonition

wch. not Answering y^r. designed End, they proceeded to Send Letters

to Other Chhes, & particularly to ye Ist. Chh in Reading, desiring   [A36]

them to back or Second ye Admonition; Accordingly I laid

ye Matter before ye Chh, Who considering ye Importance of

ye Case, desird ye Matter might be deferr'd till ye next L^{ds}:

Day: ⸺⸺⸺When ye Consideration of ye Matter being

Resum'd ye Chh not Seeing Sufficient Reason to grant y^e

Prayer of y^t. Petition ⸺ Voted in ye Negative

    At ye Same Time laid before ye Chh a Letter from ye Chh

in Tivertown, who had lately Rec^d: y^e. Gospell built an

House for Public Worship & Settled a Pastor,[93] but being

in their Infancy were Weak & therefore desird Assistance in

Order to defray their Charges: ye Chh taking y^e. Matter into

Considerat^n Voted to grant ye Desire of ye Petition, Accordingly

a Contribution was Appointed to be on ye Next Thursday Sennight

it being fast Day.

Augt. 28   L^{ds} Day Eve Stayed ye Chh. & Read a Letter from Willm: Baldwin who w^th: Other Members of ye Chh of Christ in Narragansett N^o: 2

were highly Offended wth. their Pastor, M^r. Elisha Marsh & Chh on

Various Accounts, & therefore desird Our advice in Councill w^th: many

other Chhes Call'd to sit in New Town — The Chh having heard

ye Letters Voted to gratify ye prayers of ye Petition — & accordingly

appointed Lieut^t. Parker & Capt. Bancroft as their Delegates.

Sep. 18   L^ds Day Eve ye Common Service of y^e. Sabb^h. being Over

I Communicated to ye Chh Letters Sent from ye Chh in Chelsea

                    Instalment

desiring Our Assistance in y^e ~~Ordination~~ of M^r. W^m: McClanathan

W^m: they had called to ye Pastoral Office in S^d. Chh. — The Chh

Voted to go by their Delegates Deacon Emerson Capt. Eaton

Capt. Nicolls W^th: their Pastor

NB   The Councill Met at Time Appointed, but Much being Objected

ag^st. Moral Character of M^r McClanhathan ye Councill declined

y^e. Installm^t. for present & adjourn'd to 3^d: Wednesday Dec^r

next, In Mean Time taking Necessary & prudent Measures to find

out y^e. true Character of y^e. Gent^n. Elected

1749

March Lecture Day after ye Service of y^e. Day I Stayed ye Chh,

laid before y^m: y^e. Case of John Dammon & Wife

who Notwithstanding all Endeavours to Reclaim 'em, Yet

Continued in y^r. Enthusiasticall Notions, & Uncharitible, Censorious   [A37]

frames, giving out y^t y^s: Chh & all Other Chhes in y^e. Land were but

Baals Chhes & y^e. Ministers, but ye Dragons Angels[94] w^th: Many Other

Expressions of y^e. like Nature: after Much Debate upon y^e. Case ye Chh

proceeded to Vote y^t: y^r: Conduct in y^se. things, as also in Refusing to

Vote   Attend y^s. Chh Meeting of W^ch: they had been duly Notified, was

Censurable, as Contrary to y^e. Word of G^d: & ye Bonds of ye Chh Covenant

& therefore they were forbidden ye Table of y^e. L^d: for ye present. Yet

Inasmuch as a Controversy Arose founded on y^e: Quest^n. Whether Mr Dammon & Wife were not put out of ye possess^n of y^r own Minds & Much being offerd to prove y^t y^y were at least under a <u>Dementia quoadhac</u>^95 ye Chh tho't it not proper Immediately at least to Censure y^se p^rsons but Voted to Spend Some time in prayer on y^r. acc^t: desiring also y^t. y^e. Rev^d. M^r. Clark of Salem Village, M^r. Putnam of N^o: Precinct & M^r. Emerson of Malden Might be Intreated to Assist in S^d Solemnity. — ye Time for S^d. Solemnity to be left w^th: ye Pastors ——— Hereupon Voted y^t two of y^e. Deacons & Capt. Nicolls be a Committee to Inform S^d. Dammon & Wife of ye transactions of y^e. Chh & Withal Give y^m to know y^t. y^e. Chh Expect y^r. Attendance at y^e. Time of prayer —after W^ch: ye Meeting was Adjournd for two Months for further Considerat^n

May 12th — being Lecture Day I Stayed ye Chh after Divine Service; & further Represented to y^m: y^e. Case of M^r. John Dammon & Wife who still Continued in y^r. former Offences, & Refus'd to attend ye Chh on ye Day of Prayer tho Set Apart on their Partic: Account, of W^ch: they were Duly Notify'd; & Who also Refus'd to give Account of their Conduct, at this Meeting where they were Required to give their Attendence: the Chh herupon, taking ye Matter into Serious Consideration Voted y^t. Bro^r. John Dammon & Wife obstinately persisting in their Uncharitable Language & Disorderly Behaviour, be therfore Suspended ye Communion of y^e. Chh, till they shall give Suitable Satisfaction . at ye Same Time Voted y^t. an Admonition be dispensed to John Dammon & Wife & y^t Deacon Temple Capt. Eaton Capt Bancroft & Bro^r. Eph^m. Wesson & Joseph Parker accompany ye Pastor in Dispensing S^d. Admonition.

At ye Same Time ye Case of Eben^r Parker Junr who had long liv'd in ye Sin of Drunkeness, & had been Suspended therefor was taken [A38] into Consideration at W^ch: Time S^d. Parker Offering a Confession of his Sin & pretending to be humbled therfor, the Chh so far

accepted his Acknowledgm^r: as to Vote a Reprieve from ye Sentence

of Excommmunication, W^{ch}: y^y. had formerly Voted to pass wthout

Repentance & Reformation: S^d. Reprieve to continue for ye Space

of One Month & no longer Except there were Apparent Tokens

of Repent^e. & Amendm^r: In ye Mean [time] they who had ye former

Special Watch Over him together wth: M^{ess} Josiah & Jotham

Walton were desird to Continue it.

Lecture Day   Some Considerable Time having passed ye Chh met ag^n: to Consider

Sep^r: 28 ye Case of Eben^r: Parker but he not being present tho Warnd

ye Chh Voted to protract y^r. Lenity towards him till ye Next Lecture

Day; when y^y: purpos'd to take his Affairs into Considerat^n & proceed

agst. him, without Reformat^n, Whether present or Absent

Octo 27.   being Lecture Day ~~I Movd to~~ The Chh being Met by Adjournm^t

I Movd to ye Chh - Case of Eben^r Parker, who after Some

Debates upon ye propriety or Impropriety of Immediately Considering

S^d Case at Length Voted to adjourn to thursday Seven Night

s^d Parker being Absent

following & y^t Deacon Bancroft Deacon Temple Capt. Brown

Deacon Emerson & Bro^r. Eph^m. Wesson be a Committe of ye Chh

to Visit S^d Parker & Solemnly to Urge upon him ye Necessity of

paying due Regards to ye Authority of ye Chh

    Thursday Novr 10th: The Chh being Met took into Considerat^n ye Case

of Eben^r Parker & Nothing of Importance being Offerd by him in his

Vindicat^n. Voted 1st y^t. they would Extend their Lenity to him no farther

2dly: That Conduct of Eben^r. Parker by Reason of habitual

Drunkeness aggravated by Many & Awfull Considerat^{ns}, partic: by

his Continuance in it for a long Course [of] Time & In Contradict^n. to many

Solemn promises & Engagem^{ts}: is Such as y^t. we apprehend him

unworthy of being a Member of Christs Visible Chh, & y^t therfore he be Cut off from it —— Accordingly a few Sabb[s]. following

he was Excommunicated in face of y[e] Congregat[n]

1750

March 11th:   Jacob Bancroft & Wife having been guilty of y[e] Sin of

Fornicat[n], acknowledgd y[r] Sin were Received to Charity respectively, & had

y[r]. Child Baptised

April 1 communicated to y[e] Chh Letters from a Chh in Eastham

Inviting Our presence & Assistance at y[e] Installm[t]. of y[e]. Rev[d]   [A39]

M[r]. Edw[d]. Cheever in y[e] Pastoral Office there, but y[e] Chh Considering y[e]

great Distance & y[t] Their Assistance was not of absolute Necessity declin'd

going

May 27   Having Rec[d] Letters from y[e] Chh of Ch[t]: in Northhampton

Signifying y[e] Great Difficulty they labord of in Respect of diff[t].

Sentiments Relating to y[e]. Right to y[e] Holy Supper, & Intreating Our

Assistance in Removing S[d]. Difficulty; I Com[ted] y[e] Letters to y[e] Chh

who Esteeming y[e]. Matter of great Importance Voted to Send[96]

N B: Sam[ll]. Bancroft Jun[r]: Chosen Delegate

July 22[d]   The Chh being Stayed after y[e] Service of y[e] Sabb[a]. I Comunicated

to them Letters from y[e] Third Chh in Lynn Desiring Our

Assistance in y[e] Ordination of M[r]: Joseph Roby to y[e]

Pastoral Office in S[d]. Chh: — The Chh having Voted y[r]

Readiness to Assist; Deacon Bancroft, Cap[t]. Brown Cap[t].

Sweyn Cap[t]. Nicolls & M[r]. Sam[ll]. Pool Were appointed

Delegates to Accompany y[e] Pastor

Octo   M[r]: Joseph Sweyn was dismist & Recomended to y[e]: Chh

of Christ in Wenham — at y[e] Same Time I Communicated

Letters from y[e] Chh afores[d]. desiring Our Assistance in Seperating M[r].

Sweyn to y[e] Pastoral Office there — y[e] Chh Voted to Send

Deacon Emerson Cap[t] Brown Cap[t]. Sweyn, Benj[n]. Sweyn & M[r]

John Walton Junr Voted Delegates, & also M^r. Sam^{ll}. Pool

Near ye Same Time I Communicated to y^e: Chh a Letter

from ye Rev^d M^r. Cleveland Pastor of ye South Chh in Malden

Desiring Our Assistance in Councill about ye Expediency of his

Removal to Hallifax in Chebucta^{97} to W^{ch}: place he was Earnestly

Invited. The Chh having heard his Letters Voted to Send.

NB: Capt. Brown & Capt. Nicolls Voted Delegates

Novr James Abbott & Sarah his Wife were at their Request dismist

& Recomended to ye Chh of X. at Pennicook

Decr. 9th Jacob Parker & Abigail his Wife, Children of ye Chh   [A40]

tho not Members in full Communion, being Convicted in

their Consciences of their breaking ye Seventh Com^t. offerd

their Acknowledgm^t & were ag^n. Rec^d: into Charity according to

their former Standing

1751

May Having Rec^d Letters from a Number of ye Breth^n of ye Chh

of Northampton adhering to y^r. Late Pastour ye Revd Mr Edwards

Signifying y^r. Desires y^t. we w^d Incorporate y^m. & Install

y^r. Late Pastor over y^m if we Saw meet, or Otherwise give

Such Advice as y^r. Circumstances Calld for; having also Rec^d Letters

from ye Rev^d: M^r. Edwards, desiring y^t. he might have an

Opportunity to lay his Case before a Councill, & have y^r advice,

I Read ye Letters to ye Chh who Voted to Send according to y^e

Desire of y^e. Petitioners — N B. Capt: Brown & Sam^{ll}. Bancroft Junr. Deleg:

June   Having Rec^d. Letters from a Number of ye Breth^n. of y^e

West Chh in Sudbury signifying y^r. Uneasiness wth. y^r. Pastor

Refusing y^m: a Chh Meeting tho often Requested, as also to Joyn in

& hereupon desiring Our Assistance & Councill.

Councill under y^r Difficulties — I read ye Letters to ye Chh

as also a Complaint of y^e. Grievance of y^e. Breth^n. Carryed in to ye Pastor of S^d Chh, — Upon W^ch: ye Chh Voted to Send

N B: Deacon Emerson & John Temple Delegates

July   Communicated to Chh Letters Rec^d: from ye Chh at Linebrook desiring

us to Joyn in Councill to advise y^m. in y^r: Conduct towards two Breth^n

who had Spoken to y^e. disadvantage of [the] Moral Character of y^r. Past^r

The Chh thinking ye Chh at Linebrook had Sufficient Power to deal

wth. y^r. Offending Breth^n. Refused to Joyn

Sep^r: I Communicated to ye Chh Letters wch. I Rec^d: from a Number

of Breth^n: belonging to y^e. Sec^d: Chh in Sutton, desiring y^e

presence of this Chh w^th: Others to advise y^m. under long &

pressing Difficultys — ye Chh after Some debate, Esteemd it

their Duty to Send. Accordingly Deacon Bancroft

Capt. Eaton Capt. Brown & Capt. Nicolls Were Voted

Delegates or Any two of them

Jan^y: 26   Sam^ll. Nicolls & Wife dismist & Recom^ded: to a Chh   [A4I]

of Christ in Lebanon^98 under Care of M^r. Sol^n. Williams Past^r

1752 March 22^d: Nath^ll: Bacheller Junr. offered his

Confession of ye Sin of Fornication his Wife having

been deliverd of a Child in ab^t: five Months after

Vid: ⊕   Marriage, W^ch: being Read, he was Rec^d: to Charity
  ^

May   Stayed ye Chh on ye L^ds. Day & Comunicated to y^m Letters

from a Number of Aggriev'd Breth^n. belonging to ye 2nd

Chh in Sutton Earnestly Intreating ye Presence & Assist^e. of y^s

Chh in Concurr^e: w^th: Other Chhes Calld to Sit in Council on y^e

3^d. Tuesday of May Instant. — Accordingly ye Chh very generay

Voted to Send —   N B: Deacon Bancroft & Capt Brown Delegates

⊕ Ap^l.   W^m: Bryant Junr: having bro't an Accusat^n. ag^st: his Bro^r

Noah Eaton, for false & Injurious Speaking of & Wilfull Lying as

also for hard Oppressive dealing; I calld ye Chh: together who after long Hearing & Debate Voted y^m Selves dissatisfied w^th: ye Conduct

& a Number [of] Points Articled ag^t. him,

of Bro^r: Eaton & herupon Suspended him till he Sh^d.

make Proper Satisfact^n.
         Public
Nov^r: 26   After Service of ye Sabb^a. I Read to ye Chh Letters to y^m

Signed Nathan Town & Eunice his Wife Signifying

y^t. it had pleased God to Contend w^th: y^m: by Fire by W^ch:

all y^r. Substance & provisions were Consumed, & therefore

Desiring ye Charity of ye Chh & Congregat^n in this place

to W^ch: She formerly belonged — Wherupon ye Chh after a few

Moments Debate Unanimously Voted a Contribut^n:

N Bene She was ye Daughter Of M^rs. W^m. Green

1753 March   M^r: James Parker & Wife were at y^r. Request

Dismist from us & Recomended to ye Chh at Southborô

Where they had Removed

Ap^l. 12th: Having appointed a Chh. Meeting Some Time before

for ye Choice of a Deacon, ye Chh Accordingly

Met on y^s Day, when Capt: Benj^a. Brown was   [A42]

Chosen to that Office, at ye First Vote.

    at ye Same Time Were dismissed M^rs: Abigail

Hay, now ye Wife of ye Rev^d: Mr Joseph Emerson

as also Mary Richardson, now Farley, & Recomended

to ye Chh in Groton, under ye Watch of M^r. Emerson Afors^d.

    at ye Same Time also Noah Eaton having Acknowledgd

ye Faults for W^ch he had been some Time past

Suspended, & Asking fogiveness, was Restored to Charity.

Augt. 24 Being Lecture Day I Communicated to ye Chh y^e

Case of Primus Negro Servt. to M^rs. David Green Junr.

who had for a long Time Absented himself

from ye Communion of ye Chh, but He, tho Warnd,

not Appearing, yᵉ Chh Adjournd yᵉ Consideratⁿ

     of yᵉ Case till yᵉ Next Chh Meeting

Sepʳ. 9 Service of yᵉ Sabb; being Over Elizᵃ Fowler was

     Recᵈ: into yᵉ Fellowship of yˢ Chh having been

     dismist & Recom̄ended — 2ᵈ. Chh in Woburn

Octᵒ 19 Being Lecture Day, yᵉ Chh Met by Adjournmᵗ

     to Consider yᵉ Case of Primus Negro Servᵗ. to

     Mʳˢ. David Green Junʳ: Sᵈ: Primus having

     offer'd yᵉ Reasons for Absenting himself from

     yᵉ Worship & Ordinances of X. yᵉ Chh

     Voted yᵐ Selves Unsatisfied wᵗʰ: his Reasons,

     & Suspended him from Chh Fellowship till he

     Shᵈ Manifest his Repentᵉ.

1754

March 3 John Townsend Junʳ was then at his Request

     Dismist to yᵉ Chh at Wilmington

June 2: Kendal Bryant was then at his Request

     dismissed & Recommended to yᵉ Chh of

     Christ in Concord

June 23ᵈ Having a fortnight past Communicated Letters   [A43]

     from a Number of Aggrieved Members of yᵉ

     West Chh in Sudbury, desiring Our Help & Advice

in Concurrence wᵗʰ: Other Chhes, yᵉ Chh who then Adjourn'd yᵗ they

     might be better prepard for Action Resumd yᵉ

     Consideratⁿ. of this Matter & generally Voted to Send

     yᵉ Desird Help: NB Deacon Brown Delegate.

Decʳ. 22:   One Labary who was taken Captive by yᵉ Indians

     last Augᵗ. & Carryed to Canada, having Earnestly

     Requested Help of us in Order to his Redemption

I proposd ye Matter to ye Chh & Congregation who

Voted a Contribution ye Next Lords Day

— 29   This Vote was Reverst y^s Day on Some Jealousy

& Surmises whether Labarra w^d. Ever Obtain ye Money.[99]

Feby 9   Wife of Kendal Bryant Junr. dismist & Recomended

to ye Chh of Concord.

1755

June 29   After ye Service was Ended I Com^ted to ye Chh Letters

Sent from ye Rev^d. M^r. Carnes Desiring us to Join

in Councill wth. other Chhes, in Order to a Regular

Dismission from his Pastoral Relat^n. if it Sh^d. be

Judged Expedient, Accordingly ye Chh Voted to Send

& Deacon Brown being Nominated was Accepted.

NB: ye Councill Met at Time & Place & Wrote a Letter to

ye Chh; but y^s being treated w^th: Neglect; upon Adjournm^t

Voted M^r: Carnes Might lawfully Withdraw from[100] his Chh; yet

advised him to patience & forbearance for Some Time.

Novr. 2^d   I Communicated Letters from[101] Chh. at Lynn End

desiring Our Assistance in ye Ordinat^n. of

M^r. Benjn. Adams to ye Pastoral Office there: y^e

Chh Accordingly Voted Compliance & wth y^r Pastor

Sent Deacons Bancroft Brown & Emerson &

Capt. Sweyn.

Decr 14 Maverick Smith & Wife having been   [A44]

guilty of Fornicat^n before Marriage

Confessed y^r Sin humbled y^m Selves & Were

Rec^d to former Charity

at ye Same Time I laid before ye Chh.

& Congregat^n ye distressed Circumstances of ye Family of

Benj^a Dammon a Native of y^s Town

& for Many years an Inhabit^t. of it Who

Requested Our Charity; Herupon ye Chh
     Voted
Readily a Contribut^n for him on ye Next L^ds Day.
   ^

1756

Jan^y   after Divine Service Read Letters Sent

from Woburn Desiring Assistance in ye Ordinat^n

of M^r. Josiah Sherman to ye Pastoral

Care of ye 1st: Chh of X there. Voted Affirm^e

Delegates Deacons Bancroft & Brown Sg^t

Nicolls & Capt. Eaton.

Ap^l.   Laid before ye Chh ye Desire of

Jon^a. Smith for a Charitable Contribution

on Acc^t: yt his House had been Consumed

by fire, with whose Desire ye Chh

Unanimously Concurr'd

June   Jon^a. Brown having been guilty of y^e

Breach of ye Seventh Com^t made Confess^n of

his Sin & was Restored to former Charity.

——— Meriah Negro Servt to Deacon Parker dec^d

dismist & Recom̄ended to ye Chh

in Salem under ye Care of Revd Thos. Barnard.

Augt 29 Jon^a. Bancroft & Wife having been guilty of   [A45]

ye Breach of ye Seventh Com^t. made Confess^n

of y^r Sin & were Restord to former Charity

1757

June 17: Being Lecture Day, I Stayed ye Chh after Religious

Service to Read a paragraph in ye Will of Deaon

Parker Deceased in w^ch: be bequathed a Legacy to

ye Chh to be put into ye Hands of ye Deacons &

two Other Members to be Chosen by ye Chh: Accordingly

ye Chh proceeded to ye Choice of ye Breth^n. Who

were Capt. John Goodwin & L^t. Sam^ll. Bancroft.

—— 19th: ye Service of ye Sabb: being ended, I stayed ye Chh

& Intimated to y^m. y^t ye Frowns of G^d: upon ye Land being

Many & g^t: Especially in Respect to ye long Drought w^th: w^ch.

we have been Visited & wherby ye Increase of ye Land is

g^tly threatned I tho't it highly proper y^t a day

of Fasting sh^d be Kept, to humble Our Souls before

G^od & Earnestly Seek his Favours. ye Chh Concurring

wth. me in ye Tho't, Agreed y^t Next Thursday be Kept

as a Day of Solemn Fasting & Humiliation

Novr 23 Mr Joshua Parker was at his Request Dismissed

& Recomended to ye Chh of Christ in Canterbury

under ye Pastoral Care of ye Rev^d. M^r. Coggeshall.[102]

—— Eben^r. Wesson was at his Request dismissed

& Recomended to ye Chh of Christ in Souhegin West

under ye Pastoral Care of ye Rev^d: Dan^ll Wilkins[103]

1758

Ap 29 W^m: Pool & Wife having long lain under y^e

guilt of ye Sin of Fornicat^n Were at length

Convicted in their own Consciences, made

[A46]

Humble Confess^n. of y^r Sin & Were Restord to

Charity.

May 28 Joseph Gold was then at his Request

dismissed & Recomended to ye Chh at Souhegin.

Novr. 2^d: The Chh being Call'd to Meet together

on this Day to Make Choice of a Deacon

to Supply ye Place of Good Deacon Bancroft

whom God hath Taken to himself; Made

Choice of M^r. Sam^ll. Bancroft Junr Nephew

to y^e: Deceas'd.

Decr. I Signifyed My Concurrence wth y^t

Vote of ye Chh, & M^r. Bancroft having

Accepted his Call Entred into his Office & Seat

Decr. 31 Read to ye Chh Letters Rec^d from y^e

Chh of Christ in Middleton, Desiring

Our Assistance in ye Ordination of

M^r. Elias Smith Chosen to ye Pastoral

Office in S^d. Chh. Voted in ye Affirmative.

NB. Deacon Brown, Eben^r: Nicolls Eben^r: Smith

& Isaac Smith Junr, Delegates.

Jan^y: 14. Read Letters from ye Chh in Stoneham desiring

Assistance in y^e. Installment of ye Rev^d

M^r. John Searl over ye Chh. there. Voted Affirm^e

NB: Deacon Emerson, Deacon Bancroft Capt

John Sweyn & Wm Bryant Delegates

1760

Ap W^m: Bryant & Wife dismissed to ye Chh

in Sudbury ye Pastoral Care of Revd Mr Cook

Augt W^m: Johnson & Wife Dismissed to ye Westerly

Chh in Lynn.

1761

May 17   Read to ye Chh Letters from ye 2^d Chh in ye Town

Inviting our Help at ye Ordinat^n. of

Mr Stone to y^t Pastoral Office. Voted

Affirmative.

Deacons Brown & Emerson Coll: Nickols Capt Goodwin & Jon^a [A47]

Eaton Delegates.

Oct^o Sam^{ll} Bancroft having been one of ye 2 Trustees

     Voted to take Care of ye Legacy left ye Chh by

     Deacon Parker; & he being afterwards Chosen

     Deacon; Coll^{ll} Nicolls was Voted to Supply his Place

Novr 22   Rebecca ye Widow of John Dammon Dec^d

     having made Acknowledg^t of ye Sin, for w^{ch}

     she wth her Husband had been long Suspended,

     was herupon Rec^d. into ye Charity of ye Chh

         & Congregat^n

     29 Stayed Chh after Service & Mention'd ye Applicat^n of M^r

     Melandys Family for a Contribution, in Considerat^n of y^r

     Needy Circumstances; ye Chh falling in herwith, agreed y^t.

     ye Next Thursday being Thanksgiving Day, shoud be a

     Day therfor.

     1762

Sepr Stayed ye Chh after divine Service & Read y^e

     Letters Missive from Marblehead Desiring our

     presence & Assistance at ye Ordinat^n of M^r

     Whitwell as Colleague Pastor wth y^e: Rev^d

     Mr Barnard; but being strangers to ye Gent^n

     his Experiences & Principles Voted not to Send

     1763

Sep^r —— Read ye Letters Missive from ye Third Chh in

     Salem desiring Our Assist: at ye Ordinat^n of

     Mr Huntington, to ye Work of ye Ministry; but

     being Unacquainted wth ye Gent^n his Principles,

     Morals & Experiences; Voted not to Send.

     however afterwards to Send y^t we Might Know y^m.

1764

Ap. 12 Chh Voted on Fast Day, a Contribution for Thos Hartshorn

brot low by ye Dispensat^n of Provid: ye Next Sabb:

July 15. Then John Boutell Junr & Wife Made humble Confession of y^e

Sin of Fornication & were Rec^d to Charity.[104]

At a meeting of ye first Church of Christ in   [A48]

Reading on ye 18th Day of July: 1765

after Seeking to God By Prayer the Church

1. Voted that D^e Benjamin Brown Should

   be moderator for this meeting.

2. That D^e Brown Emerson Should be ye Church's

   Clerk During the Church's Pleasure.

3. D^e Jonathan Temple D^e Samuel Bancroft

   and Eben^r Nichols Esqr weare Chosen a Com^{tt}

   to goe to Mr Hobbys and fetch the Church

   Books of Record: which Books ware Brought

   to the Church: and the Church Covenant was

   Read to the Church.

   The Church voted to Keep the 15 Day of

   August next Insuing as a Day of fasting

   and Prayer.

   The Church Platform was Read to ye Church

   at said Meeting and Left to be Considred

   afterwards.

At a meeting of ye first Church of Christ in

Reading on ye 2d Day of September: 1765

after Looking up to God by Prayer.

D^e Benjamin Brown was Chosen Moderator

for this Meeting.

It was moved to the Church whether the Church
wold Receive Members while we are Destitute
of a Pastor and it Past in ye Affermative
by a General Vote. Then it was,

Voted that the Deacons Should be a Committee
to Examen Persons that Should offer themselves
to the Communion of ye Church and Receive the
Satisfaction that they Shall Give and propound
them to the Church: and that the Persons that
Shall Give Satisfaction to the Committee: Shall
have the Covenant Given to them by Some
ordained Minister: and they Shall Give in their Rela
tions to S^d Committee.

It was then proposed whether the church would
Chouse a Comm^{tt} to Draw up a Confession of faith
by the help and assestance of an ordained minister
or Ministers and it past in ye affirmative.

Voted that Eben^r Nichols Esqr D^e Bancroft and Lt John
Temple be a Com^{tte}: for that purpos.

Voted that the Revd Mr Clark and ye Rev^d M^r ~~Samuel~~
Stone be ye Ministers to ~~asest~~ Asest ye Committee
in Drawing up a Confession of faith for ye Church.

Voted to adjourn this meeting to this Day four weaks
at two of ye Clock in ye afternoon.
                          above Sd
At the adjournment the Committee above said ^
having by the help of ye Revd Mr Peter
Clark of Danvers Drawn Up a Confession of
faith Did Present it to the Church for thare

acceptance and it was Read to them and accept

ed of them: by a Unanamos Vote.

Voted to accept of ye Platform for a General Rule of Church

Dissapline So Farr as it is agreable to the word of God.

Voted to abid by the Church Covenant.[105]

Confession of Faith.   [A50]

1. We do seriously & solemnly profess to

   believe in one eternal almighty God

   the Father Son & holy Ghost, who

   created the World by his Power, &

   governs it by his Providence, & is

   the Redeemer of the fallen World

   by his Son Jesus Christ. ——

2. We believe the holy Scriptures of the

   old & new Testament to be the Word

   of God, & adhere to Them as the only

   Rule of Faith & Practice, directing Us

   in all Matters of divine Worship, & in

   Church-Administrations, as well as in

   an holy Life & Conversation. 2 Tim: 3: 16. 17.

3. We believe, that our first Parents fell

   from that Estate of Integrity Honour &

   Happiness in which God at first
   that   fell
   created Them, & all Mankind in Them,
         ^   ^
   by their Transgression in eating the

   Forbidden Fruit; & that thereby They

   involved themselves & their Posterity in a

   State of Sin & Death;

   and that in Consequence hereof, all the   [A51]

Generations of Adam are born in a State
of corrupted Nature, destitute of original
Righteousness & Purity, & infected with
Sin properly so called so as to become
Children of Wrath by Nature — Psa: 51.5.
Rom: 5.19 Eph: 2.3.4. And that God
hath from all Eternity chosen a certain
Number of lapsed or fallen Mankind
to Life & Salvation as the End, & Faith
in Christ & Holiness as the Means — Eph: 1.4
2 Thess: 2.13. ——

4. We believe, that God, in Compassion
   to the sinful perishing State of Mankind,
   fore-ordained, & in the Fulness of Time
   sent his only begotten Son, to be the
   Saviour of the World: & that Jesus
   Christ the Son of God, became true
   & real Man, being made of a Woman,
   & in all things like unto his Brethren
   Sin only excepted; & at the same Time
   in his original Nature God over all
   blessed for ever more, being God
   & Man in one Person — John 1.14
   1 Tim: 3.6 Gal: 4.4. Heb: 2:17 Rom: 9.5, 6.

5. That Christ the Son of God having   [A52]
   in Compliance with his Father's Will
   taken on Him the Nature of Man,
   hath therein substituted himself to
   bear our Sins in his Sacrefice on the

Cross for the Expeation of them, &

humbled himself in his Obedience unto

Death for our Redemption, whereby

he has made a true & perfect

Satisfaction to the Justice of God

for the Sins of Man. ———

6. That He rose again from the Dead

on the third Day, & ascended into

Heaven as our victorious Redeemer,

& sitteth at the right Hand of God

making Intercession for Us, & having

Power given Him over all Things

in Heaven & on Earth. ———

7. That he sustains & executes the

Threefold Office of Prophet Priest

& King in his Church. ———

8. That in the Exercise of his Office as

Redeemer, and of the Fullness of Power

committed to Him; He has published   [A53]

the Gospel-Covenant: Requiring

Faith & Repentance of sinful Men,

in Order to Pardon & Salvation.

And We must look to be be pardoned

& saved only thro' the Merits of Christ,

applied by Faith as our only available

Plea before the Justice of God in

Opposition to all Works, not only Those

of the <u>mosaic</u> Law, but all Works of

Righteousness which we are supposed to

have done, or can do, either before
or after Grace received; & the only
solid Ground of the Imputation of the
Righteousness of Christ to Us for our
Justification is our Union to Christ
by Faith, & not Works of Obedience
'tho' a lively Faith uniting to Christ
will be ever followed with Works of
Gospel-Obedience.— Rom: 3.25. Tit: 3.5.
Phill: 3.9. Rom: 8.1. ──────

9. We believe the holy Spirit is given thro'
the Merit & Intercession of Christ to make
Application of his purchased Redemption to
Men's Souls;
and that his gracious Influences are [A54]
necessary to a Life of Faith & Obedience
& particularly the regenerating & renewing
Power & Grace of the holy Spirit is
necessary to quicken Sinners naturally
dead in Sin, impotent & averse to all
spiritual Good; & to lead them into the
Life of God: And his gracious Aids are
to be sought & depended on by Believers
in all their Acts of the spiritual Life,
whereby They are enabled to persevere
to Perfection. ──────────

10. That Christ hath instituted a Gospel-
Ministry, & the two Sacraments of
Baptism & the Lord's Supper as the

outward Means of the Application of

Redemption - to be observed in his Church,

'till his second Coming. ————

11. We believe another Life after this Life,

& that Christ will come again, & raise

the Dead, & judge the World; & that

We must all appear before the

Judgement-Seat of Christ. ————

12. That at the last Day, the Wicked   [A55]

shall be adjudg'd to everlasting

Punishments, & the Righteous to Life

eternal. ————————————

The above calvinistic Articles

of Faith We receive as being

agreeable to the Word of God

& the common receiv'd Opinion

of these Churches. ————

on the 30th Day of Sep[t]ember 1765

The above Confession was acepted by the Church

as their own beleafe by a Unanamos Vote

and that it Should be Recorded in the church

Book.

—————————————————

At a meeting of the first Church of Christ in Read

ing upon the 18th Day or September 1766

a
Decon Benjamin Brown moderator.

Voted That the Church Doth mak choice of Mr John

Lotrop to be the Pastor of this Church Provided

his principals of Religion and meathod of Church

Government agree with this church: ~~then it was Voted to adjoyrn~~
~~the meeting to the~~ Voted that the Deacons with Coll
~~Ni~~ Nichols and Mr John Temple and Mr Nathaniel
Emerson be a Committee to Joyn with the Rev^d
Mr Joseph Emerson of Malden the Revd Mr Robbe
of Lynn and the Revd Mr Stone to Examen M^r
John Lotropt: with Regard to his principals of
Religon and meathod of Church Goverment and
at the adjournment of Said meeting which was
on the 25th Day of September 1766 the Comm^tte
above Said made thare Report to the Church and
the Church acepted of the Report of Said Commi^tte
and Renewed thare Choice and
Voted That the Church Doth make choice of Mr
John Lotropt to be the Pastor of this Church.

[A56]

At a meeting of the first Church in
Reading February the 24: 1767
~~Mr Jo~~ the Revd Mr Joseph Roby
Chosen moderator.

1 Voted that the Church is greaved that
So many of their Breathen Do not
meet with them at this time

2 Voted that the Church Send an affection^ate
message to those Breatheren that have
absented themselves from the meeting
this Day. Particklulerly to those Bre
theren that are Dissatisfied with Mr Latrop
and Desire their Attendance at the adjorn

ment of this meeting

3 that Deacon Emerson Deacon Bancroft

and Mr Timothy Pratt be a Committee

to goe to these Bretheren and Cary y^e

message of Church to them.

4 Voted that this meeting be adjourned to   [A57]

next ~~fry~~ fryday 2 of ye Clock at this place.

At a meeting of the first Church of Christ in

Reading upon the ninteenth Day of November

1767: De͞con Benjamin Brown was Chosen

moderator

Our Brother Thomas Parker came before the

Church and acknoliged he had been guity of y^e

Sin of Intemperence: and Expressed his Sorrow

theirfor: and that he wold Indever a Reforma^n

for the future: the Church took it Into Considration

and So left it for the Present.

Debate
Then after a Considrable upon the Dificultys
^

that are amungst us the Church proposed to Ad

journ the meeting and to Send for the Rev^d

Mr Stone for our assestence: as Moderator

the Church then Voted to Send to the Revd Mr Stone

to Assest us at the Adjoyrnment of this meeting &
  and to be moderator
then Voted to adjoyrn this meeting to the first

munday after the thanksgiving: (viz: the 7th Day

of December next[)]

Voted that all matters of complaint that are

to come before the Church Shall be Exhibited

in wrighting: and a Coppy of the Complaint

Sent to the Person or persons Complained off.

At a meeting of ye first Church of Christ in [A58]

Reading on the first Day of Sepember 1768

Deac^n Sam^{ll} Bancroft Chosen moderator.

The Church then Past this Vote following.

That wareas we have for a considrable time

Past Lived in a neglect of the Lords Supper by

means of Some perplexing Circumstances ~~that~~ which have

attended our affairs we Unitedly humble ourselves

before God for our Sinfull neglect & Implore

forgiveness: through the Blood of attonment &

grace for the future to honnor Christ bya carfull

Att on all his ordinances and our purpos is by ye endance[106]

Leave of Providence to attend the holy Supper

with all Convenient Speed hoping thare to meet

with Christ and Sit togather as frends and

bretheren forbaring one another and forgiving

one another as God for Christs Sake forgiveth us

At a meeting of the first Church in Reading April ye 18: 1769 [A59]

the Revd Mr Elias Smith was Chosen Moderator

1   it was then Put to Vote whether the Church wold

hear Mr Caleb Prentice four Saboths upon Probation

and it Past in the affermitive 34 yeas 25 nays

2   voted that Brown Emerson Col Nichols John Smith

Josiah Walton & Jonathan Eaton be a Committee to wait

upon Mr Prentice and Lay before him the Votes of ye Church

the meeting was then adjoyrned to ye next munday Com: fortnit at the adjornment it was put to Vote whether ye Church

~~Will~~ will at this time Give Mr Caleb: Prentice Libarian

at Cambridg a Call to the work of the ministry in this

Place and it Past in the Affermitive 39 yea: 26 nay

3ly Voted that Brown Emerson Coll: Nichols & Capt Goodwin

be a Com^ttee to wait upon Mr Prentice and Lay before him

the Votes of ye Church

---

of X
at a meeting of ye first Church in Reading on the 7
^

Day of August 1769: Brown Emerson Moderator

1. It was Voted Unanomosly that the Church Doth
of Cambridg
Renew: their Call of Mr Caleb Prentice to be the
^

Pastor of this Church and Minister of this Parish

2ly Voted that Coll: Nichols Brown Emerson & Capt Goodwin

Shall be a Committee to wait upon Mr Prentice and

Lay before him the Votes of ye Church

Notes

1. Pagination begins with p. 4.

2. MS damage at upper right corner; conjectural reading supplied from typescript, p. 2.

3. MS damage to lower right corner; reading supplied from typescript, p. 3.

4. This is the first of several cues in the succeeding pages that directs the reader to members in half-way membership, recorded on odd-numbered pages, and members in full membership, recorded on even-numbered pages.

5. The remainder of MS p. 7, nearly half of the page, is blank.

6. Here follows a parenthetical note in shorthand ending with the written-out words "beagles opened," in which the scribe apparently recorded the "Senseless Jest." A beagle, the title of a sheriff's officer or bailiff, also connotes a noisy, shouting person.

7. The remainder of MS p. 49 (p. 121), nearly half a page, is blank.

8. Reference not completed.

9. There is little doubt that there is a lacunae in the MS, since the document following—the church covenant first composed in 1644—takes up in the middle of a third point. That the next two leaves were tipped in is suggested by the fact that they are not paginated. On MS p. 49 (p. 121), the circumstance is explained: Rev. Richard Brown notes that the church covenant was in "a loose paper." For that reason, he transcribed the full text of the covenant on MS pp. 50-51 (pp. 121-24).

10. The names listed on this page were written in a different hand.

11. Here entries are written in another hand. This list recapitulates that on MS p. 31, with the exception of the very last name, Mary Burt.

12. *Propositions Concerning the Subject of Baptism and Consociation of Churches, Collected and Confirmed Out of the Word of God, By a Synod of Elders and Messengers of the Churches in Massachusetts-Colony in New-England . . .* (Boston, 1662).

13. Here begin the entries written by Rev. Jonathan Pierpont.

14. Pierpont took up the practice of dividing the page into columns, the left side for recording half-way members and baptisms, and the right for recording full members.

15. The tabulations of church members at the tops and bottoms of MS pp. 33-37 are in the hand of Richard Brown, probably upon his assuming the pastorate in 1712, so that he could have an accurate running total.

16. No first name provided.

17. Illegible deleted entry.

18. No first name provided.

19. This entry was written in a different hand, probably by one of the deacons. Subsequent entries were written by Richard Brown.

20. With the exception of MS pp. 49, 51, and 53, Brown left odd-numbered pages blank beginning at this point. William Hobby continued this practice; the final odd-numbered blank page is p. 81. For the sake of continuity, blank pages will not be noted.

21. Shorthand.

22. Every name has beside it, either preceding or following it, an "X" that was probably made by Richard Brown in compiling and checking his list of members. The notations beside the first three males in the left column are likely to denote Brown as pastor ("S" for "Shepherd"?) and the following two as deacons.

23. This word is in shorthand.

24. Actually, there are 26 listed under Charlestown, bringing the total to 237.

25. This word is in shorthand.

26. This entry is written in a different hand, mostly likely that of a lay officer; entries in William Hobby's hand begin on the next page, MS p. 71.

27. This word is in shorthand.

28. This word is in shorthand.

29. This word is in shorthand.

30. This word is in shorthand.

31. This word is in shorthand.

32. This word is in shorthand.

33. The last word, apparently written in at a later time, is a conjectural reading, possibly meaning "Joseph Gold's [son] Daniel" (compare following entry).

34. The Maonites were a tribe that lived in the wilderness of Maon; see I Sam 23:24.

35. Entries in William Hobby's hand cease at this point; entries through MS p. 92 are in a different hand, probably that of one of the church deacons.

36. I.e. brought over, subtotal.

37. At this point, membership lists for the pastorate of Caleb Prentice commence, but these are omitted. For minutes of church meetings beginning in 1712, one must go to the rear of the book and read backwards.

38. This word in shorthand.

39. This word in shorthand.

40. This word in shorthand.

41. This word in shorthand.

42. This word in shorthand.

43. This word in shorthand.

44. This word in shorthand.

45. This word in shorthand.

46. Killingsley, Conn.

47. This word in shorthand.

48. The remaining two-thirds of the page is blank.

49. This word in shorthand.

50. This word in shorthand.

51. This word in shorthand.

52. Coventry, Conn.

53. This word in shorthand.

54. This word in shorthand.

55. This word in shorthand.

56. Revs. Thomas Symmes of Bradford and Samuel Fiske of Salem First Church.

57. This word in shorthand.

58. This word in shorthand.

59. On Sept. 4, 1724, Thomas Blanchard and Nathan Cross of Dunstable were taken by Indians to Canada. Though Reading contributed towards their ransom, the two apparently worked off most or all of their redemption in one year's time by building a sawmill for their captors. The fact that the Reading records mention "Blanchard Children" may mean that another, unidentified Blanchard was taken or that Cross was misidentified. Emma Lewis Coleman, *New England Captives Carried to*

Canada Between 1677 and 1760 During the French and Indian Wars (2 vols., Portland, Me.: Southworth Press, 1925; rep. Bowie, Md.: Heritage Books, 1989), II:167-68.

60. This word in shorthand.

61. This word in shorthand.

62. This word in shorthand.

63. On the significance of 1727 earthquake for church membership, see introduction, pp. 45-46.

64. This word in shorthand.

65. This word in shorthand.

65. The remaining half of MS p. 17, and the entirety of p. 18 in this series is blank.

67. This word in shorthand.

68. This word in shorthand.

69. Rev. Edward Holyoke, pastor of Marblehead Second Church, 1716-37, afterwards installed as president of Harvard College.

70. The remaining two-thirds of the page is blank.

71. Rev. John Lowell, pastor of Newbury, 1725-67.

72. This word in shorthand.

73. MS p. 22 of this series is blank.

74. Brown did not finish the entry; William Hobby's handwriting begins at this point.

75. David Hall, pastor of Sutton, 1728-89.

76. *I.e.* Mendon, whose pastor from 1716-68 was Rev. Joseph Dorr.

77. Rev. Benjamin Colman of the Brattle Street Church, Boston.

78. Windham, Conn., whose pastor was Rev. Samuel Mosely from 1734-91.

79. Rev. Daniel Fuller, pastor of Willington, Conn., 1728-58.

80. East Haddam, Conn.

81. Rev. Joseph Torrey, pastor of the Congregational Church in South Kingston, R.I., 1732-91.

82. Rev. James McSparren (1709-57), priest at St. Paul's Church, Narragansett, 1721-57.

83. Otherwise known as the Massachusetts Convention of Congregational Ministers, still in existence today.

84. Rev. Samuel Osborn (1685-1774) had been pastor of the First Church in Eastham, 1718-19, then pastor of the Second Church in Eastham (Orleans), 1719-38. See J.M. Bumsted, "A Caution to Erring Christians: Ecclesiastical Disorder on Cape Cod, 1717 to 1738," *William & Mary Quarterly* 28 (1971): 413-38.

85. *I.e.* Amherst.

86. Then in Massachusetts, now in Maine.

87. The newly settled pastor of Framingham was Matthew Bridge (1721-75); in 1747, a Separatist Church was formed in that town.

88. The pastor of Bradford (a part of Haverhill) from 1726-65 was Joseph Parsons (1702-65).

89. Apparently referring to the departure of some members from the First Church of Woburn to form the Third or Separate Society there, under the ministry of Josiah Cotton (1703-1780), who was installed in July 1747.

90. Rev. Aaron Cleveland (1715-57), pastor of Malden, 1747-50, then converted to the Church of England.

91. Edward Cheever (1717-1794), pastor of Lynn Third Church, or Saugus, 1738-48; and then of Eastham, 1751 until his death.

92. On John Dammon, see introduction, p. 37.

93. Tiverton, R.I.; the pastor of the First Congregational Church from 1746-78 was Othniel Campbell (1696-1778).

94. A conflation of two traditions: Dagon (mentioned in I Sam. 31:10) and his son Baal, a Philistine deity; and Bel and the Dragon (Apocrypha, Dan. 14).

95. Temporary dementia.

96. On Edwards and his dismissal from Northampton, Mass., see introduction, pp. 50-51.

97. Nova Scotia.

98. Lebanon, Conn.

99. *I.e.* whether the money would actually ever reach Labaree. Peter Labaree was a French Huguenot, a carpenter by trade, who lived in the settlement of Charlestown (No. 4). He was taken captive, along with several others, on Aug. 30, 1754. His Indian captor sold him to the French in Montreal, who demanded 500 livres for his ransom. The ransom was paid, but no opportunity for a trade coming in the meantime,

Labaree finally escaped in May 1757. He became a landowner in New Hampshire, married and had a large family, and died in 1803. Coleman, *New England Captives Carried to Canada Between 1677 and 1760 During the French and Indian Wars*, II: 312-13.

100. This word in shorthand.

101. This word in shorthand.

102. Rev. James Cogswell (1720-1807), pastor of Canterbury, Conn., 1744-71.

103. Rev. Daniel Wilkins (1710-83), pastor of Amherst, 1741-83.

104. Hobby's entries end at this point. Entries on MS pp. 48-49 and 56-59 are in a different hand, probably that of Benjamin Brown, one of the deacons.

105. The covenant is written in a different hand from that which precedes and follows.

106. This word, including the interlineation, is written in a brighter ink, possibly spelling out an abbreviated form.

The Rumney Marsh
Church Records

1715-1757

The Churches sent unto for their Countenance & Assistance by their Delegates, Elders & Messengers, were the Old North-Church at Boston, the Church of Lynn, the Church of Reading, & ye New-north Church at Boston

The sermon was preached by Mr Thomas Cheever.

After the Sermon, they proceeded to Gather the Church: the Revd Doctour Cotton Mather, who was chosen to manage & Moderate the whole affair, having briefly declared to ye whole Assembly the Occasion of the present Solemnity, did publickly read the Covenant, by which the persons more immediatly Concerned did Coalesce into a Church-State, for the enjoyment of all Special Ordinances, & for the performance of all the Duties, which the Lord Christ hath prescribed unto his Disciples, in such Churches &c, desiring the Brethren to stand up & manifest their Consent thereunto openly, which they did accordingly.

After follows an exact copy of the Covenant, with the Brethrens names.

We, whose names are hereunto Subscribed, apprehending our selves called of God to Combine together, in order to the forming of a Church-state among us for the observation & enjoyment of all the especiall Ordinances; which we are persuaded will be a Singular Service for our generation; Under a deep sense of our Unworthiness to be so highly favoured of the Lord, to transact personally with God, unless the Lord, and acknowledging our utter inability to keep Covenant with God, unless the Lord by his Spirit & Grace inable us thereunto; admiring that free & rich grace which Triumpheth over so great Unworthines, with humble dependance upon him for his grace & assistance, do make & renew our Covenant with God, & one with another, as follows.

In the first place, we do declare & profess our hearty belief of the Christian religion as contained in the holy Scriptures, which God hath given unto man, to be the only, perfect, sufficient, & perpetuall Rule of his faith & life, heartily resolving by the help of divine grace to conform our lives to the Rules of our holy Religion.

And we do this day give up our selves to that God whose name alone is Jehovah, Father, Son, & Spirit, the only true & living God, & Avouch him this day to be our God, chusing & cleaving unto him as our God & Father, our portion & chief good. We give up our selves also to our Glorious Lord Jesus Christ, who is the Lord our Righteousness adhering unto him as the only Head of his Covenant people, & take him for our Only Redeemer & Saviour, our Prophet, Priest, & King, & for our Captain & Leader to bring us to eternal blessedness, likewise we profess our Everlasting & indispensable Obligation to Glorify God in all the Duties of gospel Obedience, as becomes his Covenant people, forever engaging by the help of Christ to endeavour to keep our selves pure from the sins of the times, and to observe & attend the Duties of a Church-state, and of a Society Confederated for Obedience to, and enjoyment of him in all Gospel Ordinances.

Rumney Marsh Records Book, MS p. [1]. Courtesy Boston Museum of Fine Arts.

Rumny-marish Church-book:

1715:

The[1] Churches sent unto for their Countenance & Assistance by their
Delegates, Elders & Messengers, were the Old North Church at Boston,
the Church of Lynn, the Church of Redding; & ye New-north Church at Boston.

The sermon was preached by Mr Thomas Cheever.

After the Sermon, they proceeded to Gather the Church: the Rev^r Doctor
Cotton Mather, who was chosen to manage & Moderate the whole affair, having
briefly declared to ye whole Assembly the Occasion of the present Solemnity,
did publickly read the Covenant, by which the persons more immediately Concerned
did Coalesce into a Church-State, for the enjoyment of all Special Ordinances, & for
 the performances of all the Duties, which the Lord Christ hath prescribed unto his
Disciples, in such Churches &c, desiring the Brethren to stand up & manifest their
Consent thereunto openly, which they did accordingly.
Here follows an exact copy of the Covenant, with the Brethrens names.

We, whose names are hereunto Subscribed, apprehending our selves called of God
to Combine together in order to the forming of the Church-state among us for [y^e][2]
observation & enjoyment of all the especiall Ordinances; which we are pers[waded]
to be a Singular Service for our generation; Under a deep sence of our Unwo[rthines]
to be so highly favoured of the Lord, to transact personally with so Glorious a [Being]
and acknowledging our utter inability to keep Covenant with God, unless the Lord
by his Spirit & Grace inable us thereunto; admiring that free & rich grace which
Triumpheth over so great Unworthines, with humble dependance upon him for his grac[e &]
assistance, do make & renew our Covenant with God, & one with another, as follows.
In the first place, we do declare & profess our hearty belief of the Christian relig[ion]
[as] contained in the holy Scriptures, which God hath given unto man, to be the only pe[rfect,]
[s]ufficient, & perpetuall Rule of his faith & life, heartily resolving by the help of div[ine]

grace to conform our lives to the Rules of our holy Religion.

And we do this day give up our selves to that God, whose name alone is Jehovah,

ffather, Son, & Spirit, the only true & living God, & Avouch him this day to be our Go[d,]

chusing & cleaving unto him as our God & ffather, our portion & chief good.

We give up our selves also to our Glorious Lord Jesus Christ, who is the Lord our Righteou[sness,]

adhering unto him as the only Head of his Covenant people, & take him for our Only Redee[mer]

& Saviour, our Prophet, Priest, & King, & for our Captain and Leader to bring us to eternal blessed[ness.]

Likewise we profess our Everlasting & indispensable Obligation to Glorify God in all the

duties of gospel Obedience, as becomes his Covenant people, forever engaging by the help of

[C]hrist to endeavour to keep our selves pure from the sins of the times, and to observe & attend

[t]he duties of a Church-state, and of a Society Confederated for Obedience to, and

enjoyment of him in all Gospel Ordinances. At[3] the same time we

give our Offspring with our selves up unto the Lord,

humbly adoring the grace that we & our Children may

be looked upon as the Lord's, promising by his help

to do our utmost in the Methods of a Religious education,

that they may be the Lords. Moreover we do give up our

selves to one another in the Lord, engaging to walk by faith

as a[4] Church of Christ in the faith & Order of the Gospel, so far as [the Lord hath or shall reveal][5]   [2]

unto us, (& particularly as is held out in the Platform sett forth by these Churches unto [which]

for the substance we declare our adherence) promising in brotherly love to watch over one

another, & to avoid all sinfull stumbling blocks, and contentions as much as possible; and to

submit our selves to the Discipline & Government of Christ in this his Church; and to

the Ministerial teaching, guidance, & Oversight of the Elder, or Elders thereof, in

all things agreable to the Rules of Christ in his word, and conscienciously to attend the

Seals & censures, and all the holy Institutions of Christ in Communion with one another,

desiring also to walk with all Regular & due Communion with other Churches.

And all this we do, flying to the blood of the Everlasting Covenant for pardon of [our]

many failings, desiring to depend humbly upon the Grace of God in Christ, to en[able]

us to a faithfull discharge of our Covenant duties both to God & one another: & [where]
we shall fall short, humbly to wait upon his Grace in Christ, for pardon, acceptance,
and healing for this own name sake. Amen.   a true copy

                                        Attest Thomas Cheever.

John Tuttle	William Halsy
John ffloyd sen[r]	Daniel ffloyd
Edward Tuttle sen[r]	Asa } Halsy's mark
[El]isha Tuttle	Thomas Cheever

[After th]e Covenant was read & the Brethren had manifested their consent thereunto,
[D[r]] Mather did declare unto them, that they were now acknowledged by the Delegates of the
Churches, as one of their Sister Churches, & that they were intrusted with the powers a[nd]
priviledges which Christ had given unto his Churches; of which this was one special priviledg[e]
to choose their Own Officers: He therfore desired them, that, as they had formerly chose[n]
M[r] Thomas Cheever for their Pastour, if they did continue in the same mind, and also did
desire that the s[d] M[r] Thomas Cheever might now be Ordained & Solemnly sett apart to the
Pastorall Office & charge over them, they would manifest it by lifting up their hands, which they [did.]
Whereupon they proceeded to the Ordination. The Charge was given by D[r] Cotton Mather.
The Rev[d]: M[r] Jeremiah Shepard: M[r] Richard Brown & M[r] John Webb did Assist & joyn
in Imposition of hands. The right hand of ffellowship was given in the name of
the Delegates of the Churches, by the Rev[d]: Jeremiah Shepard, both unto the [Rev[d]]
Mr Thomas Cheever as the Pastour of y[e] Church; & unto the Church as a Sister C[hurch]

                    After all a psalm was sung: & y[e] Assembly dismissed
                        with a blessing by the new Ordained Pastour.

                    The names of the Members of y[e] Church at Rumny-marish.   [3]

{ Thomas Cheever. Pastour.   Jacob Halsy.
{ Elizabeth Cheever, since deceased.   Mary Halsy, wife of Asa Halsy.

              since deceased.
{ John Tuttle sen[r]: Deacon   { Samuel Watts
                      ^

{ Martha Tuttle. since deceased.

{ Lᵗ: John Floyd, since Deceased

⎰ Rachel Floyd. since Deceased
      back to Lynn Church

{ Edward Tuttle senʳ since[6] dismissed.
this woman was not dismissed from Lynn Church
~~Abigail Tuttle~~

Elisha Tuttle senʳ. since deceased.

William Halsy

Daniel Floyd

Asa Halsy. since deceased

John Floyd junʳ.

{ Samuel Tuttle. since deceased.

{ Abigail Tuttle

{ Ensign Joseph Belcher. since deceased.

{ Hannnah Belcher
        since deceased.
Sarah Halsy. wife of William Halsy

Abigail Halsy, wife of Jacob Halsy.

Thomas Burdit senʳ: of Maldon: since deceased

Mary ffloyd wife of John ffloyd junʳ: since
           deceased
Moses Hill, of Maldon. since deceased

John Chamberlane

Hannah Chamberlane, since deceased.

Mary ffloyd wife of Daniel Floyd.

Hannah Skinner, widdow, of Maldon since
           deceased
        since deceased
Hannah Lewis wife of Isaac Lewis

Mehetabel Davis.

Abigail Halsey widdow of Abraham Halsy

July 8ᵗʰ: 1739: Hannah Chamberlane. Susannah Cham
           berlane

{ Elizabeth Watts
John[n] Leath
              junʳ: of Maldon
Elizabeth Sprague wife of Jonathan Sprague

Abraham Skinner: dismissed to yᵉ Church in Woodstock
Thomas Skinner: of Maldon since deceased
Mary Skinner. since deceased
Joseph Whittemore, since[7] deceased[8]
Elizabeth Whittemore

Nathan Cheever   the 2ᵈ Church in Woburn
Susanna Richardson of Maldon: since dismissed to
Joseph Burdit.   of Maldon
William Sargeant of Maldon; since deceased.
{ Thomas Burdit   of Maldon since dismissed
{ Mary Burdit   to yᵉ South Church in Matoun
Elisha Tuttle.
Richard Whittemore.
Jeremiah Whittemore this couple were afterwards
Patience Whittemore dismissed to West-town Ch:
Eleanor Leath, wife of John Leath.
Ruhamah Tuttle, widdow of John Tuttle junʳ:
Jacob Chamberlane: since deceased.
Mʳ Hugh Floyd, since deceased.
Eleanor Floyd.
Rebeccah Hinckson since deceased
Patience Davis
Ruth Whittemore, yᵉ wife of Joseph Whittemore
{ Benjamin Whittemore
{ Sarah Whittemore .
since deceased   since deceased
Joseph Whittemore. Thomas Eastis. William Tuttle.
Sarah Halloway, wife of Joseph Halloway.
Thomas Brintnal, since deceased.
Sarah Leath, wife of ffrances Leath of Woburn.
Joanna Tuttle.
Mehetabel Lamson.
Benjamin Floyd. since Deceased.
Mʳ Edmund Bonman. dismissed to Falmouth; since deceased
Susannah Harndel: since deceased.
Joannah Halsey.
Samuel Floyd & Joannah his Wife.   Wife
Nathanael Oliver: Ensign Thomas Prat & Mary his
David Whittemore & Allis his Wife dismissed to Lichfield
Abigail Halsey daughter of Deacon Jacob Halsey
Mᵗˢ Abigail Halsey Wife of Elder Halsey. Samuel
Maxwell. Abigail Eustace, wife of Thomas Eustace.
Mary Halsey Wife of John Halsey. Mary Parker
Wife of John Parker. Sarah Halsey Wife of Samuel Halsey

At a Church Meeting appointed: Novemb: 9th: Mr John Tuttle was chosen to the Office [4]

of a Deacon; who accepted the same.

At the same meeting, it was agreed that One fflagon, two platters, four cups, one bason

with table cloath & one napkin should be bought for the use of the Church; Mrs Tuttle

wife of Deacon Tuttle was desired to buy the same, Mr William Halsey was desired to

be assisting unto her in that affair: & the Charges to be paid by the Church.

It was also agreed at the same meeting to have the Sacrament of the Lords-supper

upon the last Lords-day in Novemb: instant: and the next time upon the last Lords-day

in ffebruary: and afterwards once in six weeks: untill the cold & short days:

It was also agreed that the Charges of the bread & wine for ye Sacrament should be

paid, by a contribution to be made every Sacrament day: and that each Communicant

should give six pence a time during the first year; the Overplus to be reserved as

a Church-stock in the hands of the Deacon.

Attest.   Thomas Cheever Pastour.

named
1715 Novemb: 6th: A child of Asa Halsey, baptized Joseph.
^

[1]715/16 March: 11: Baptized 2 Children of Elisha Tuttle sen^r: A son named Jabez: & a Daughter: Hannah.

[1]716. John ffloyd jun^r: was received to full Communion with the Church: on March: 25^t:

April: 1st: A child of John Floyd jun^r: baptized: named John.

Same day: Samuel Tuttle & Abigail his wife were received to full Communion

April: 29: Ensign Joseph Belcher & Hanna his wife were received to full Communion

Same day, s^d Hanna Belcher was baptized.

May: 6^t: Sarah Halsy was received to full Communion; wife of William Halsey.

—— 13 Three Children of Ensign Joseph Belcher were baptized, their names

　　　were Nathanael. Jame. & Hannah.

—— 27 Abigail Halsy, wife of Jacob Halsy was received to full Communion

June 10 A Child of Samuel Tuttle baptized: named Abigail.

Same day A Child of Jacob Halsy baptized: named Abigail.

July 8th: Thomas Burdit sen^r: of Maldon was received to full Communion; and was

Baptized at the same time.

Novemb: 4th: Mary ffloyd wife of John ffloyd jun[r]: was received to full Communion.

Decemb :16th: A Child of Asa Halsey baptized named Hannah.

March: 31st: 1717: Moses Hill of Maldon was received to full Communion.

May: 26th: A Child of Nathaniel Richison baptized, named Rachel, by virtue of the

> Communion of Churches, y[e] Mother of the Child being a member of Woburn C[hurch.][9]

June: 16: John Chamberlane & Hannah his wife were received to full Communion.

1717   [5]

July: 21st: Five Children of John Chamberlane were baptized, their names were

> Sarah, Abigail, Elizabeth, Hannah, Mary.

August: 4th: Mary ffloyd wife of Daniel ffloyd received to full Communion.

September: 27th: At a Church-meeting appointed to deal with our brother Edward

> Tuttle for disorderly forsaking the ffellowship of the Church, (he having absented
> from the Sacrament of the Lords-supper three several times one after the other)
> and to know the reason of the same; he gave no other reason but this, he was
> dissatisfied because I refused to baptize one of his Grand Children, viz, a
> Child of his Son John Tuttle; he was told that could not be allowed for a
> sufficient reason, for as much as I had openly & fully declared my judgment
> in that matter before we Signed our Church-Covenant; he gave in a
> written acknowledgment, in which he owned the irregularity & disorder of his
> former absence, expressing his sorrow for the same, & desiring forgivnes both
> of God & the Church for his offence, & promising to return to the Commu-
> nion of y[e] Church according to his Covenant duty, &c: Hereupon the
> Church declared their satisfaction therein, & so y[e] matter was lovingly ended.[10]

> Attest.   Thomas Cheever Pastour.

Octob: 20: Hannah Skinner, widdow of Abraham Skinner of Maldon, was

> received to full Communion.

Edward Tuttle his confession and acknowledgement, that wherein I have given
any just matter and occasion of Offence to any particular person in this Church

or to the whole Church in generall, either directly or indirectly (for in so doing

I offend & sin against God) I am sorry for it & do repent & I do desire

and ask forgivenes, first of God through the merits of his Son; and then next

of the Church, & so of every particular person in the Church against whom

I have offended.

this is a true copy of the acknowledgment given in to the Church, at

the Church-meeting: Septemb: 27th:

Attest   Thomas Cheever Pastour

March: 16   1717/18: Hannah Lewis wife of Isaac Lewis was received to full Communion.

April 13 -   A Child of Asa Halsy baptized, named Abraham.

May 4th   Mehetabel Davis was received to full Communion.

June: 1st: A Child of Ensign Joseph Belcher baptized, named Jonathan.

June: 22d: A Child of Isaac Lewis baptized, named Abijah.

June: 29:   Edward Tuttle senr: was dismissed back to ye Church of Lynn upon

his desire, he was always uneasy & therefore ye Church readily voted his

dismission that we might have no farther trouble with him.

1718
July: 6t   Abigail Halsey of Maldon, widdow of Abraham Halsey,was received to full   [6]

Communion, & was baptized at the same time.

A daughter of sd Abigail Halsey baptized at the same time, named Abigail.

July: 13th: A son of Moses Hill baptized, named John.

———   Same day a son of John ffloyd junr: baptized, named John.

August: 10th: Jacob Halsy was received to full Communion.

——— 24   Mary Halsy, wife of Asa Halsy was received to full Communion.

Octob: 19   Samuel Watts & Elizabeth his wife were received to full Communion.

—— 26   A Child of Samuel Tuttle baptized, named Elizabeth.

Same day a Child of Jacob Halsey baptized, named Elizabeth.

1718/19
Jan: 25:   Elizabeth Sprague wife of Jonathan Sprague junr: of Maldon was received to full Com=
munion.

Febr: 1st: A Child of Samuel Watts baptized, named Richard.

— 22   John Leath was received to full Communion.

March: 1st: A Child of John Leath baptized, named John.

May: 24th: Abraham Skinner, Thomas Skinner, & Mary Skinner all of Maldon

were received to full Communion, and were baptized at the same time.

———-- Same day a Child of Jonathan Sprague junr: of Maldon baptized, named Hannah.

When Abraham Skinner abovenamed first offered himself to our
Communion, & before he was publickly propounded, I stayed the Church,
and acquainted them with his desire; and because there had some years
since been a charge brought against the sd Abraham Skinner for stealing
or carrying off a post from the parsonage land in Maldon, the Church did
appoint, severall of Our Bretheren, viz: Lt: John ffloyd, William Halsy,
Daniel Floyd, & Thomas Burdit to enquire into that matter, who accordingly enquired of Deacon John Greenland of Maldon, William Serjeant
and others, and reported unto the Church, That they found the sd Abraham
Skinner had been charged, prosecuted, & condemned by the Court for stealing
or carrying off a post as aforsd, upon the single evidence of one Thomas
Parker of Maldon; & this being directly contrary to the Law of God, 19: deut:
15: 18: Mat: 16: 8: john: 17: the Church judged that the forsd matter was not
sufficient to barr his being received to Communion, nor could they look upon
the sd Abraham Skinner duely convicted of the crime he was charged with.
The Church was the more confirmed in this their judgment, because the sd
Parker had weakned his own Evidence by contradicting it. Which thus appeared
When sd Parker was about joyning to the Church of Maldon, the
aforenamed Abraham Skinner gave in a charge against sd Parker in writing,
a copy of which charge follows.

Maldon December ye 30 day 1713:

To the Reverend Mr David Parsons pastor of ye Church of Christ in Maldon.
I the Subscriber, hearing that it is the desire of Thomas Parker to joyn to
the Church of Maldon, Sir I thought good to acquaint you, that I have known
this Thomas Parker to be guilty of falsifying or lying, which is a breach of the

ninth Commandment, the which I can prove: ~~Thoma~~ Abraham Skinner.

Here follows a copy of the evidences to prove the charge against Parker,
which being brought to me, I thought good to enter them in Our Church book
that our proceedings in this matter may be clear. [7]

Hannah Skinner & Mary Skinner both of Maldon being of full age do testify &
say, that they did both of them sometime in ye moneth of January in ye year 1710
then hear Thomas Parker of Maldon say, that he being by some persons charged
with the stealing of postes on the parsonage land in Maldon, said he had con
fessed the stealing of one post & no more, but at the same time said, he had taken
or stolen more, but would never confess them to those he had made his former
confession unto: and they farther say that ye s^d Thomas Parker did then with
tears confess & say, that Abraham Skinner was now ~~charged~~ complained of for the
stealing the postes that he had stolen or carryed away.

Thomas Skinner & Mary Skinner both of Maldon, of full age do testify & say,
that they did sometime in the moneth of March in the year 1711, then hear
Thomas Parker of Maldon solemnly protest & say, that he could not, nor would not
take any Oath referring to the postes, that were carried or stolen off the
parsonage land in Maldon, that should any wayes be to the dammage of
Abraham Skinner, for said he if I should swear that I did ever see Abraham Skinner
carry, or bear of any post, or posts off the parsonage land, I should take a false
oath: but at last did say, he could not tell what he should swear, till he came
to the Court.   true copy: June 10th: 1710.

Pr **Thomas Cheever.**

July 5th Joseph Whittemore & ~~E~~
Elizabeth his wife were received to full Communion.
s^d Joseph Whittemore was baptized at the same time; also a Child of
s^d Whittemore baptized at the same time, named Edmund.

Sept: 20th: ffour Children of Thomas Skinner were baptized, their names were
Thomas, Abraham, John, & Joseph.

Same day a Child of Jonathan Sprague jun.: of Maldon baptized, named Jonathan.

—— 27th   A Child of Abraham Skinner baptized, named Abraham.

Oct: 4   Nathan Cheever was received to full Communion.

—— 11   A Child of Isaac Lewis baptized, named Mary.

—— 25   Susanna Richardson of Maldon widow was received to full Communion.

Novemb: 1st: A Child of Nathaniel Richardson baptized, named Nathan.

—— 8   A Child of Thomas Skinner named Benjamin, baptized.

Same day a Son of Susanna Richardson baptized, named Biel.

——15   A Child of John Chamberlane baptized, named Susanna.

1719/20:
March 13   A Child of John Pratt of Maldon, who married Mehitabel Davis, baptized, named Mary.

April: 3d: Joseph Burdit of Maldon received to full Communion.

June: 3d   At a Church-meeting appointed to choose a Deacon, one or more: Deacon Tuttle by reason of his weaknes of body desiring to be released from his office: it was in the first place carried by a Major Vote to choose two Deacons, first one, and afterwards a second; ~~According~~ and that there should be a Majority of the Voters to make a choice. Accordingly, when their Votes were brought in for the first Deacon, our brother Mr John Chamberlane was chosen by a Majority of the Voters. When the votes were brought for the second Deacon there was not a Majority of the Voters for any person, till the third time of Voting & then our brother Mr Samuel Tuttle was chosen by a Majority of the Voters: Lt John Floyd & Asa Halsy & Jacob Halsy were as was then thought; but afterwards there appeared some mistake appointed to treat with the beforenamed persons and to make report to the Church, whither they did accept & would serve in the Office of Deacons, as soon as conveniently they could.   Attest   Thomas Cheever Pastour

Ipswich: 16 july: 1719:   The second Church of Christ in Ipswich, to the Church of Christ   [8]
in Rumny-marsh sendeth Greeting, & wish that Grace, Mercy, and
Peace may be multiplied unto you from God our heavenly ffather
and our Lord Jesus Christ.

Revd & Beloved.

These are to signify to you, that we have a very mournfull Case to lay before you, scil.[11]

the Deplorable Condition, which our Beloved Sister Church in ye Town of Wenham, is

lapsed into. For that according to our present View the s^d Church seems to us, either

Obstinately bent upon a design to subvert the ancient Constitution of these Churches,

or through the prevalency of some temptation are rushing upon their own Confusion,

which God of his infinite mercy prevent. Now R^d & Beloved brethren, under so awfull

a prospect, we hold our selves in duty bound to express, & open their condition to your

selves & other Churches in order to their Relief, if God will succeed us. Therefore

these are to notify you, that upon a Complaint exhibited to this Church, by Mr William

Rogers member of ye s^d Church in Wenham, wherein he Complains of great injustice

done him in ye s^d Church &c: Whereupon we sent a Delegation of prudent men to

Represent us, with Instructions to make farther enquiry, & Administer a word of advice,

if they judged the Complaint sufficiently evidenced & just. The s^d Church in Wenham

has all along, since our first sending to them in this present case, Manifested much

Obstinancy, & put great contempt upon the Proceedings of this Church, & thereby have

upon
plainly trampled & indignified the Constitution of the Churches, of which we shall give
        ^

a fuller account when the Churches sent to shall Convene at the time & place appointed.

Yet Beloved! Our Delegation, notwithstanding all slights put upon them, have with great

patience & stability of mind pursued duty for the good of the Church & Partie, but the

s^d Church has been very Obstinate & we are without hopes of their Compliance, but by this

way we are now taking. ~~with them~~ That R^d & Beloved, these presents are in the Name

of Christ, farther to Carry on the Process against the s^d Church in Wenham, according

to the Direction given by the Rule for the third way of Communion in these Churches.

Therefore we now more fully acquaint you & other Churches, that ye s^d Church is still under

brother by their
offence, for that having injured their Male-administrations, yet have Obstinately refused
                ^

to comply with their duty, under all the steps we have taken & offers made, by our Delegates

for his relief & their healing. The Admonition, which has been drawn up in very Christian

and proper terms sent & left among them for their use & direction, no improvement is made

of it by their Pastor according to its intent, but he rather Meditates, as we judge, in

Combination with some of the brethren how to defeat the whole Process: wherefore we now call upon your selves & other Neighbour Churches to joyn with us in Seconding of the Admonition which has been dispenced. We have with submission to Divine providence appointed to meet you at Wenham upon the 29th day of this instant July, at ten of the clock before noon: the house for the Elders & Messengers to meet at in the Morning, upon their first coming into the Town, is the house of Mr Samuel Kimbal. Thus, Revd: & Beloved! having offered to your Cognisance a case of such great importance, wherein the Glory of Christ is so peculiarly embarqued, and the Constitution of his Churches is in such imminent peril, we doubt not, but you will readily come into the Service, by sending, as we now Pray & desire you, your Elder or Elders & other Messengers to joyn in Concert with Our selves & other Churches sent unto, for the support of our Action, reinforcing our Admonition, & carrying on our Process till it should come to a final issue. So recommending all that shall be involved, & so great an example, by our most Ardent Prayer to the Grace & Conduct of our Blessed Lord.

> We rest your loving Brethren in the bonds
> of ye Gospel. John Wise Pastour
> by Order of sd Church of Christ in Ipswich
> A true copy: Attest Thomas Cheever

To the Revd Mr Thomas Cheever
Pastour, to be Communicated to the
Church of Christ in Rumny-marish.
Pr Mr Saml: Kimbal.

I received this letter July 18th, and communicated it to the Church the next Lords-day, and the Church readily Voted to comply with the desire of Ipswich 2d Church, and chose Lt: John Floyd & Mr William Halsy to accompany me & attend that Service

> Attest   Thomas Cheever Pastour.

Here follows a copy of ye Result of the Council of Churches called by the second   [9]
Church in Ipswich, to Assist & advise in the case of Mr William Rogers Member of
the Church of Wenham, he having complained of injustice done him by sd Church of

Wenham, unto the 2ᵈ Church in Ipswich, & desiring that they would make enquiry in order to his relief according to the third way of Communion directed in the Platform.

July 29ᵗʰ 1719:

The Delegation of five Churches, viz: the 2ᵈ Church in Ipswich, the Church in Rumny-marish, the Church of York, & the two Churches in Glocester, regularly met at Wenham, this twenty ninth day of July 1719, & then & there having supervised the case of Mʳ Wiliam Rogers, relating to the Suspension, he sustains under the Censure of the Church of Christ in Wenham, & finding ~~that~~ the Admonition dispensed by the second Church of Christ in Ipswich, to the sᵈ Church in Wenham to be just. Yet considering the great importance of the matter now before us, & being desirous & willing, that the sᵈ Church in Wenham might have farther time offered to them, to reconsider what has past, and the imminent peril they are in of incurring the displeasure of the Churches in the Association, if they will abide a full process: and considering that they have obstinately refused to attend on the process commenced against them hitherto. We have therefore adjourned to the last wednesday in September next ensuing, & then to meet at the house of Mʳ Samuel Kimbal, when & where the sᵈ Church of Wenham shall have oportunity to offer any just reasons, why the sᵈ Admonition should not be fully executed upon them: and order that they be duly Notified by the Moderatour of this Delegation viz: the Pastour of the sᵈ Church in Ipswich: and moreover we also appoint, that the sᵈ Moderatour draw up in form, after the best manner he can to suit the Occasion, our final Resolve in the case & have it in readiness for us.

Voted by yᵉ sᵈ Delegation: as attest   John Wise moderatour.

Wenham: Sept: 30ᵗʰ: 1719:

We, the Delegation of five Churches, viz: the Second Church in Ipswich which did begin the Process, the Church of Rumny-marish (the Church of York not appearing the weather being bad) & the two churches in Glocester, being now met by adjournment in Wenham abovenamed: After very Solemn & humble addresses unto God for direction in this great

concern devolved upon us by his wise providence, we now proceed.

ffirst, We sent a Notification to the Church of Christ in Wenham on the 15th of this

instant, wherein was set forth, that the Delegation of the s^d five Churches, formerly

mett in the Town of Wenham at Mr Samuel Kimbal's on 29th of July last, to super

vise the case of Mr William Rogers, relating to the Suspension he was under from the

s^d Church in Wenham, did then & there find & declare, that the Admonition dispensed

by the s^d 2^d Church in Ipswich to the s^d Church in Wenham, in order to the restora

-tion of the s^d Rogers was just, & also the s^d Church in Wenham was in the s^d Notifi

cation Directed to attend on the Delegation now mett, but the s^d Church refusing to

submit to the s^d Notification, & still persisting in their Obstinacy, We now in the name

of Christ, & in right of the Churches we represent, proceed to draw up a more formal

and final Result in the case, we therefore declare our judgment & sentence in ye following articles

ffirst, That the Management of the 2^d church in Ipswich towards the Church in Wenham is

well & sufficiently founded in the Canon of these Churches, and the process of ye s^d Church

is to be justified from what the Platform of our Church discipline says about the third

way of Communion of Churches, & therefore the s^d process is agreable to the way of Order,

and tends greatly to the promotion of Union, peace, truth, holiness & mutual edification in

and to the establishment of the Churches, and is a laudable & proper example for us, & all

other Churches in the Consociation to follow, and imitate one towards another in such like case.

Secondly. We therefore condemn the Church in Wenham for slighting & rejecting the Process,

& method taken with them by the s^d 2^d Church in Ipswich; the s^d Church in Wenham has

thereby put high contempt upon the Constitution of these Churches, notwithstanding they did

so solemnly & publickly upon the Pacification, promise for the future to Submit to the third way of [10]

Communion in the Platform, & by their s^d contempt have begun such a rupture & breach in

their alliance & gospel order, which, if not check't & stopt in time, tends to the utter

ruine and subversion of the Noble frame & constitution of these famous, ancient, & flourish

ing Churches. And therefore we farther declare that our judgment is, that the s^d Church

in Wenham, they continuing in fellowship with these Churches, & all other Churches in

this grand Association, are bound by the Canon at their utmost peril to Submit to such
a method when taken with them by any Neighbour Sister Church upon such or the like cause.

sufficient

Thirdly. Thus having abundant reason to justify the 2^d Church in Ipswich in their proceeding
& having fully supervised the case of s^d Mr William Rogers, we do now in Concert with
the s^d Church declare, that ye s^d Mr Rogers has not given any just offence to the s^d Church
of Wenham, by any groundless or injurious charge against his Pastour, on 31st of january 1716/17
in those words of Opposition for which he was Suspended, in that they were sufficiently
evidenced unto us to be true. Therefore we now more formally & publickly Justify the
s^d Admonition dispensed on the 19th of May 1719 by the s^d Church in Ipswich to the
Church in Wenham, in favour of s^d Mr Rogers as aboves^d.

ffourthly. In consideration, that the s^d Church in Wenham hath all along manifested great
Obstinacy, & now also after due patience & long waiting for their Compliance, the s^d
Church still continue very inflexible & obstinate, therefore in the Name of Christ &
of the several Churches we represent, these presents are to set forth & declare, that
we the s^d Delegation having joined our selves, do in concert execute, set on, and second
the s^d Admonition, & for that end do now advise, direct, & Admonish the s^d our much
pitied & greatly beloved Sister Church in Wenham, that after such a long and unjust delay, they do now release their s^d brother William Rogers from the s^d suspension, and
restore him to Communion with the s^d Church in Wenham, & by all due means & brotherly deportment towards him establish him in the perswasion of their brotherly love to him,
and also we still continue to advise the s^d Mr Rogers, upon the Churches receiving him
to their fellowship. that he suppress all hard resentments towards his Pastour, & brethren, notwithstanding the unkindnesses & injustice he has met with from them. 12: rom:
1: cor: 13: And for the present relief of s^d Mr Rogers, while the s^d Church shall deliberate, we grant a permit to the s^d Rogers for Occasional Communion with any of our
Churches. ffinally thus hoping our s^d beloved Sister Church in Wenham will well consider how they have swerved from the rule of Charity & justice in the case of their
s^d brother Rogers, & also revise what ruptures they have made in the Order of these
Churches, & also we hope & pray that the Grace of God may be sufficient for them,

and influence their minds under the present awfull crisis they are reduced to, and

dispose & bow their hearts to comply with their duty, in the reasonable & just di-

rections that we have laid before them, & so prevent those other more terrible

parts of the process with remain yet to be fulfilled; but if not, God assisting, we

are resolved to execute the same, & that by pursuing every step to a final issue

according to the direction of our Platform.

Voted. nemine non consentiente

John Wise moderatour.

Wenham Octob: I[st]: 1719:

We the Delegates of five Churches, (the Church of York being not here, the weather being

bad) having mett at this time by Adjournment at the house of M[r] Samuel Kimbal in Wenham aboves[d],

and our Sister Church in Wenham remaining very obstinate, & still continuing to resist the regular

Process carried on against them in the case of M[r] William Rogers; having found on the 29th of July

last, & then declared the Admonition dispensed by the 2[d] Church in Ipswich to the s[d] Church in

Wenham to be just, from the sence of duty incumbent on us, & faithfulness to Christ, & his Churches, and

a due regard to justice we have seconded, & this day farther administred the s[d] Admonition to the s[d]

our Sister Church in Wenham, as does more fully appear in the Instrument of Execution we have publish-

ed against the s[d] Church, reference thereto being had. And farthermore considering how much the

well being of these Churches doth depend upon the careful conduct, wise & good management of this

important business, which God in his holy & wise providence hath at this juncture devolved on the

Churches we represent, & nextly on our selves, we now in due form make a farther pause, & shall

still wait a convenient space of time for the Submission of the s[d] Church in Wenham, expecting their   [11]

complying with their duty, as set forth in s[d] Admonition, that has been reinforced, seconded, & published

against them as aboves[d]. And moreover considering at what distance several of us dwell, & also that

the time of the year is hastning on, that may make it more difficult for travel, we therefore judge

it meet to make some suitable precaution in the business, that is to say, if the s[d] Church in Wenham

shall fully, & in due time comply with the s[d] Admonition, then the Delegation of the s[d] five

Churches is dissolved; but if not, we shall continue in being as a representative body, God helping of us, & shall proceed with the process, & our next step will be to draw up & publish our forbearing Communion with the s^d Church of Wenham for our s^d five churches: & then we shall farther also do & perform such other acts as are agreable with the canon & government of these Churches, in order to, & in hope of the repentance & full compliance of the s^d Church in Wenham. And for the future we leave the affair, as it is now stated, to the conduct & management of the Delegates of the three Nearest Churches in the s^d Delegation to draw up in form what may be farther need-full, & transmit the same to the Delegates of the other Churches concerned for their appro-bation, & also if there be Occasion for it, to determine on time & place when, & where a grand Council of Churches shall be Convened, as the Platform doth direct; and also to fix the number of Churches, & who shall be Cited through the whole Consociation, in order to the Definitive sentence in this case. And moreover before we dismiss this present Session, we de-clare, that upon issuing out the Sentence of forbearing Communion with the Church of Wenham for our s^d five Churches, which God prevent, if it be his holy will, by bowing the hearts of our s^d Dear Sister Church to a compliance; but if otherwise, & the s^d Sentence be pronounced by us as above is provided, then we think due care should be taken to grant Occasional Commu-nion to other innocent Members of the s^d Church of Wenham, & especially such as do, & have born due Testimony against the Corruptness & Obstinacy of the fores^d Church of Wenham, they signifying & setting forth that they have so done, & this provision is made for the ease of the innocent, until the Grand Convention of Churches shall be made in this case, & then to proceed to a more full Renunciation of all right of Relation to, & acts of ffellowship, as the Platform doth more expressly direct to, with the s^d Church. ffinally, we the s^d Delega= tion having made the best provision we can in so great a Concern, do now leave it to the s^d three Churches as aboves^d to take care in all points for the future, & do what is meett according to their best discretion in the case relating to the s^d Church of Wenham and the s^d Mr Rogers, & to give to the Delegates of the other two Churches an account of things from time to time for their approbation, before any thing of moment as aboves^d be fully Executed.

Voted   nemine non consentiente

John Wise moderatour.

A copy of the result, which the Delegation had unanimously voted & published, was sent by

    several of the Members of the Delegation, to the R^d: Mr Gerrish Pastour of the Church

    of Wenham, & left with his wife, he not being to be spoke with by them.

The s^d Mr Gerrish refused to communicate to his Church the result of the Delegation, &

    see whither they were willing in compliance therewith to restore their brother Mr Rogers,

    which was justly grievous & dissatisfactory to many of his Church.

                following
On the sixth of January the s^d Mr Gerrish died, the difference in Wenham not made up.

After the death of Mr Gerrish, the Church found their difference not being made up was a

barr to their Obtaining another Minister, & thereupon began to endeavour to put an end

to their long continued difference, & after some meetings & essays at last at a Church

meeting they voted to restore Mr Rogers to their Communion, & to revoke what had past

in the Church formerly against him, & that an account of their doings should be sent

to R^d Mr Wise, moderatour of the Delegation or Council that had met at Wenham,

under the hand of Mr Prescot, whom the Church of Wenham had chose to be Moderatour

of their Church meetings & to keep their Church records till they had a Pastour settled,

and that seeing the end is obtained, which was aimed at by their process, & Mr Rogers restored

that they would now cease all farther steps: &c: After R^d Mr Wise received an account of

the Church in Wenham's restoring Mr Rogers to their fellowship, he communicated the same

to the Delegates of the 5 Churches who declared their acceptance, & so a period put to

any farther steps: and the Delegation was declared dissolved.

To ye R^d Mr Thomas Cheever   [12]

Pastour of the Church of

Christ at Rumny-marish.

January 14th 1719/20

Honoured Rev^d: & Beloved.

It having pleased the most Glorious Head of the Church, after, as we

hope, our most earnest, humble & Solemn Supplications unto him, on a day of

fasting & prayer for his gracious Guidance & Assistance, in a matter of so great importance, to Direct us of the New-North-Church in Boston by a very

considerable Majority of Votes, to Invite the Revd Mr Peter Thacher late

of Weymouth, to the Pastoral Office among us, and to Incline him to accept

of our Invitation. We have agreed upon Wednesday the 27th of this present

January (God willing) to fix him in the full Exercise of s^d Office among us.

We therefore humbly & earnestly intreat the Presence of your Revd Pastour

with such Messengers, as you shall think proper to send with him, to Concurr

with the Elders & Messengers of Several other Churches in Exercising such

Acts of Communion with us, as the Solemnity of the ~~Ser~~ Occasion may call for.

We earnestly ask your Prayers, that Grace, mercy & peace from God our

Father, & from Our Lord Jesus Christ may be multiplied upon us, & upon

our Offspring, & with our humble beseeching the Throne of Grace, that

the same inestimable blessings may descend on you in a most plentiful

manner.

We Subscribe Your in the faith

and fellowship of the Gospel.

John Webb, in the name and at

the desire of the Church.

To the Rev^d: Mr Thomas Cheever

to be Communicated.

You are desired to meet at the

Pastours house by Nine of the clock

in the Morning.

I communicated this letter to the Church on 17th jan:

who readily complied with the desire of Our Sister Church

and chose L^t: John Floyd, Mr William Halsey, & Mr John

Chamberlane to accompany me and concur with the other

Church or Churches that should attend that service.

True copy. Attest Thomas Cheever Pastour

After our return I acquainted the Brethren, whom I sent for to my house,

and who gave me a meeting all except two or three, with what we had done

as to the installing yᵉ Revᵈ: Mʳ Peter Thacher in the Pastoral Office at

the New-North Church, together with the reasons of our doings therein, who

declared their approbation of the same.

Attest Thomas Cheever Pastour

1720   [13]

June 17ᵗʰ   A Church meeting to choose a Deacon, one or more: What was done the former meeting

June: 3ᵈ was dropped because of great uneasiness; it was in the first place Hurried by a

unanimous Vote to choose but one Deacon at present: and when their Votes were

brought in, there was not a Majority the first time for any person: when their

Votes were brought in yᵉ 2ᵈ time: our brother Mʳ John Chamberlane was chosen

by the Majority of Voters

Attest Thomas Cheever Pastour

July: 3ᵈ   Mʳ William Sarjeant a member of Maldon Church, having a dismission from that

Church, unto the Church of Christ at Rummy-marish, was received to full Communion.

August: 7ᵗʰ Thomas Burdit junʳ: of Maldon & Mary his wife were received to full Communion.

Oct: 2ᵈ   A Child of John Leath baptized, named Samuel.

Oct: 23   ffive Children of Thomas Burdit junʳ: were baptized, their names were

Thomas, Jacob, Jabez, Joseph, Mary.

Nov: 7ᵗʰ   At a Church meeting to choose another Deacon to be joyned with Deacon John

Chamberlane. When their votes were brought in, our brother Mʳ William Halsy

was chosen by a Majority of Votes & voters: our brother Chamberlane was not

present, it was therefore proposed & assented to by the Church, that their accepting

the Churches call to sᵈ Office should be manifested by their sitting in the Deacons

seat. And whereas at the last Church meeting about making some allowance to the

Deacons for their trouble yearly, as also to make allowance to the Churches Delegates sent to Wenham & to Boston &c. Deacon Tuttle declared openly that he desired

nothing for the time he had served the Church in the Office of Deacon. After

which it was unanimously Voted that no allowance should be made to the Deacons

nor to any others out of the Church-Stock but with the knowledge & consent of

the Church, & that the Deacons should give account of their doings in their

Office unto the Church once in a year, to present any dissatisfactions or mistake.

Attest Thomas Cheever
Pastour

Nov: 13: A Child of Abraham Skinner baptized, named William.

Dec: 4th: A Child of Samuel Watts baptized, named Elizabeth.

———— 20 A Church meeting, in which the Church Covenant was read, showing that we fixed upon

Congregational principles, according to the Platform sett forth by these Chur-

ches, in which both the power of the Elders, and the liberty of the Brethren

are so sett out, as that no Church act is compleat & perfected without the con-

sent of both: when it was put to Vote, whither the Church did consent to and

were willing to abide by the s^d first settlement & Covenant, there was an

unanimous consent manifested by lifting up the hand. Afterward upon debate

with reference to the former Church meeting notwithstanding it appeared that

Mr William Halsy had a Major vote to the Office of a Deacon, because of

the fierce opposition made by three or four of the Brethren; upon the motion

of another Brother, that we might for the present rest contented with but

one Deacon viz: Mr John Chamberlane, till spirits were better composed; to

prevent further Contention & for peace it was Voted that Mr Chamberlane

should serve alone in the Office of a Deacon for the present, and passed with

but little opposition: and the s^d Deacon Chamberlane declared his accept-

ance for the present, & agreed to go to receive the Churches Vessels & stock,

if any, of Deacon John Tuttle.

Attest   Thomas Cheever Pastour.

A copy of Deacon Chamberlane's receipt given to Deacon Tuttle.

Received of Deacon John Tuttle, the vessels belonging to the Church at Rumny-marish

being two flagons, six cups, & two platters, with the table-cloth & a bottle; as also the Church

stock, being three pounds, seventeen shillings & six pence in bills & eleven shillings ten pence

half penny in pennys & half pence, ~~being~~ amounting to in the whole 4ll: 9s: 4d 1/2: I say received for the

use of the Church, this 2d day of ffebruary 1720/21

Pr me John Chamberlane

a true copy; Attest   Thomas Cheever Pastour.

1721
[14]

April: 16:   A Child of John Floyd junr: baptized, named Mary.

July: 9:   A Child of William Halsy's baptized, named Ebenezer.

Aug: 13   A Child of John Pratt of Maldon who married Mehitabel Davis, baptized named John.

—— 27   A Child, of John Whittamore a member of Maldon Church, baptized named John.

Sept: 17   A Child of Ensign Joseph Belcher baptized, named Sarah.

Nov: 12   A Child of Samuel Tuttle baptized, named Abigail.

—— 19   A Child of Deacon John Chamberlane baptized, named Lydia.

1721/22

Jan: 28:   A Child of Isaac Lewis baptized, named Nathan.

Feb: 18:   Elisha Tuttle was received to full Communion, being dismissed to this Church from

the first Church in Lynn.

Feb: 20th: Deacon Chamberlane laid his accounts before Lt: John Floyd. Mr Wm: Halsy, & Mr

Saml: Watts who were appointed by ye Church to assist me in attending that

service according to a former Vote of the Church: Novemb: 7th: 1721: and the Churches

stock in his hands appeared to be five pounds eighteen shillings & eight pence.

Attest Thomas Cheever. pastour.

March: 4th The Church was staied after meeting to appoint,

a time on the week day to consider of what should then be laid before them,

they appointed the Next Wednesday seven-night, to meet at One of ye Clock in the

afternoon at my house. which will be ye 14th of this instant March.

14: At the Church Meeting after the Church were acquainted that Deacon Chamberlane's accounts were fair & clear and what stock was in his hands, it was voted that the s^d Deacon should buy a book to keep his accounts in for the future, & pay for the ~~Chu~~ book of the Church records; and that he should gett the Windows in the Galleries of the Meeting house mended, and provide hooks & staples that are wanting to secure the s^d Windows for future. and also to take care of said Windows as their should be need for the future, and these things to be paid for out of the Church-stock in his hands: it was likewise Voted that the land belonging to the Meeting-house should be fenced in with a good board fence, and to be paid for by the Church; Mr Samuel Watts, Jacob Halsy, & John Leath were chosen a Committee to take care for the doing of it, as also to make steps at the South-door.

This last Vote being afterwards objected against by Several of the Brethren was laid by:

Attest   Thomas Cheever pastour.

At the Meeting aboves^d, it was proposed to the Consideration of the Church with respect to the Difference & distance that does still continue between the Church and Severall of the Inhabitants in this place; Whither some Overtures for peace should not be made by the Church, unto our afors^d Dissenting Neighbours & Friends; After much debate pro and con: and after the Objections made by some were answered, and the unhappy effects of the Want of peace, how mischievous it might prove in after times; as also the great blessings of Peace, & ye special blessing pronounced by Our Saviour unto peace-makers. and after Some of the Brethren declared that Some of the Principal of Our Dissenting Neighbours & ffriends had manifested a desire of peace. The Church Unanimously Voted to send in the following words their proposal to Our s^d dissatisfied Neighbours, to be Directed to Lt: John Brintnal to be Communicated to the rest

the proposal made follows over leaf:

I Communicated both the letters on the other side to ye Church on Feb: 25^t: who readily Complied with the Desire of the Committee; & also the desire of Our Sister Church in the East end of Watertown; & chose D^n: John Chamberlane, L^t: John Floyd: Ensign Joseph Belcher, M^r W^m: Halsey, & Mr Samuel Watts, to

Accompany me, & Assist in Common Council with the other Churches that should

meet for that Service at Watertown at the time appointed. L^t: ffloyd, & Mr Belcher

did not appear; but the other three Brethren gave their attendance, where we mett

with eight Churches, as by ye Records of ye Scribe in my keeping may appear:

Attest Thomas Cheever Pas^r: the Result of ye Council follow's overleaf:[12]

To ye Rev^d: Mr Thomas Cheever   [15]

Pastour of ye Church of Christ

in Rumney-Marish to be Commu-

nicated to ye Church there.

To our Brethren of ye Church of Christ in Rumny-marish

Rev^d: & well beloved.

Wheras we of ye Committee of ye Church, and the rest of ye Society belonging to the

Middle-part of Water-town, have unanimously made Choice of the Rev^d: Mr Robert

Sturgeon, to be our gospel Minister, who has seen good to accept of our Call to

settle in that work.[13] These are humbly to request your Presence, & Assistance, by your

Elders & Delegates, in setting him apart for that work, according to the practise

of the Churches in New-England, & desiring your prayers for us, remain

yours in the Fellowship of the Gospel.

Dated at Watertown: this 15th ffebruary: 1721/22	Caleb Church
The time y^t we have appointed for our	John Parkhust
Ordination is the first Tuesday but one	Simon Tayntor
being ye 27 day of this instant.	Thomas Straight
	Joshua Biglow
	Edward Harrington
The place, where the Elders & Messengers	Samuel Pearce
are to come to, is Mr Samuel Pearce's.	Ebenezer Wellington.
	Committee.

Copia vera.

Attest Thomas Cheever Pas[r]:

To the Rev[d]: M[r] Thomas Cheever, Pastour

of y[e] Church in Rumney-marish to be

Communicated to the Church.

Watertown. Feb: 23: 1721/2

The Church of Christ in y[e] East end of Watertown to the

Church of Christ in Rumney-marish Sendeth Greeting:

Rev[d]: & Beloved

We received notice this week, of a Letter sent to you, to Desire your Assistance in the

Ordination of M[r] Robert Sturgeon, to a Church in Watertown: what Church is intend-

ed we are at Uncertainties, but suppose they may be Some persons partly of the

Eastern, & partly of the Western precincts in Watertown, who endeavour to impose

upon you: for there is such a party in the Town, who have for some time had M[r]

Sturgen preaching among them, & seem to have been Clandestinely carrying on

a Design to embarrass y[e] Affairs of y[e] Town, which were lately Established by the

Act of y[e] General Court. We also desire you to send your Pastour & Messengers to

Assist in a Common Council, with the Pastours & Messengers of other Churches, on

Tuesday next, to hear what may be Offered unto you, by those who first sent ~~for~~ to you

and by Agents for both of the Precincts of y[e] Town, Reasonably hoping you

will bear due Testimony against all Disorders.

We are your very loving Brethren in the ffellowship of the Gospel.

Henry Gibbs, Pastour

in y[e] name & with the

consent of the Brethren.

You are desired to meet at eight of

the Clock in the Morning at the

house of the Rev[d]: M[r] Gibbs.

Copia vera.

Attest   Thomas Cheever. Pastour.

At a Council, of Nine Churches, Assembled at Water-town, at the Desire of the   [16]

Eastern Church in s^d Town, A part of which Council being also Convened

at the Desire of Such as Attend on the Publick worship of God in the Middle-

Meeting-house in s^d Town. On Febr: 27: 1721/2. To advise & determine on what

should be Offered to them, relating to the Ordination of the Rev^d: M^r

Robert Sturgeon.

After humble Supplication to heaven, and an impartial hearing of what was

offered to us, by all Parties, we advise & Determine as followeth

Imprimis   Whereas there are a Number of Persons in s^d Water-Town, who by a private Sub-

scription and Pretended gathering of a Church, have Attempted the Settlement

of the s^d Mr Robert Sturgeon as their Gospel Minister, We are of Opinion,

that the Proceedings, of the s^d Subscibers relating to Mr Sturgeon's Settle-

ment, are Contrary to the Designe of the General Court Act, relating to the

Division of Water-town into two Precincts.

2.   We also are of Opinion, that the afors^d Proceedings are not agreable to the

good Order, & practise of the Churches of Christ in New-England, neither are

those, that call themselves a Church, to be Owned as such for the reasons

beforementioned.

3   Wherefore we Determine & Declare, that the Ordination of no Person on

the forementioned or the like foundation Ought to be Proceeded in.

4   And whereas the Western Precinct have Erected a Meeting-house, which it is

supposed & hoped will in a very little time be fitt for the Publick Worship of

God, and upon hearing of what hath been alledged, We are of Opinion, that

it will be very Conducible to the peace of Water-town, that the Eastern

Precinct do proceed to Erect & finish a Meeting-house on School-house-hill, within

a year at farthest from this time, & accordingly, we earnestly advise them thereun.

5   Whereas Mr Joshua Warren with Others, in the behalf of the Subscribers for M^r

Sturgeon's Settlement, have asked the Advice of this Council concerning the

Maintaining of Preaching, in the Middle Meeting-house in Water-town; till One

is provided on School-house hill; the Council judge it Advisable that there be

Preaching ~~at the~~ s^d Middle Meeting house, until according to the Order of the

General Court, the Meeting house be fitted for the Worship of God in the

Western Precinct, and farther we cannot see reason to advise.

And we pray the God of Peace to give you peace always by all means.

Thomas Cheever Moderatour

in ye name & with the

Consent of the Council.

Copia vera.

Attest Thomas Cheever.

This Result of the Council I read unto the Church, the Sabbath

after, being 4th March:

Attest Thomas Cheever pastour.

1721/2   in Rumney-marish   [17]
March: 14: The Church of Christ, to Our Dissatisfied Neighbours & Friends in Rumney-marish
        these, Directed, by the Vote of the Church, to L^t: John Brintnal to be Communica-
        ted to the rest.

Whereas there hath been, & is still an Openly continued distance & difference

between the Church of Christ in this place, & some of the other Inhabitants, which

we think cannot but be Uncomfortable both to them and Us, as well as displeasing

unto Our Glorious Lord. We have therefore, (upon serious Consideration of our said

differences with the uncomfortable effects, as also from some intimations give us by

Some of our Brethren, that Some of Our s^d Neighbours & friends were Desirous of peace,

to let it appear that We are desirous of a good peace with all Our Christian Neigh-

bours & friends,) agreed to make this Overture, unto Our Dissatisfied Neighbours and

ffriends, that they would be pleased to let us know, what are the hinderances unto a
peace on our part, that so we may remove them, if we judge them capable of being
removed, that for the future there may be a better understanding among us, that we
may live & love as Brethren, & the interest of Christs Kingdom may be the better
promoted among us, to the good not only of the present but Succeding Generations.
We would earnestly pray Our dissatisfied Neighbours & friends to let us hear from
them with all Convenient speed.

March: 14: 1721/2 Rumny-marish.

Thomas Cheever Pastour

in y[e] name of the Brethren.

To Lieut[t]: John Brintnal
to be Communicated.

April: 29: The Church was staied and the following letter read unto them:

Watertown. April: 27: 1722.

The two Churches in Watertown, viz: the East & West part thereof, to the Church of Christ
in Rumny-marish, Wish the Multiplication of Grace, mercy & peace from God the Father
through Our Lord Jesus Christ.

Reverend & Beloved.

The very difficult Circumstances of our Town in General, & each of these Churches
in it, are such (though the holy & Sovereign Providence of God) that we Eminently stand
in need of Direction & Assistance for giving light & Restoring peace unto us, from the
Neighbour Churches in Communion with us. The Occasion whereof is the Coming of a
Gentleman lately from Ireland into our Town, viz: M[r] Robert Sturgeon, who has been ende-
vouring to Constitute a Third Church in the Town, in a very factious & Schismatical
manner. We having used all the more Private Methods to prevent the Growth of these
Disorders: and also called a Reverend Council, who by their Elders & Messengers Condemned the Proceedings of said M[r] Robert Sturgeon & his Party; yet he & they

bidding defiance to all these Methods have gone on with great Resolution. We have
in this case no better Remedy than to call in farther Council; and we do it the rather,
because this Schisme is like to be a spreading Leprosy through all the Churches in the land
except timely Suppressed. We therefore the Afflicted Brethren in Watertown entreat
your Assistance by your Elders & Messengers on the Next Tuesday to Meet in Council
on this important matter, that by the blessing of God upon this Institution of his,
Our present Disorders may be Redressed, and all such bold Attempts for the future
on the Order of the churches in this Province Discountenanced; whereby also the
Supream Authority of the land in Civil Respects has been Oppugned, as you will
be more particularly enformed, when Present with us. Desiring your instant prayer
on our behalf, We are your very loving Brethren in the Fellowship of ye gospel

   Henry Gibbs, Pastour of ye East Church in Watertown.

   Jonathan Sanderson Deacon of ye West Church in Watertown

1722   [18]

Your presence is desired at Nine
of the Clock of ye afors^d day at
the house of L^t: Coolidge.

       The Churches of Christ to be added to those
       that have been formerly on Our Spot, are the
       Old Church, ye Old North, ye Old South and
       Mr Colmans in Boston, & ye Church in Dorchester.

To the Reverend Mr Thomas Cheever
Pastour of the Church in Rumny-marish
to be Communicated to ye Church.

       Copia vera. Attest Thomas Cheever Pas^r

The Church upon hearing the letter, readily Complied with the Desire of
Our Sister Churches in Watertown, & Voted that L^t: John Floyd, together
with Our Brethren Deacon John Camberlane, Mr William Halsey, & M^r

Samuel Watts, who were of the former Council at Watertown, should

Accompany me, and attend that Service at time & place appointed.

Attest: Thomas Cheever Pastour.

When the time came, Lt John Floyd & Mr Samuel Watts gave their Attendance

with my self at the place appointed, where we mett with the rest of the

Churches who were desired to meet in Council by their Elders & Messengers,

the result of the Council here follows.

May: Ist: A Council of fourteen Churches, Convened at Watertown, on Tuesday, May: Ist,

1722, upon the desire of the two Churches there, complaining of Disorderly

proceedings among Several people in the Town; After solemn invocation of

the Glorious Lord, and through Examination of the Matters laid before us,

(which the Persons, principally Complained of in the Town, declined to Attend,

when fairly Notified,) have declared, as followeth.

I   We apprehend the Neighbours, who have Combined, & Subscribed to fform a third

Congregation in the Middle of Watertown, have done what has a tendency to

Defeat the good intentions of Our Nursing Fathers in the Civil Government;

Whose Directions for the Establishment of two Precincts, & Churches in Water-

Town, appears to us evidently Calculated for the general Welfare of the Place,

the interest of Religion, the period of Contention, & the reasonable Ease of

the Inhabitants; and their Attempts that way are therefore to be blamed, and

are such as may not expect Countenance from the people of God: <u>I: Peter: 2:</u>

<u>13. 15:</u> <u>I. Cor: 10. 37:</u> <u>13: Rom: I. 2:</u> <u>14: Rom: 19:</u>

2   It appears, that the small Number of Brethren, who have attempted the Formation of a

new Church in Water-town, were Guilty of much Disorder, and Violated their solemn

Church Covenant, when they Signed their Private Covenant before they either

had, or asked a Dismission from the Church to which they belonged: and y^e Є

Church have had weighty reason to decline the granting them a dismission

from them, when they afterwards requested it. We hereby declare, that they are

❧ 253 ❧

still to be considered as Members of that Church, who may treat them as
Offenders, & liable to their holy Discipline, on this occasion: and they are not
to be Owned as a Distinct Church in Water-town. <u>10: Heb :25:</u> <u>I: Peter: 5. 5:</u> <u>17: Ezek: 18. I</u>

3   It appears that Mr Robert Sturgeon, to qualify himself for purposes which he had
frequently promised not to prosecute, Obtained for himself an Ordination at a
Private house in Boston, from the hands of three Ministers lately arrived from,
and two of them returning to Ireland, and this without the advice, or knowledge
of any of the United Ministers in Boston, or any other Pastours or Churches that
we can learn in the Province; & also without any proper & previous publication of
what was intended: and that afterward in a Private house from the Single hand
of Mr Magregory Minister of Nutfield,[14] he received an Enstalment in the Pastoral
Charge of some of the beforesaid Brethren, as a Church in Watertown; whereupon he
has gone on to the Publick actions of a Pastour to a Flock there. These proceedings we judge to be full of irregularities, and carry in them a very undue ~~imp~~
imputation upon the Churches in this Countrey, & threaten the introduction of
the utmost confusion among us, and are a very ill requital of the brotherly-kindness wherewith
Strangers from North-Brittain, & Ireland have been embraced & honoured among us; and   [19]
require a publick testimony to be born against them; and in this testimony a Rebuke
appears to be peculiary due to Mr Magregory, whose Conduct has expressed so much
temority, presumption, and intrusion, as is greatly offensive unto us, nor may he expect
the regards due to a Minister in our Churches, until we have received suitable
satisfaction from him, for the insult he has made upon the good order of our Churches, particularly his acting in defiance of the late Council of Watertown.
<u>13: acts: 2. 3.</u> <u>I: tim: 5. 22:</u> <u>I: Cor: 14: 33. 40:</u>

4   As we cannot but commend our Brethren in the Western precinct of Watertown for
their proceeding so far as they have done, in Erecting of their New Meeting-house
as also in their Seasonable Remonstrances to Mr Robert Sturgeon, & his party;
adding our advice, that they take all speedy & proper Measures for the Settlement
of all Ordinances among them, to which we pressingly exhort the Neighbours, who

have Subscribed to a Separate intention, to fall in with a due concurrance; so we
encourage our Brethren, in the Eastern Precinct, to do what they have by the late
Council been directed unto, either by obtaining a Removal of the Middle Meeting
house to School-house hill, or building a New one there.

5   We do with all Solemnity Admonish the Brethren, who have been trying to sett
up a third Church in Watertown, together with the Person, whom they have so unad-
visedly Owned as their Pastour, to repent of & desist from their Disorderly, and
Schismatical proceedings, lest it become yet more Manifest unto all men, that the
Glorious Lord, who walks in the midst of the Golden Candle-sticks, & who hates the
work of them which turn aside, & who is terrible ~~out of~~ from his holy places, is dis-
pleased at the way which they have taken. We particularly declare, that M[r]
Robert Sturgeon has no right to the Office of a Pastour among them, and ought no
longer to preach, nor exercise any part of the Ministry in the place where he
now is, and that the people ought not to Countenance it: and that we judge him
unworthy to be employed in any of the Churches, till he has made a publick
satisfaction. To conclude, we exhort M[r] Sturgeon and his Adherents, that they
yield a ready & willing Compliance with the Admonition, which we give unto them
in discharge of our duty, to our Glorious Lord, and unto them, and unto all our Churches: and expect that they will not treat this with the same Contempt which
they have cast upon the advice, & determination of the late Council of Churches
in this place, as they would not expose themselves to a farther & more awfull
Censure upon their Offences.

Finally Brethren be of one mind, live in peace, and the God of love and
       peace shall be with you.

    a copy   Cotton Mather Moderatour.

July: 15:   A Child of John Floyd jun[r]: baptized, named Jacob.
—— 29th:   Eleanor Leath wife of John Leath was received to full Communion.
Sept: 16:   A Child of Samuel Watts baptized, named Elizabeth.

Octob: 7:   A Child of John Leath baptized, named Elijah.

———- -21st   Richard Whittamore was received to full Communion, & baptized at the same time.

Dec: 23[d]:   Jeremiah Whittemore was received to full Communion, & Patience his wife.

1722/3:
Jan: 20   A Child of Nathan Cheever baptized, named Nathan.

Feb: 19:   Deacon Chamberlane laid his accounts before M[r] William Halsy, M[r] Sam[l]: Watts & M[r] Jacob Halsy

who were appointed by the Church to Assist me in that Service, and the Church-Stock in his

10[s]: 6: glazier	hands, (beside twenty shillings & six pence laid out by him according to a Vote of
3[s]: my book	the Church, for mending the Meeting-house Windows & for y[e] Church-books)[15] [was found]
7[s]: y[e] Deacon	to be six pounds, ten shillings & a penny: 6[L]: 10[s]: 1[d]:
Book: 20[s]: 6[d]:	

1723:   [20

June:23[d]:   Ruhamah Tuttle, (Widow of John Tuttle jun[r]) was received to full Communion.

July: 24th:   A Child of John Pratt of Maldon, (who married Mehetabel Davis) baptized, named Sarah.

August: 10th: A Child of Jeremiah Whittemore baptized, named Jeremiah.

Octob: 13 A Child of Deacon John Chamberlane's baptized, named Lois.

——— 20   A Child of Abraham Skinner baptized, named Isaac.

Dec: 1st: The following letter was read unto the Church:

To the Rev[d]: M[r] Cheever, Pastour

of y[e] Church of Christ in Rumny-marish.

From the Church of Christ in Reading North-precinct, to the Church of Christ in

Rumny-marish, Grace & Peace be multiplied to you from God y[e] Father & our Lord Jesus Christ.

Rev: & Beloved. Whereas nine of y[e] Brethren of this Church have apprehended themselves to

be much aggrieved by their Pastour, in being denied y[e] Priviledges of the Brother-hood; and in

his partiality in y[e] Administration of the affairs belonging to this Church of Christ: which

matters of grievance are manifested by sundry positive articles, in a writing drawn up &

signed by them, & delivered by them to him their Pastour: and we being apprehensive of our

present uncapacity to put a peaceable issue to this Difference among our selves. We, viz:

the Pastour, the Dissatisfied Brethren, with the other part of the Church do earnestly desire the presence & Assistance of your Rev^d: Elder, with two of your Messengers, on

Tuesday ye 26^t of Novemb, and if Thanksgiving should be in that week, then we shall

expect you, on 3^d of Decemb, which is the Tuesday following, to hear & Determine the

matters of Difference among us.

So commending you to the grace & blessing of God in our Lord Jesus Christ, & desiring

your earnest prayers to God for us.

    We rest, yours in the faith & fellowship of the Gospel.

Reading Novemb ye 12^{12} 1723

                                      Daniel Putnam

                                      Pastour

                                      in the name & with ye consent

                                      of ye Brethren.

The Churches that are sent to, are ye first of X in Church

Marble-head, ye 1st Church in Reading, ye Church in Woburn,

the first Church in Salem, ye Church in Rumny-marish, the 2^d

Church in Andover, the Church in Billericah:

afterwards ye Church in Lexington was sent to, in the stead of Woburn Church, ye Rev^d:

Mr Fox not being well: & ye Church in Salem-village in stead of Reading first Church.

The Church upon hearing the letter, readily Voted to comply with the desire of our

Sister Church in Reading North-precinct, & Ensign Joseph Belcher, & Mr William Halsy

were chosen to Accompany me & attend that Service at the time appointed.

When the time came, Mr William Halsy accompanied me to Reading, (Mr Belcher

had a Son to be buried that very day the Council was to meet) where we mett

with the rest of ye Elders & Messengers of the Churches desired to meet in Council.

        The Result of the Council here followeth.

At a Council of seven Churches, held at the North-precinct in Reading, on Decemb: 3^d

1723, to hear and Determine the matters of Difference there, between y^e Rev^d: M^r

Daniel Putnam, and Some of his Church, that call themselves aggrieved. The Rev^d: Mr Putnam, & the whole Church, before the Opening of the Council, laying them= selves under Obligation to sit down satisfied by the Judgment of this Council.

Whereas, (after having earnestly sought to God for direction) having publickly heard, [and]^17 privately Considered all, that the Several aggrieved Brethren had to alledge [against] the Rev^d: Mr Putnam, with his Answers, the testimonies, and the Votes [of the Church relat]ing thereto. We do find

[1   That the several Charges ma]de by the aggrieved, against the Rev^d: Mr Putnam as to his Administrations, are groundless and unjust.   [21]

2   That the Aggrieved have greatly departed from the Platform, in chapter tenth;^18 in their Carriage towards the Rev^d: Mr Putnam.

3   That although the Aggrieved Brethren have something Softned their Charges against their Pastour, by saying that it is their Opinion that such things were a breach upon their priviledges, and to ask farther light in these matters; Yet it is plain, that they are too positive in their Opinion, and too sharp in the expressing thereof, and sometimes use severe expressions & heavy insinuations.

4   That the Rev^d: Mr Putnam did Use some sharpness, as well as extent of Speech, which the Aggrieved look upon as grievous; which, though he had great Provocation, yet had better have been let alone.

5   That Deacon Thomas Taylor ought to humble himself before God, and to the Pastour, & Church for his Disorder, & Opposition to his Pastour, which he hath manifestly discovered in a day of temptation; and for the future demean himself to the Pastour and Church with much humility & circumspection, lest he should again give Disturbance to the Church of God, and that so doing, the Pastour and Church receive him into their good Opinion, and Charitable affection.

6   That the aggrieved Brethren, & especially Capt: Thomas Briant, having unjustly charged the Rev^d: Mr Putnam, as they do in their paper, and have done more so in their publick reports, do therefore Manifest the sence of their evil, in taking up and spreading such evil reports of an Elder without cause, by humbly asking forgive=

ness of God, & of their injured Pastour; and in their future carriage submit them= selves peaceably & orderly to the Ecclesiastical Administrations of him, who is sett over them in the Lord.

Finally, We earnestly entreat by the Gentleness and meekness of Christ, that both Pastour and people make it their sincere endeavour, to forget and forgive all that hath past as grievous to them; laying aside all heart-burning, & evil surmisings, and harsh speeches of, and to one another; and carry themselves with all gentleness, tenderness, meekness, humility, love & charity, preserving the Unity of the Spirit in the bonds of peace, that the God of love & peace may be with them.

A true copy.   Thomas Cheever Moderatour

with the Unanimous consent

of the Council.

I read this Result of the Council publickly, on the next Sabbath, being 8th December.

1723/4
Jan:19th: A Child of Isaac Lewis baptized, named Joseph.

Feb: 9:   Jacob Chamberlane was received to full Communion.

——- 10   Deacon John Chamberlane laid his Accounts before Ensign Joseph Belcher, & Mr Samuel Watts who were appointed by the Church, to Assist me in that Service, and the Church-stock in his hands was found to be, Seven pounds, seven shillings, & eight pence: 7ll: 7s: 8d:

March:15:   I stayed the Church, and propounded to ye Church, (which I had propounded before to Severall of the Brethren in private, who very readily consented to the Motion) that upon days of publick fasting, and also on days of publick thanksgiving for the future we might have a Contribution for the poor. I mentioned several things to show that acts of Charity and alms are a very special part of Christianity, & when performed rightly are acceptable unto God. The Church readily as to ye greater part came in to the proposal, and Voted that what should be gathered on such. Occasions, should be kept by it self in the Deacons hands, and be sacred to the forenamed use, & should be disposed of to Objects of Charity when such

Objects should appear; with the knowledge and Consent of the Church: and they agreed [22] to begin the next Publick fast, which is to be on the twenty sixth day of this instant March; and that Notice should be given hereof to the Congregation, if any of them would come in to this good proposal; which was done accordingly the Sabbath before the ffast.

Attest   Thomas Cheever. Pastour.

1724

March: 26ᵗ: On this day a Contribution was made for the poor, according to the before na-med Vote of yᵉ Church, & several of the Congregation came into it, and though it was a foul day, there were thirty shillings gathered, & four pence.

April: 5ᵗ: Mʳ Hugh Floyd, & his wife, having their dismission from Maldon Church, to the Church at Rumny-marish, were received to full Communion.

Same day. A Child of John Floyd baptized, named Mary.

June: 7ᵗʰ: A Child of Jacob Chamberlane baptized, named Samuel.

July: 12: A Child of Samuel Tuttle baptized, named Tabitha.

August: 2ᵈ: A Child, of William Thompson, recommended from Ireland, baptized named James.

——— 9 A Child of Samuel Watts baptized, named Edward.

Octob: 4ᵗʰ: A Child of John Pratt of Maldon, who married Mehetabel Davis, baptized, named Anne

——— 18: Rebeccah Hinckson was received to full Communion.

Nov: 5ᵗ: Thanksgiving day, stormy day: the Contribution amounted to twenty ~~one~~ shillings & 9 ~~some~~ pence

——— 29 A Child of Thomas Wait junʳ, (who married Abraham Halsey's widow) baptized, named Ebenezer.

1724/5

Febr: 16: At a Church-meeting Deacon John Chamberlane laid his accounts before the Church, and the Church Stock in his hands was found to be: 8ˡˡ: 17ˢ: 9ᵈ.

At the same, John ffloyd as Executor to his ffathers Will, paid a legacy of ten pounds, given to the Church by his ffather in his last will, into the hands of Deacon Chamberlane in behalf of the Church; and it was Voted by the Church that the sᵈ ten pounds should be laid out in a silver cup for the Use of the Church, with the sᵈ Lᵗ: John ffloyds name upon it, as his gift, & that Deacon John Chamberlane should get it done as speedily as might be.

At the same Meeting it was agreed that we should have the Sacrament in the winter, and that from & after the next Sacrament day which will be on the last Lords day in ffebruary, it shall be observed Once in six weeks throughout the year, and that it should be proposed the Next Sacrament day for the Concurrence of Our Maldon Brethren. & This was proposed & consented to upon 28th of ffebruary. At the same Meeting after some Debate about the matter, it was Unanimously Voted & agreed, that the Contribution for the Poor upon publick fast days, & thanks givings should be Continued, & that Notice should be given, the next time when the Proclamation was read, to the Congregation, that the Church did allow them to Nominate some meet person to be joyned with Deacon John Chamberlane

to take ~~the care & charge~~ an account of what should be collected at such times.

Attest Thomas Cheever.

—— 28   A Child of Elisha Tuttle baptized, named Jacob.

April: 1st: Publick fast, the Contribution amounted to thirty ~~one~~ shillings.

June: 27:   Patience Davis was received to full Communion.

Oct: 28:   Publick thanksgiving, very warm. The Contribution amounted to thirty five shillings.

1726
March: 13: A Child of Samuel Tuttle baptized, named Samuel.

—— 24   Publick ffast, the Contribution amounted to twenty five shillings & threepence.

—— 29   Deacon Chamberlane laid his accounts before my self with Several of the Brethren, & the Church stock in his hands was found to be 10ll: 16s: 7d:

April: 10:   A Child of John Leath baptized, named Eleanor.

July: 24:   A Child of Isaac Lewis baptized, named Lydia

Sept: 18:   A Child of Jacob Chamberlane baptized, named Elizabeth.[19]

Novemb: 10: Publick Thanksgiving. The Contribution was appointed for Ebenezer Hill of Maldon, who, having a sore leg for several years, which the Doctours at last judged incurable,

1726   unless his leg was cutt off, [(]which was done the 7th of this moneth) petitioned Our Church   [23]
(5:10:11)
and Congregation for our Charity: there was gathered about five pounds ten shillings.

Nov: 20.   A Child of Thomas Wait junr: baptized, named Mary.

—— 27   A Child of John Floyd baptized, named Sarah.

Dec: 25th   Jeremiah Whittemore & Patience his wife, upon their desire were dismissed by a

Vote of the Church, to the Church of Christ in West-town, alias Weston.

1727

March: 19   A Child of Samuel Watts baptized, named Anne.

———- 20   At a Church-Meeting after much Debate, it was Voted ~~that~~ that the Contribution for the

Poor upon the next ffast day, which is appointed to be on the 30th of this instant March

shall be for Mrs Marbles Daughter Hannah who has been a considerable time Under the

Doctours hand having a dangerous humour in her Mouth & throat: &c: and that Notice hereof

should be given to the Congregation the Sabbath before, if they had any thing to

Object against the Churches proceeding in this matter.

At this Meeting Deacon Chamberlane laid his Accounts before the Church; and the

Church Stock in his hands was found to be: 11^{ll}: 11^s: 5^d: And at the same time

1727   The Stock in his hands for the Poor was found to be: seven pounds, one & 4^d 7^{ll}: 01^s: 4^d

March: 30   The Contribution, which according to the forenamed Vote of the Church was appointed

ffast: for Hannah Marble, (& of which Notice was given to the Congregation) amounted to: 3^{ll}: 12^s: 9^d

three pound &c:

April: 9th: A Child of Elisha Tuttle baptized, named Elizabeth.

Octob: 15th. The Church was stayed & the following letter read unto them.

Boston. Octob: 10: 1727.

To the Church of Christ, whereof the Reverend Mr Thomas Cheever

is the Pastour.

The old Church in Boston sendeth Greeting in our Lord Jesus.

Reverend, Honoured, & Beloved.

We presume you are not unacquainted that We have sometime since

Chosen, & called our Worthy Brother Mr Charles Chauncey to the

Pastoral Office among us. Now these come to inform you, that we

have appointed Wednesday, the twenty fifth of this instant October

to be the day for his Ordination. At which solemnity we desire your

presence & help, by your Elder & Messengers, to joyn with others in

Council on that important Occasion, agreeable to the known approved

Custom of these Churches. And beseech you in the mean time to assist

us by your fervent prayers, in preparing for so great a transaction,

that we may have the Gracious smiles of Heaven on our proceeding

& experience much of the promised presence of our Ascended Saviour

& Head in the midst of us. The same we wish to you & to all

the Churches. Grace be with you & Peace to the Brethren, with

Faith & Love which is in Christ Jesus. Unto whom be glory in the

Churches World without end. Amen.

The Delegates are desired to meet

at Mr Foxcrofts house by nine a clock

in the morning of s^d day.

Thomas Foxcroft Pastour

in the name of the Church

Copia vera. Attest Thomas Cheever.

The Church readily complied with the Desire, & chose D^on: John

Chamberlane, Mr Hugh Floyd, Mr William Halsey, & Mr Samuel

Watts, to accompany me, & Assist in that Service, at the time &

place appointed. At which time ye Rev^d: Mr Charles Chauncey was

Ordained to the Pastoral Office in s^d Church. Attest

Thomas Cheever

1727:   one   [24]

Nov: 9:   Publick Thanksgiving: The Contribution for the Poor amounted to thirty ~~one~~ shillings ~~& six pence~~

26   Ruth Whittemore was received to full Communion.

Dec: 31:   Benjamin Whittemore & Sarah his wife were received to full Communion.

1727/28:

14 Jan: A Child of Mr Macurdin's, (who brought a testimony from Ireland) baptized, named Abraham.

21:   Joseph Whittemore, Thomas Eustis, & William Tuttle were received to full Communion.

ffebr: 28th: At a Church Meeting appointed to Consider how the contributions for the Poor should be

drawn out, as Occasion should require. It was, after some debate, unanimously agreed to choose three of the Church besides Deacon Chamberlane to be a Committee,

and that Notice should be given to the Congregation, if they think meet to Choose

an equal number to joyn with the Committee, chosen by the Church, and that this

Committee of the Church and Congregation shall have full power to drawn out, and

dispose of what is, or shall be collected, for the Poor, according to their best

judgment and prudence, until the Church shall see cause to alter this Method

when some other or better Method shall appear: (but if the Congregation do not

see cause to Choose a Committee, after some reasonable time of two or three

moneths allowed for the consideration of this proposal) then the Committe of

Church shall have the power of drawing out and disposing of the money afors[d]

and give account of their acting in this affair to the Church once in the year:

at the same time M[r] Samuel Watts, M[r] Jacob Halsey, & M[r] Samuel Tuttle were

Chosen to be joyned with Deacon Chamberlane as a Committe for the end afors[d],

and accepted.

At the same time, Deacon Chamberlane laid his accounts before the Church, and

the Church Stock in his hands was found to be twelve pounds & five pence,

out of which twenty shillings was disbursed for mending the Meeting house windows,

so the Church stock in his hands is but eleven pounds & five pence: 11[ll]: 00[s]: 5[d]

and there was found, eight pounds, twelve & four pence in his hands for the Poor: 8: 12: 4

Attest Thomas Cheever Pastor.

March: 10. A Child of John Leath baptized, named Sarah.

Same day Sarah Holloway, wife of Joseph Holloway was received to full Communion.

21:    Publick ffast. The Contribution for the poor amounted to twenty two shillings & some pence.

31:    Three Children of Benjamin Whittemore baptized. named Benjamin. Jacob. Sarah.

——   Two Children of Joseph Holloway baptized same day. named Martha. Mary.

June 16   Thomas Brintnal received to full Communion.

August: 11: A Child of Capt: Nathaniel Oliver baptized, named James.

Sept: 8:   A Child of Jacob Chamberlane baptized, named Phebe.

—— 22   A Child of Joseph Whittemore baptized, named Hannah.

Octob 20. A Child of Samuel Tuttle baptized, named John.

some pence.

Nov: 7:   Publick thanksgiving. The Contribution for the poor amounted to thirty nine shillings &

— 10th: Sarah Leath, wife of ffrancis Leath of Woburn, received to full Communion.

March: 2d A Child of Samuel Watts baptized, named Rachel.
  1728.9:

Same day, a Child of John Grover, (his wife a member of the New-North Church,

in Boston) was baptized, named Edmund.

—— 4th   At a Church meeting, appointed to receive the account of the Committee chosen

to draw out & dispose of the money collected for the Poor. The sd Committee did

give an account of five pounds drawn out & disposed of, viz: three pounds to

the Widow Lamson, & twenty shillings in wood to Widow Marble, & as much to

her daughter the Widow Tuttle. The Church were well satisfied with what

they had done. And chose the same persons, to be a Committee for the same

purpose, for this year ensuing. The Church also Voted, that Notice should be

again given to the Congregation, if they think meet to choose an equal Number

to joyn with the Committee chosen by the Church for the business aforsd, and

that Notice be given the next Lords day for Church & Congregation to meet

at the Meeting house, the Wednesday next after. Attest: Thomas Cheever Pastror.

At the same time, Deacon Chamberlane laid his accounts before the Church,

and the church Stock in his hands was found to be: eleven pounds, seventen, & 7d:

11: 17: 7:

9   Joanna Tuttle, daughter of Edward Tuttle junr:, received to full Communion.

16   A Child of James Brintnal, (his wife a member of Charlstown Church) baptized: James.

20   A publick ffast: The Contribution for the poor amounted to about twenty nine shillings.

1729   [25]
May:25t: ~~The Chur~~ I Communicated the following letter to the Church:

Woburn May 19. 1729.

To the Church of Christ in Boston, whereof ye Revd: Mr Thomas Cheever is

the Pastour, Grace, mercy & peace be Multiplied. &c

The church & Town of Woburn having made Choice of Mr Edward Jackson to

be our Minister, and over us in all matters of ye Lord; & God having inclined his heart to accept our Invitation. We earnestly desire our presence, & Assistance by your Reverend Elder & Messengers, to meet with the Rev^d: Elders & Messengers of other Churches, & joyn with them in putting Mr Jackson into the sacred Office of a Pastour over us, according to the Gospel Directory. And humbly asking your most solemn & fervent prayers to the God of all Grace on our behalf, for a good issue of all our Difficulties, & for ye Success & prosperity of ye Gospel among us. We remain Yours in the faith & fellowship of the Gospel.

By order & consent of the Major part

of the Church & Town of Woburn.

William Lock

George Reed

Samuel Blogget.

The day appointed for Ordination
is Wednesday June 4th next. You are desired
to meet on Tuesday June 3^d at the house of
Mr Jonathan Pool Esq in Woburn at One of
the clock afternoon to prepare matters for Ordination.

The Church readily Complied with the desire, & chose D^n Chamberlane, William Halsey, & Samuel Tuttle, to accompany me & attend that Service. Afterwards Deacon Chamberlane Came to me & Desired to be excused from the Service;

June: 1st: I stayed the Church & acquainted them with the desire of Deacon Chamberlane & his reasons, whereupon the Church chose Mr Hugh ffloyd & Mr Samuel Watts. &c

June 3^d I went to Woburn with those four Brethren accompanying of me, where we mett with the Elders & Messengers of Lexington, Redding, Chelmsford, Billerica, Newtown, and Brookline Churches. When we were formed into a Council, we advised to the most probable Methods we could think of for the Accomodating the differences among them, and laboured with Mr Fox & those that held with him, & also with those who did adhere to Mr Jackson, & who were those that had called this Council, & were by far the

greater part of both of Church & Town, almost two to one, but our advice had not complied with: whereupon the Council came Unanimously into this Vote.

We judge it not advisable to proceed forthwith to Ordination under their present Circumstan ⌐ces.

       The result of a Council of 6 Churches called & Convened at Woburn June 3^d 1729

      to Consider & advise with respect to the Ordination of Mr Edward Jackson &c

After Solemn & earnest prayer to God, the God of all Wisdom & Grace, for Divine direction

in the very difficult & arduous affairs before us, & upon the most mature thoughts on the

perplexed state of affairs in Woburn, We did Solemnly & Unanimously advise to the most

probably Methods, we could think of, towards an Accomodation of their unhappy difference

which were not mutually complied withall: whereupon we thought it unpracticable to pro-

ceed to Ordination under their present Circumstances. But we with bowels of com-

passion beg of the Contending parties to leave off strife, & contention, & yet pursue

the Methods proposed, or any other that can be thought of, more likely to Compose, &

heal their unhappy differences, that if it be possible they may yet live in love and

peace, that the God of love & peace may yet be & abide with them.

                          Thomas Cheever Moderatour

                              in the name & with

                            Consent of the Council.

Sept: 21: 4 Children of ffrancis & Sarah Leath of Woburn

        baptized, their names were, Benjamin, Robert, Ebenezer, Mary.

Octob: 5: A Child of Benjamin Whittemore baptized, named Esther.

 Nov: 2^d A Child of John Floyd baptized, named James

               of Christ   [26]
       To the Church in Rumny-marish, Greeting.
              ^
       R^d & Dearly Beloved.

       Whereas there is a Number among us, who call themselves aggrieved Brethren, and as they say have pro-

ceeded to extraordinary & uncommon means in Deposing, upon a Delinquent Offices, and which

still as they say has involved them in several difficulties, and for their Publick Vindication, &

to hear & advise upon the reasons & Regularity of their Ecclesiastical proceeding, & to direct to peace & good Order; have by their letters missive Convened 7 Churches upon the case, who by their Elders & Messengers in form of an Ecclesiastical Council, taking the Case into their Consideration, have Adjourned to the first Tuesday in September next, at nine of the Clock in the Morning to meet at the house of Lt Coolidge at Watertown, withall adding, that the Subscriber be with Convenient speed acquainted with it, with liberty to adde a like Number of Seven Churches to make up a Council, and also to lay before s^d Council what may be matter of Grievance to him. We beseech you therefore R^d & dearly Beloved to pitty us under our great calamities. To pray for us, that the God of all Grace would restore good Order & peace among us; and afford us ye Assistance of your R^d: Elder, or Elders & such Messenger or Messengers as you shall think fit, to joyn in the aboves^d Council at time & place, with such other Churches, as we have sent to, to make up our Numbers to hear, advise, & direct in the aboves^d case, & in what else may have been amiss in their Conduct; and shall be Regularly laid before the Council. That the Great Shepherd of ye sheep, through the blood of the Everlasting Covenant, would make you perfect in every good work, working in you that which is well pleasing in his sight, is the hearty prayer of yours, in the faith & fellowship of the Gospel.

Leicester. August: 4th 1729.

David Parsons. Pastour

with the consent of the Church.

To the R^d Mr Thomas Cheever
Pastour of ye Church of Christ
at Rumny-marish, & to s^d Church.

The Churches sent to by Mr Parsons, were Mr Barnards, & Mr Holy Okes, Mr Prescott's, Mr Appleton's, Mr Williams of West-town, & Mr Coaks of Sudbury, & Rumny-marish.[20]

August: 24th. I read the letter to the Church, & ye Church consented to send our beloved brethren, Mr Joseph Belcher. Mr Samuel Watts. Mr William Halsey. Mr Jacob Halsey & Mr Thomas Brintnal, to accompany me & attend that Service.

Sept: 2^d: The afors^d Brethren appeared, & attended ye Service at Water-town on the first day of y^e

Council. Mr Belcher & Mr William Halsy desired to be excused from farther attendance.
Mr Jacob Halsy did not attend the last day of ye Council: But Mr Watts & Mr Brintnal
attended ye whole time. The Council sat at Watertown four days & then adjourned to Boston, to meet upon. Sept: 16.

Sept: 16: The Council mett at Boston according to Adjournment, & sat four days in Mr Colman's
Meeting house, and drew up their Result, & then Dissolved.
Mr Watts, & Mr Brintnal attended ye whole time; ye other Brethren but part of the time.

The agrieved Brethren at Leicester, being ye Major part of the Church, had deposed their
Pastour, for Several crimes which they charged him with, under three general heads.
first of Male administration. 2^d: Of Delinquency. 3^d: Of immorality: and they branched
these heads into Several Articles: 8 under the first: 3 under ye 2^d: under ye 3^d head they charg
ed him with Slander in 4 articles: and fraudulent dealing: & lying in 4 articles.
they themselves in their letters Missive call their action extraordinary & uncommon, and
well they might; the like was never done in this land before; The Council of Churches
called by the Agrieved Brethren, Were Mr Colman's, Mr Thachers, & Mr Checklys of Boston,
Reading, Medfield, New-town & Oxford. here follows ye Result of the Council.

At a Council of 14 Churches, called by ye R^d: Mr David Parsons, & the agrieved Brethren at Leicester, Convened at Watertown Sept: 2^d: 1729. & after by Adjournment at Boston,
Sept: 16. following: to hear & judge of the Reasons & Regularity of the Proceedings of the
agrieved Brethren: & also what was matter of Grievance to Mr Parsons, & such other things
as should be regularly laid before them. After a long & full hearing of both parties
and repeated Supplications to the throne of Grace. We came unto the following Result.

ffirst: With respect to the Several Articles of Charges brought in against Mr Parsons.
ffirst as to the head of Male administration.

I: It doth not appear, there was any Male-administration of Mr Parsons, in appointing
the Sacrament.

2: That Mr Parsons telling the Agrieved Brethren, that he did not desire their presence, when he   [27]
called the rest of the Church to ask, Whither they had best to call a Council upon the

agrieved's request, was not excluding them from Church priviledges: and that Mr Parsons calling that part, (the Minor part), of the Church with himself the Church, and taking their advice, as referred to in the Evidence relating to the calling of the Council, We cannot judge to be a Male-administration.

3: As to the 3^d article referring to Mr Read's admission, if dropt by Mr Parsons just after his receiving the Result of the former Council, and before the Brethrens Vote of Deposition, as he declares, We think it ought not to have been alledged as an article against him.

4 That Mr Parsons was guilty of Male administration, in admission of the Members referred to in the fourth article. Yet it is the Opinion of the Council, in considera-tion of their Solemn Covenant with God & them, that the s^d Brethren be looked upon, and accepted by the Church in Leicester, as Members in full Communion.

5 We judge that the Agrieved Brethrens absence from the publick Worship, the Lords day after their receiving the Result of the former Council, was very blame worthy; yet Mr Parsons was also blame worthy, in not referring to another Lords day, the readmission of those Members.

6. As to bringing cases of private Offence before the Church &c. We apprehend, that as to one of these, viz: L^t: Newhals; it having been transacted before the Churches renewal of Covenant, the Brethren should not have made it a charge upon him. As to the other case of Mr Thomas Richardson, it having been made a publick talk, Mr Parsons apprehended it might supersede a private dealing; which though a mistake & unadvised in him; yet he having issued the Matter; We also apprehend that the Brethren should not have proceeded farther in it.

7. As to the seventh article of Charge, viz: Mr Parsons commanding the Deacon out of his seat &c, though Mr Parsons provocation at time was very great & aggravated, yet we judge, the Expressions (as in the words of the evidence) were very rash, & carry in them a power, which does not belong to a Pastour, according to the Constitution of these Churches.

8. That it does not appear, that Mr Parsons laid, any Charge against the Brethren,

as alledged in the eighth article: yet supposing Mr Parsons had done, as they say,

We cannot look upon it a Male administration under their Circumstances.

    Secondly, as to the head of Delinquency.

1   That it does not appear, that Mr Parsons was guilty of any Culpable Delinquency

with respect to the first article, considering their Circumstances, but rather gave

a just answer to them, who desired him to lead them in the Choice of a Ruling Elder.

2   As to the 2^d charge. We apprehend the State of the Church was such at that time

that Mr Parsons acted prudently in proposing, & endeavouring to issue the matters

of Difference in another way.

3   That Mr Parsons does not appear guilty of any culpable Delinquency in the case of Slander.

    Thirdly. As to the head of Immoralty:and ffirst. Slander.

1.   That we cannot tax Mr Parsons with Slander, in calling a certain Meeting a Cabal,

considering his explanation of himself, as to his acceptation of the Design of said

Meeting, & the time & Occasion of Using the word, and that he professeth he

designed no reflection upon religious meetings.

2.   That it does not appear Mr Parsons is guilty of Slander, as charged in the 2^d article.

3.   It does not appear, Mr Parsons was guilty of Slander, according to ye charge in 3^d article.

4.   We judge it a rash & injurious expression of Mr Parsons, to call a number of the Church

a Mob. Secondly as to fraudulent dealing.

It is Unanimously agreed, that there does not appear any fraudulent dealing in Mr Parsons

with respect to the bond or Note from Mr Newhal, or with respect to the Deeds of Quitclaim.

    thirdly. As to lying.

It is Unanimously agreed, that it does not appear to this Council, that Mr Parsons was

guilty of lying, in the four several articles charged against him, though we think he

should have been more considerate & cautious in the expressions in his letter to

the R^d Doctour Mather.

Secondly. After all that hath been heard & debated. It is Unanimously agreed, that the R^d M^r [28]

David Parsons, hath not been guilty of any such Crimes, as render him unworthy of the

Gospel Ministry, or of the Ministry in the Church of Leicester.

Thirdly. That although this Council are very desirous to Assert & Preserve the power of Particular Churches, to Depose, or Disclaim their Officers according to the Rules of Congregational Discipline, as laid down in the Platform: Yet we judge the Agrieved ffraternity
in the Church of Leicester were guilty of great irregularity, in proceeding to Depose
the R^d Mr Parsons, as they have done. And in as much as they did it, so soon after the
sitting of a Venerable Council, (which after hearing most of their Charges, and
Differences, were farr from advising to any such thing; and without seeking farther,
and waiting longer for the advice of another Council; as also contrary to the advice
and perswasion of many Worthy persons in a private way. Therefore We judge the R^d
Mr David Parsons is still the Regular Pastour of the Church in Leicester.

Fourthly. With respect to the Articles of Charge & Grievance laid before us by Mr Parsons;
Several of which he withdrew.

    1. ffirst, we judge, (as a former Council did) that the R^d Mr Parsons hath been shamefully
treated, with respect to his Support, for the time past; and do earnestly recommend
it to the Town of Leicester, to pay those Arrearages, that have been so long due, and
to provide for his Support for the future: and do all that becomes Christians, on
their part, to Secure unto Mr Parsons a just & full title to his lands in Leicester.

    2. We cannot but bear Our Testimony against such Unreasonable, & Unjustifiable actions,
as that of Opposing Mr Parsons his going into his Pulpit on the Lords day, & setting
up another in Opposition to him, in such an unseemly way & manners though they
might be led into it from their Misapprehension of things.

    3. We judge it the Duty of the Agrieved Brethren & people of Leicester to Return from
their Private Assembling on the Lords day, to the Publick Worship of God under the
Ministry of the R^d Mr David Parsons.

    4. We judge that Deacon Southgate ought not to Withhold the Churches Vessels from
the Use of the R^d Mr Parsons, and the Church.

Fifthly. Having thus given Our thoughts, upon the several matters laid before us, We do, as
in the fear of God, and tender mercies of Our Lord Jesus Christ, earnestly beseech
Our Beloved Brother in Christ the R^d Mr David Parsons Seriously & with grief to lay

to heart the broken State of his fflock; and to consider how far any rashness in his
words, and hastiness in his actions may have been Offensive to his Brethren, in the
day of darkness, & temptation that has passes over him, and be humbled for them.
And we do earnestly Recommend to him a just Regard to the Tenour of the Platform
of the Church Discipline, in the Allowance of the proper power of the Brotherhood pursuant
to their Church Vote. We do also with the same earnestness Exhort, & perswade the
Beloved Agrieved Brethren of the Church of Leicester, seriously to Consider, how far
they have suffered themselves, in the day of Temptation through some mistaken conception of things, to be led into Uncharitable thoughts of, & rash & unjustifiable carriage toward their Pastour: as also how far a too Groundless Spirit of Opposition to their
Pastour, may have hindred the growth of the Church, and the Success of the Gospel
among them, and deeply to afflict & humble themselves therefor.

And now Brethren, We would call upon you all with the greatest meekness & Concern of Soul, to
remember the Solemn Obligations you have brought your selves under before God, and this
Council, to hearken to Our Christian advice, and return to each other, in the love and spirit of
the Gospel, and receive one another in the Lord: and put away from you all bitterness, and
wrath, clamour, & evil speaking, with all malice, as becomes the Disciples of the Meek and
lowly Jesus: to love one another, to put on, as the Elect of God, bowels of mercy, kindness,
humbleness of mind, long-suffering, forbearing One another, & forgiving One another, as
we hope, God for Christs sake hath forgiven you, and above all put on Charity, which
is the bond of perfectness. 13: john. 34. 35: 12: Romans. 9: 1: Corinth: 13 chapter. 5: galat. 19-22:
4: Ephes. 2. 3. 30. 32: 3: Coloss: 12. 13. 14: 3: james. 6: 14 to 18: 1: peter: 4: 8:

a true copy.

Signed in the Presence, and at
the desire of the Council.
Benjamin Colman Moderatour.

1729/30
ffebruary 22[d]: Mehitabel Lamson was received to full Communion.

1729:
~~April 2~~   & some pence.

Novemb:13: Publick thanksgiving. The contribution for the Poor amounted to thirty seven shillings

1730
April: 2: Publick ffast. The Contribution for the Poor, thirty ~~one~~ shillings ~~& 4 pence~~.

1730
April:13: At a Church meeting appointed to receive the Deacon's accounts &c as also to choose [29]

another Deacon. Ensign Joseph Belcher, Mr Samuel Watts, & Mr Jacob Halsey were

chosen a Committee, to be joyned with the Deacons, for drawing out and disposing of

the money Collected for the poor; and also, to agree with some fit person to look

after the Meeting house.

At the same time, Our brother Mr William Halsey was chosen to the Office of a

Deacon by a Majority of Votes, & Voters; he Objected his unfitness, but it was left to

his serious Consideration, and that he should Manifest his acceptance of the Churches

call to s^d Office, by sitting in the Deacons seat. the Churches stock in the Deacons

hands was found a penny short of what it was last year: 11^ll: 17^s: 7^d: Out of which the

Deacons were ordered to buy a case for the Cushion to preserve it from dust.

Aug: 2^d A Child of Joseph Whittemore baptized, named Abigail.

—— 16 A Child of John Leath baptized, named ffrancis.

named John
Sept 20. A Child of Benjamin Brown of Boston, (his wife a Member of Mr Welsted's Church) baptized,

Nov: 12. Publick Thanksgiving. The Contribution was appointed for Mrs Lamsons daugh-

ter, under dangerous circumstances by a swelling in her neck the Doctour speaks

very doubtfully of her: there was gathered, about five pounds, eleven shillings, odd pence.

22 A Child of Jacob Chamberlane's baptized, named Edmund.

Jan:10: Benjamin Floyd received to full Communion.
1730:31:

ffeb: 21. A Child of Benjamin Whittemore baptized, named Hezekiah.

March: 14. A Child of Daniel Watts baptized, named Elizabeth.

—— 25: Publick ffast. The Contribution for the poor amounted to twenty nine shillings & some pence

31: At a Church Meeting to receive the Deacons Accounts: the Churches Stock in the

Deacons hands was found to be seventeen shillings, two pence more than last year.

At the same Meeting upon the fame of abusive carriage of Elisha Tuttle and his

wife to their Mother & Sister, after some Debate, the Deacons were appointed

to go to them & to Desire them to forebear coming to the Sacrament the
Next time: & also to enquire into the matter & see what Evidence there was
to lay before the Church at their next Meeting appointed on the seventh day of
April next. & also to Order s^d Tuttle & his Wife to Attend ye Church at that time
At the same Meeting. Mr Saml: Watts, Mr Jacob Halsey, & Mr Samuel Tuttle were
Chosen a Committee to be joined with the Deacons for drawing out, and
disposing the Money Collected for the Poor.

April: 7:   The Church mett according to Appointment, Elisha Tuttle & his Wife were at the
Meeting; the Evidence of their Mother & Sister was distinctly read once & again,
which they solemnly affirmed, as in the presence of God, to be the truth; but s^d Elisha
Tuttle & his Wife denied what they were charged with: & their behaviour before the
Church was not such as was expected by the Church, whereupon the Church thought
it best to referr the matter to another time, & that they might have time to Consider
their former carriage to their Mother & Sister.

May. 2:   Three Children of Benjamin Floyd baptized: their names were Benjamin, Mary, & Sarah.

—— 23   A Child of Thomas Eustis baptized, named Sarah.

July. 2^d   At a Church Meeting Elisha Tuttle & his Wife gave satisfaction to ye Church.

Oct: 28:   Publick Thanksgiving. The Contribution for ye Poor amounted to thirty one shillings, & some ^pence

Jan: 2:   A Child of Samuel Tuttle's baptized, name Mary.
1731/32

—— 16:   A Child of John Leath baptized, named Jedidiah.

Feb: 6:   A Child of Benjamin Whittemore baptized, named Phebe, & a Child of John Halsey baptized, named ^Sarah

—— 13.   A Child of Elias Whittemore baptized, named Elias.

March: 26:   A Child of Joseph Whittemore baptized, named Samuel.

April: 6^t.   A General ffast, a very storm day; ye Contribution for the Poor, but ten shillings, some pence

9   Mr Edmund Bowman was received to full Communion

May: 19:   At a Church Meeting to receive the Deacons Accounts. The Churches Stock in the Deacons
hands was found to be: 13^ll: 09^s: 11^d: At the same time an Account was given of what the
Committee had drawn out for the Poor, which the Church approved of, & the Church
Voted the same Committee that were chosen last year to Continue this year.

At the same Meeting Elisha Tuttle, being sent to by the Church, came and being asked the reason of his withdrawing from the Communion of the Church, after Considerable debate, he Owned that he had done wrong in his Withdrawing, and that he was Sorry, he had neglected so long without asking a dismission. Upon which the Church declared that they would be satisfied, with what he had declared, for the time past; provided he did return to his duty.

Attest Thomas Cheever
Pastour.

April: 23 A Child of Mr Levinston baptized, named Mary.

1732 [30]

June: 4: Susannah Harndel was received to full Communion & baptized at ye same time.

May: 30: 1732.

To the Church of Christ at <u>Rumny-marish</u> in Boston, Whereof ye Rev^d: M^r <u>Cheever</u> is the Pastour, the Second Church of Christ in Boston sendeth Greeting: May Grace, Mercy, & Peace be multiplied unto you from God our Father, & from Jesus Christ our Lord. Rev^d: Hon^d: & Beloved.

Having by earnest & repeated Prayer with Fasting sought unto the ever blessed, and allsufficient God, & our Saviour, to repair the great Breach that has been made upon us, We have chosen our Worthy Brother M^r <u>Samuel Mather</u>, to the Pastoral Office among us: and his heart having been inclined to accept our Call, We have appointed that Wednesday the Twenty first day of the Next moneth shall, God willing, be the Time for his publick & Solemn Separation to that sacred Charge, by Prayer & Imposition of the hands of the Presbytery as the Gospel directs.

Now therefore we humbly ask the Presence & Assistance of your Rev^d: Pastour, & such other Delegates, as you shall think meet to send with him, to joyn in Council with the Rev^d: Elders & Messengers of several other Churches, for such acts of Ecclesiastical Communion as the Occasion of the Day shall require. And we conclude with imploring your ardent and incessant prayers for us; That we may enjoy the smiles of our Ascended Saviour upon our Proceedings. & that the God of Peace, who brought again from the Dead our Lord

Je[s]us ~~Christ~~ that great Shepherd of the sheep, through the blood of the everlasting

Covenant, may multiply the blessings of it upon us, & upon our Children, & make us perfect

in every good work to do his Will, working in us that which is well pleasing in his sight,

through Jesus Christ, to Whom be Glory in all the Churches, World without end. Amen.

Yours in the Faith & Fellowship of ye Gospel.

Joshua Gee Pastour

with ye Consent of ye Church.

The Delegates are desired to meet

at my Dwelling house at Nine of the

Clock in ye Morning of s^d day.

June: II:	I read this letter to the Church, & the Church
	consented to send Our beloved Brethren Deacon Chamberlane, Deacon Halsey, Mr Joseph
	Belcher, Mr Samuel Watts, Mr Jacob Halsey & Mr Thomas Brintnal to attend that Service.
	The Brethren appointed, accompanied me at the time & place appointed being
	the twenty first of June, When the Rev^d: Mr Samuel Mather was Ordained to the
	Ministry of the Gospel, & to the Pastoral Office in the 2^d Church of Boston.
Sept: 3:	A Son of Mr Samuel Watts baptized, named Bellingham.
Octob: 22:	A Child of Ebenezer Pratt baptized, named Tabitha.
Novemb: 5^t:	A Child of Jacob Chamberlane baptized, named Nathanael.
Octob: 26.	Publick Thanksgiving. The Contribution for the Poor amounted to 37^s & some pence.

1733
March: 4:	A Child of Benjamin Floyd baptized, named Ebenezer.
	A Child of Samuel Pratt baptized at the same time, named Rebeccah.
— 11th	Hannah Halsey, daughter of ~~Asa~~ Halsey, was received to full Communion.
— 29	A General ffast:
July: 8th	A Child of John Brintnall baptized, named Thomas.
— 29	A Child of Daniel Watts baptized, named Sarah.
Sept: 23:	A Child of Thomas Eustis baptized, named Abigail.

Novemb: 4: Samuel Floyd, & Joannah his Wife were received to full Communion.

———- 11: Two Children of Samuel Floyd baptized, Tabitha, Joannah.

——— 18   Nathanael Oliver admitted to full Communion.

———- 22: Publick Thanksgiving. The Contribution for the poor amounted to 46ˢ & some odd Pence.

Decemb: 9. A Child of Samuel Floyd baptized, named Samuel.

1733:34
Feb: 3.   A Child of James Brintnal baptized, named Samuel.

——— 10.   A Child of Joseph Whitemore baptized, named Mary

March: 1ˢᵗ: A Church Meeting, to receive the Deacons accounts. The Churches stock in Deacon

           Chamberlanes hands was found to be twelve pounds, eleven pence, the which because

           of his removal to live at Pullen-point, he desired the Church to receive it, which

           hey did, & gave Deacon Chamberlane a receipt by their Pastor: The Church then

ll s d   deposited sᵈ: 12ᴸ: 11ᵈ in Deacon Wm: Halseys hands, so that the Church's Stock in sᵈ
12: 0:11
03:17: 0   Deacon Halseys hands, with three pounds & seventeen shillings which he had in
01: 0: 0

           his hands before, & twenty shillings given by Deacon Chamberlane, amounts in

           the whole to sixteen pounds, seventeen shillings, & eleven pence. There is also

           in the hands of Deacon Halsey four pounds, sixteen shillings & five pence of the   [31]

           money Contributed for the poor.

           At the same Meeting Capt: Samˡ: Watts, Mʳ Jacob Halsey, & Mʳ Samˡ: Tuttle were desi-

           red to Continue as a Committee in conjunction with the Deacons for drawing out

           and desposing of the money Collected for the Poor. Attest: Thomas Cheever Pastour.

March: 24: A Child of Elias Whittemore baptized, named Timothy.

April: 4:   A General ffast

——— 14.   A Child of John Leath baptized, named Mary.

           The 2ᵈ Church at Boston, to the church of Christ
                       at Rumny-marish, Sendeth Greeting.

           Reverend, Honoured & Beloved.

           We cannot doubt, but you have been greatly Afflicted to hear of the

           Scandalous Differences, & Divisions that have arisen & prevailed for some years

in the first Church of Christ at Salem. But we are now particularly to inform
you, how far we have Proceeded on this Melancholy Occasion, & to ask your Assistance in the farther prosecution of our Duty, hoping that our United Endeavours
may, by the blessing of God, be Instrumental to heal their Divisions, to remove their
Scandal they have given, & to produce the desirable fruit of Peace & Brotherly love.

We received an Epistle from a Considerable Number of the Brethren of that Church
Dated Dec^r: 20: 1733: representing to us, what Occasion there was for some of Christs
faithful Servants to endeavour, according to the Order & Discipline professed in our
Churches, that the woful effects & Consequences of their Divisions might be
removed and prevented.

Upon this Occasion we had several Meetings, to Commend the Divided Church to the
God of Peace, & to seek his gracious Direction, and Consult about our Own duty. And
apprehending our Selves bound not only to seek & accept help from other Churches,
when we need it, but also Charitably to offer help to other Churches, when we take
notice of troubles, divisions, & scandals at any time permitted to arise, prevail and
continue long among them. We therefore Determined by our Elders & other Delegates
to Visit the first Church in Salem, in order more fully to Understand their case,
& to know what might be our farther Duty relating to it.

We informed them of our Design, in a letter directed to the Rev^d: Mr Fisk, to be Communicated to the Church, beseeching them to give Our Messengers an Opertunity to confer
with them at Salem upon the 2^d day of February past. But our letter not being Communicated to the Church, we could have no Answer from them. However we received
separate letters from the Rev^d: Mr Fisk, & from a Number of the Brethren in the same
sentiments with him; which, though written with a Design to discourage our Coming
to them, rather Confirmed us in a perswasion, that we were called to Testify our
Communion with the first Church in Salem, according to the Method prescribed in
our Platform of Church discipline, commonly called the third Way of Communion
and agreably to the Advice of a Council of Churches Assembled at Salem in the Sum-

mer past. Our Delegates were accordingly sent to Salem, that they might more particularly enquire into their Case, & stir up that Church to use the proper means for
healing their sinful & mischievous Divisions. And, though the Rev^d: Mr Fisk refused
to give them an Oportunity to confer with the Church, yet they found upon enquiry
that the first Church in Salem, during the long Continuance & under all the sad
effects of their Scandalous Divisions, have never met together (though it had been
once & again requested by a Considerable Number of the Brethren) to consult about
their duty, & the Means of Peace, under such awfull frowns of God upon them. Where
upon our Delegates, as directed by us & in our Name, Signed a letter of Brotherly
Admonition to the first Church in Salem, & Waited on the Rev^d: Mr Fisk, entreating
him to accept & communicate it; but he once and again refused our letter, declaring
he would have nothing to do with a letter that came in the third way of Communion: so that we were denied the Priviledge of Communion with Our Brethren
the first Church in Salem, either by letter or by conference.

When we received from our Delegates an Account of what they had done in our Name
and how they had been treated by the Reverend Mr. Fiske & a Number of his Brethren, who
appear to justify him in his Arbitrary Conduct, We were of Opinion, that nothing far- [32]
ther could reasonably be demanded of us, before we called in the help of other Churches
to joyn with us, in Seconding our Charitable Admonition, as directed in the Platform
of our Church discipline. But being desirous to act with all the gentleness & mo-
deration becoming the Gospel, & to have a Testimony for us, in the Consciences
of all our Brethren, who may hereafter be acquainted with our Proceedings, We
concluded not to take any farther Step, in the third way of Communion, before we
had made another Application to the Rev^d: Mr Fisk, Accordingly we wrote to
him March 5^t, inclosing a copy of our letter of Admonition which he had before
refused, & beseeching him to act as becomes an affectionate & faithful Pastor, and
thereby to take away from us the Necessity of calling the help of other Churches,
which we let him ~~understand~~ know we should think our duty, if we heard nothing
to prevent it, within a Moneth from the Date of our letter. But we have received

no answer from him.

This is a Summary account of our past Proceedings, & of the present unhappy State of things in the first Church of Salem. Religion is still in bleeding, dying circumstances, by reason of their Divisions; the Church Neglects to use the proper means for healing of them: and the Pastour, abetted by a considerable number of the Brethren refuses to let us have Communion with the Church, either by letters or by conference, and will not receive our Admonition.

We have therefore met together again to consider our Duty, & have determined, as the reason of the thing, & our Ecclesiastical Constitution directs, to call in other Churches to joyn in Seconding our Charitable Admonition.

Rev^d: Honoured & Beloved. As we think the Honour of Christ, the Communion of our Churches, & the Welfare of Souls are very nearly concerned; We desire the Counsel and Assistance of other Churches in the Management of this important affair: And by these Presents, we entreat you to joyn with us, & assist us in the Management of it, by sending your Elder & other Delegates, to meet our Delegates, and the Delegates of some other Churches at Salem, upon Tuesday the twenty third day of this Moneth at ten of the Clock in the forenoon; where they may have the Case more particularly laid before them, & will, we doubt not, be convinced of their Duty to joyn with us in Seconding our Charitable Admonition, which we hope, by the blessing of God, may serve the Cause of Christ in the first Church in Salem, and among all our Churches.

Wishing that Grace, Mercy, & Peace from God the Father, & our Lord jesus Christ may be multiplied unto you. We remain

> R^d: Hon^d: & Beloved
>
> Yours in the faith & fellowship of the Gospel.

Joshua Gee	in the name & at the desire of the Second Church of Christ in Boston.
Samuel Mather	

Read

April: 9th: 1734: This letter was ~~read~~ at a Meeting of the Brethren

of the Second Church in Boston, and Voted to be sent to the Church

under the Care of the Revd: Mr Cheever at Rumny-marish to be

Communicated. P.S: It was thought the Charge of Providing for the Delegates

who are sent in the third way of Communion, could not reasonably be expected

from any but the Churches that send them. Our Brethren therefore Voted, that the

necessary charges of Our Delegates should be defrayed out of the Churches stock:

Copia vera: Attest Th: Cheever.

April: 14: I read this letter to the Church: And they readily complyed with the business, and

Consented to Send our Beloved Brethren. Deacon Chamberlane, Deacon Halsey, Capt

Samuel Watts & Mr Jacob Halsey, with my self to Attend that Service.

Deacon Chamberlane at his desire was excused; the other three attended the Service.

1734: [33]

Ap: 28: A Child of Thomas Campbel baptized, named Mary: his Wife a Member of Maldon Church.

This 28th of April, I acquainted the Church, that we according to their Vote Went to

Salem, the 23d of this instant, Where we mett the Delegates of the Second Church

in Boston, and the Delegates of the third Church in Boston, & the Delegates of the

first Church in Gloucester. After we were formed into a Council, the Delegates of

the Second Church in Boston laid before us the Case of the first Church in Salem,

from a considerable Number of letters, & other Papers, as also their Charitable Admoni-

[-tion] to the sd first Church in Salem, whereby it did plainly appear to us, that there had been

Scandalous Contention in the first Church of Salem of long Continuance, & that

they had Neglected to use proper means for healing their Divisions. Whereupon We

were convinced it was our Duty to joyn with the Second Church in Boston, in Seconding

their Charitable Admonition. Here follow's a Copy of what was done by the Council.

To the first Church of Christ in Salem.

Revd: Honoured & Beloved.

We the Elders & Messengers of the third Church in Boston, the Church in Rumney-
marish, & the first Church in Glocester being called together at the Invitation of
the Second Church in Boston, & having heard an Account of the State of the first
Church in Salem, as it appears from a considerable number of letters, & other papers
laid before us by the Delegates of the Second Church in Boston, together with the
Charitable Admonition of the s[d] Church to the first Church in Salem for their Neglect of the Means of Peace, under their Scandalous Contentions; & having used our best
Endeavours, to enquire into the State of the first Church in Salem, that so we might know
Our farther Duty towards s[d] Church & discharge it. We, the Elders & Messengers afors[d],
being Convinced, that there has been a Scandalous Contention, for a long time in the first
Church in Salem, & that the s[d] Church has Neglected to use the proper means for healing
their Divisions, as also that the Second Church in Boston had just Reason to give an
Admonition to the first Church in Salem for that their Neglect, & that the s[d] Second Church
in Boston has given the s[d] Admonition with Regularity, prudence, & tenderness; and We
the Elders & Messengers of the Churches beforementioned, having used repeated but unsuc-
cessful Application to the Rev[d]: M[r] Fisk for a Conference with him & his Church, as
well as proper endeavours to obtain a Conference with a considerable number of the
Brethren of s[d] Church, & being now fully Sensible of the just Occasion of Uniting
with the Second Church in Boston, in Seconding their Admonition Charitable, both because
the first Church in Salem still continues in Contention, refuses to hearken to the Admonition
given them, & still neglects to Use the means of Peace.

We therefore, together with the Delegates of the Second Church in Boston, now declare unto you
R[d]: Hon[d]: & Beloved, that your Conduct is in our judgment very Scandalous, unbecoming your
holy Profession, & just matter of Offence to all the Churches of Our Lord Jesus Christ
through the land; and that we think Our selves called, in Obedience to him, & Charity
to your Souls, to bear a Testimony against it, according to the Order & Discipline
professed in our Churches. Dear Brethren, We appeal to you; Whither the Churches
of Our Lord Jesus Christ are not required, to be at peace among themselves, to warn
them that are unruly, to Withdraw themselves from every Brother that walketh dis-

orderly, to Mark them which cause divisions & Offences and avoid them: to maintain
Brotherly love, & to follow after the things, which make for Peace, and things
wherewith one may edify another. And for a Church of Christ in your Circumstances to behave themselves as you have done, that is not so much as Once to meet
together, to humble your selves before God under his awfull frowns upon you, and to
seek his Direction, & consult about your own duty, when broken to pieces by Contentions
which for years together have dishonoured Christ, obstructed the good effect of the Word
preached, Weakned the interests of Our holy religion in your Church & Town, & been a
grievous hinderance to the Spiritual comfort of edification of many of your Brethren
under the Ordinances of the Gospel. Dear Brethren, let your own Consciences judge & declare   [34]
whither this be to adorn the Doctrine of God our Saviour, whither this be not to give Satan
the great Adversary of Christ & our Souls, Oportunity & advantage to undermine, & weaken
the interests of pure & undefiled religion among us; & whither this be not just matter of
Offence to Neighbour Christians, who have any hearty Concern for your spiritual welfare, & the flourishing of Christs Kingdom by the power of godliness among you.
Unless the holy Spirit of God hath in a very awful manner withdrawn from you, We are
confident that upon serious consideration & self reflection you will judge & humble your
selves before the Lord.

We the Delegates of the Churches abovementioned, do therefore in the Name of the
Lord jesus Christ solemnly Admonish & exhort you, Our Dear Brethren, to repent of this
sinful Neglect of the Means of Peace, which argues the want of a becoming Concern
& Zeal for the honour of Christ, & the welfare of your own & others Souls. We exhort
you to set apart a Day to humble your selves with Fasting before the Lord, to implore
his pardoning mercy through the blood of the Everlasting covenant, & to seek his
grace, that may enable you for the future to adorn your holy profession. And we advise
& beseech you to Meet together as a Church of Christ, & guarding against every evil
disposition towards one another, prayerfully to Consult about your Duty, & to call in the
help of other Churches as it may be needful, in order to promote Peace with truth
and holiness among you.

Whenever you shall in these Methods return to your Duty, & set your selves in an exemplary manner, to make use of the proper means for healing your Scandalous Division, & for removing & preventing the Woful effects & consequents of them: We, the Delegates of the Churches beforementioned, in the Name of the churches whose Delegates We are, do assure you, Brethren, that they will stand ready with joyful hearts to testify before all the Churches, their having received satisfaction for the Offence you have given, & their readiness to exercise towards you all those Acts of Communion, which are due to a Church walking in the Faith & Order of the Gospel, and adorning the profession of Christianity. But in their Name we are likewise to Assure you, Brethren, that if you shall Obstinately & impenitently persist in such a Neglect of the means of Peace, which is just matter of Offence to all the Churches of Christ, they will in Obedience to him, and in love & faithfulness to you, think themselves bound to forbear Communion with you, and to proceed to make use of the help of a Synod, or Council of Neighbour Churches, walking orderly, if a greater cannot be had, for your Conviction: hoping it will please the Glorious Head of the Church to succeed the Endeavours of his Faithful Servants for healing your Divisions, removing the Scandal that has been occasioned by them, & preventing their Woful Consequences, which we have reason to apprehend.

And now, Dear Brethren, suffer us to apply our selves to you, as the Apostle to the Church of

I:Cor:I:IO. Corinth: We beseech you by the Name of Our Lord Jesus Christ, that ye all speak the same thing & that there be no Divisions among you, but that ye be perfectly joyned together in the same

2:Cor:13:11: mind, & in the same judgment. Finally, Brethren, farewell, be perfect, be of one Mind, live in peace, & the God of love & Peace shall be with you. Amen.

Signed at Salem: April: 25ᵗ: 1734:
Unanimously Voted by the Elders & Delegates
of the Churches here convened, that this Admonition
be presented to the Revᵈ: Mʳ Fisk Pastor of
the first Church in Salem, to be Communicated:
and that One Pastor & one Delegate of each
of these Churches be a Committe to present it.

Tho: Cushing: jun.	Thomas Cheever. Mod^r
Samuel Watts	John White
Edward Procter	Joseph Sewall
Dan: Henchman	Thomas Prince
William Halsey.	Joshua Gee
James Pierpoint.	Samuel Mather.
Joseph Allen	Edward Hutchinson
Graften Feveryeare.	Josiah Willard
William Larrabee	Nath: Saltonstall
Jacob Halsey.	James Sayword
	Nathanael Coit

Copia vera. Attest Thomas Cheever.

Memorandum. When the Committe went to present
this Admonition. Mr Fisk was gone from home;
the young woman of the house would not receive it; when told that it might be she was
ordered not to receive it. She answered, she would not say she was not: in our Return
we saw Deacon Osgood & would have given him the letter for Mr Fisk, but he also
refused to receive it.

Attest Thomas Cheever.

May: 5^t: Ensign Thomas Pratt, & Mary his Wife were received to full Communion. [35]

15: At a Church-meeting appointed to deal with our William Tuttle for drunkenness
he Offered an acknowledgement which was read; and after Considerable debate about his
acknowledgment, whither it were sufficient for his being restored to the Communion of
the Church at the Lords table from which he had absented himself for a considerable
time, it was Concluded on the Negative, for these reasons: first, becaus he had con-
tracted a habit of drunkenness by frequent acts; & also because he had often made
great promises of reformation to such of the Brethren as had dealt with him about
his sin, but all were soon forgotten: & also because he did not offer his acknowledge-

ment untill he knew the Church had appointed to deal with him. Upon the whole

the Church concluded he should be Suspended from the Lords table for some

time to see Whither his seeming repentance were attended with fruits meet for

repentance & a reformation: the Sentence of Suspension was formally pronounced.

Attest Thomas Cheever.

26. A Child of Capt. Samuel Watts baptized, named Bellingham.

June: 9. Five Children of Ensign Thomas Pratt baptized; Thomas. Daniel. Benjamin. John. Edward.

At night I acquainted the Church with the result of the Council, upon their Adjourn-

ment to Boston May 28th; who on May 30th Unanimously concluded, that Our Churches ought

to make use of a Synod, or Council of Neighbour Churches Walking Orderly, for the convic-

tion of the first Church in Salem, according to the Direction of our Platform together

27 Churches sent to.

with the Several Churches which they agreed to call in, and read the copy of the

letter to be sent to these Churches. The Church Voted, that their former Delegates

should attend this Service untill the matter were brought to an issue.

Attest. Thomas Cheever.

—— 16. A Child of Benjamin Whittamore baptized, named Rebeccah.

Sept: 8. David Whittemore & Alles his Wife were received to full Communion.

—— 15. A Child of Mr Levinston baptized, named John.

—— 22 A Child of David Whittemore baptized, named David.

July: 16. Nineteen of ye 27 Churches, called in by the 4 Churches, met at Salem by their Elders &

other Delegates, on the 16 of July, Who after they had formed themselves, having chosen

ye R^d Mr Nehemiah Walter of Roxbury their Moderatour & Mr John Barnard of Marble-

head Adjutant Moderatour, & made their Rules for their Voting by Churches; sent for

the 4 Churches to lay the Case before them which they did, and answered severall

Objections made against their proceedings. Several Ministers & some other Delegates

Withdrew, because the Councel refused to take M^r ffisks proposals to his agrieved

Brethren into their Consideration & among the rest Mr Barnard withdrew, whereupon

the Councel Chose R^d: Mr Jeremiah Wise of Berwick Adjutant Moderatour in his

stead; there remained 15 Churches, & when the letter of advice was read, it was voted
Unanimously by those 15 Churches, the 4 Churches being joyned made up the Number
of 19 Churches. The Council justifyed ye proceedings of ye 4 Churches; and adjourned to
Octob: 15: When & where the Councel being met at Salem, took M^r ffisks proposals
under their Consideration & made their Remarks upon them which were publickly
read in the Meeting house; & afterwards published their Result also in the Meeting
house: there were 17 Churches when the Result was Voted: then ye Council Dissolved.

Nov: 7: Publick thanksgiving. the Contribution for the poor above thirty shillings.

Dec: 8: Just before ye Administration of ye Sacrament, William Tuttle, who was Suspended from the
Lords supper, May: 15: was restored by a Vote of the Church to their love & Communion.

Octob: 15: The Council of Churches came into the following Result:

The Council of Churches here convened, having Examined & maturely Weighed
the case of the first Church in Salem, & having reinforced the Repeated Admonition
to the first Church in Salem, by leaving with them in July last a letter of Advice
for the Conviction of that Offending Church; & having offered other proper
Methods for that end, which have proved ineffectual. The Council now declare
their Apprehension and judgment; that the first Church in Salem has slighted
all the Means that have been used with them, nor has complied with their Duty
as a Church, in any one particular. As therefore the s^d Church, notwithstanding
a long Series of Reproofs, Admonitions, Advice, & other means upon the account of
their Open Offences, still remains Obstinate, nor resolved, or even disposed to Reform
the evil of their ways, We the Council afors^d think our selves called to bear
Witness against the Male-administration of that Offending Church, according   [36]
the Direction of our Platform of Church-discipline.

Accordingly, In the Name of Our Ld Jesus Christ, We protest, declare, & publish
that this Church is become Obstinate & impenitent in Scandal, & has justly exposed
it self to a Sentence of Non-Communion from Our several Churches. Having
made which Declaration, We farther proceed to declare to all, the Churches of

Our Lord Jesus Christ through this Province, that the first Church in Salem
has justly forfeited the priviledge of Communion with these Churches & deserve to
be deprived of that priviledge. However the Council conformably to the Pattern [of]
Our great Saviour, who has compassion on the ignorant, & on such as are out of the
way, think & make known, that the Churches to which we respectively belong, may
out of Tenderness & Compassion delay to pronounce the Sentence of Non-Communion
for the space of three Moneths after the Date of this Our Declaration.

And if after this patient & tender Delay of this Sentence, it shall not appear to our
respective Churches, that the first Church in Salem have repented & betaken themselves
to the use of proper means of peace & healing, We then advise, that Our Churches, approving and accepting the judgment of the Council, Declare the Sentence of Non-communion respectively concerning them, and that they withdraw themselves from participation with them at the Lords-table, & from such other Acts of holy Communion
as the Communion of Churches doth otherwise allow & require. And we do advise all
the Churches of Our Lord Jesus Christ through this Province; out of a religious care
to keep their Own Communion pure, to pronounce the same Sentence of Non-communion
concerning that Obstinate & impenitent Church, & to Withdraw in the same manner from them.
And in as much as there are Several Members of that Offending Church, viz. Benjamin Lynd,
James Lindal, Benj: Marston, Benj: Lynd Junr Esq, Col Thomas Barton, John Bickford, Henry
West, Samuel Ropes, George Daland, Saml: Giles, James Grant, John Archer, Miles Ward jun^r:
Benjamin Lambert, John Bickford jun^r: James Odel, Capt: Joseph Hathorn, Samuel Osgood, Capt.
Jonathan Gardner
who do not consent to the Offence of the Church, but in due sort bear their testimony against
it, We advise Our respective Churches, & all the Churches of Christ through the Province,
to receive them to wonted Communion, for we apprehend them to be innocent persons in
that Church, who therefore should not suffer with the Offenders; and farthermore we advise, that if such innocent persons withdraw from the fellowship of their Own Church and
Offer themselves to the fellowship of another, they may be received into it, as if they
had been orderly dismissed from their own church. In the name & by the Direction

of the Council.

Salem: Octob: 18: 1734:   Jeremiah Wise Moderator.

1734/5
ffeb: 21: At a Church Meeting appointed to consider what we had to do farther in the case
of the first Church at Salem: after the reading of some letters, & the proposals made
by M^r ffisk to his aggrieved Brethren, with the remarks of the Council upon them, and
also the Result of the Council; and some debate; the Church Voted their approving and
accepting the judgment of the Council; I then read the following declaration and
the Church Voted it without any contradicting, & that it should be publickly read the
next Lords day, which was done accordingly. Attest. Thomas Cheever.

23: A Child of Daniel Watts baptized, named Daniel.

We the Church of Christ in Rumny-marish, having upon the call & invitation of
the 2^d Church in Boston, sent Our Elder & other Delegates, to meet with the Delegates
of the s^d 2^d Church in Boston, and the Delegates of some Other Churches, at Salem upon
the 23^d of April last, when & where they mett with the Elders Delegates of the 3^d Church
in Boston, & the first Church in Glocester; and having the state of the first Church
in Salem laid before them by the Delegates of the 2^d Church in Boston, together
with the Charitable Admonition of the s^d Church given to the first Church in Salem,
for their Neglect of the Means of peace under their Scandalous Contentions; being
fully satisfied that there has been a Scandalous Contention for a long time in the first
Church in Salem, and that s^d Church has Neglected to use the proper means for healing
their Divisions; and that the 2^d Church in Boston had just reason to give an Admonition
to the first Church in Salem for that their Neglect; and that they had given their
Admonition with Regularity, Prudence, and tenderness, and being fully sensible of the
just Occasion of Uniting with the Delegates of the 2^d Church in Boston, in Seconding their Chari- [
table Admonition, both because the first Church in Salem still Continues in Contention, refuses
to hearken to the Admonition given them, & still Neglect to Use the means of peace:
Accordingly Our Delegates, with the Delegates of the third Church in Boston, & the first
Church in Glocester Uniting with the Delegates of the 2^d Church in Boston, made their Ap-

plication to the Rev.^d: Mr Fisk, that he would allow them a Conference with him & his Church upon the Melancholy Occasion; and when this was absolutely refused; they joyned in Second-ing the Admonition of the 2^d Church in Boston, as both the reason of the thing, & the Plat-form of our Church discipline, agreably to the Rules of Gods word directed. And having

journeyed

to meet at Boston on May: 28: that they might know, whither their Admonition had the desired good effect on the first Church in Salem, it then appeared by letters & testimonies received from 21 aggrieved Brethren at Salem, that the s^d letter of Admonition had been once and again refused by the Pastor, with repeated declarations that he would neither hear, nor receive it; so that the first Church in Salem appears to continue Obstinate & impenitent under Scandalous Divisions, & refuses to hearken to the Charitable Admonition of Neighbour Churches. Whereupon the Delegates of the 4 abovementioned Churches were Unani-mously of Opinion, that their Churches ought to proceed to make Use of the help of a Synod, or Council of Neighbour Churches Walking Orderly, for the Conviction of Our Brethren of the first Church in Salem. Accordingly by their letter they Called in a great Number of Churches, to meet at Salem on the 16th of July.

When we received from Our Delegates an account of what they had done in Our name, and what they had farther concluded upon, We were well satisfied therewith, and Voted that Our former Delegates should attend this Service, untill it were brought to an issue. The Major part of the Churches, that were sent to, did met at Salem, on the 16th of July, by their Elders & other Delegates, & having formed themselves into a Council, by choosing R^d: Mr Nehemiah Walter of Roxbury their Moderator; they sent for the Delegates of the four Churches abovenamed to lay before them the Melancholy case of the first Church in Salem; the Steps they had taken, & what they had to Offer, for the Justification of their Apprehension, that that Church is Obstinate & impenitent in Scandalous Division among them: which when they had done, and Answered Several Objections made against their proceedings; The Council justified the Proceedings of the s^d 4 Churches, & desired the 4 Churches to joyn with this Council, in their farther proceeding, as by their Votes [appear].[21] When the 4 Churches were joyned with the Council, the Council reinforced the repeated [Admo-] nitions given to the first Church in Salem, by leaving with them a letter of Advice for [their]

Conviction, & Adjourned to 15th of October.

The Council met again at Salem according to Adjournment, Octob: 15: and having Exam[ined]
& Maturely Weighed the case of the first Church in Salem, as they say in their Result
and having Offered other proper Methods for their Conviction, which proved ineffectual, the
Council declared their Apprehension & judgment, that the first Church in Salem hath
Slighted all means that have been used with them, nor have complied with their Duty, as
a Church, in any one particular: and farther declared that as the s^d Church, Notwithstanding
a long Series of Reproofs, Admonitions, & advice & other Means, upon the account of their
Open Offences, still remains Obstinate, We the Council afors^d think Our Selves called [to]
bear Witness against the Male-administration of that Offending Church according to [the]
Direction of Our Platform of Church discipline Accordingly in the Name of Our Lord Je[sus]
Christ, We protest, Declare, and publish that this Church is become Obstinate & impenitent [and a]
Scandal and hath justly exposed it self to a Sentence of Non-Communion from Our several
Churches. Having made which Declaration; We farther proceed to Declare to all the Chur[ches]
of Our Lord Jesus Christ through this Province; that the first Church in Salem hath ju[stly]
forfeited the Priviledge of Communion with these Churches, & deserve to be deprived of the
priviledge. However the Council, conformably to the pattern of Our great Saviour, who hath
compassion on the ignorant, and on such as are out of the way, think & make known, that the [Chur-]
ches, to which we respectively belong, may out of tenderness & compassion delay to Pro[nounce]
the Sentence of Non-Communion for the space of three Moneths after the Date of this our
declaration: and if after the patient & tender delay of this Sentence, it shall not appear [to]
our respective Churches, that the first Church in Salem have repented & betaken themselves
to the use of proper means of peace and healing, We then advise, that Our Churches
approving and accepting the judgment of the council, do Declare the Sentence of Non commun-   [38]
on respectively concerning them, and that they Withdraw themselves from Participation with
them at the Lords table, and from such other acts of holy Communion, as the Communion of
Churches doth otherwise allow and require.

We the Church beforenamed declare, that we approve and accept the judgment of the Council, and having waited four moneths, to see wither the first Church in Salem have repented, and betaken themselves to the Use of proper means of peace & healing, but no such thing appearing, We now Proceed to declare the Sentence of Non Communion concerning them. Accordingly, in the Name of Our Lord Jesus Christ, We do solemnly publish & declare that we will not hold Communion with the first Church in Salem, neither by participation with them at the Lords table, nor any other act of holy Communion, as the Communion of Churches doth otherwise allow and require. And in as much as there are Several Members of that Offending Church, named in the Result of the Council, who do not consent to the Offence of the Church, but do in due sort bear Witness against it, We will receive them to wonted Communion. Voted by the Church ffebr: 21: nemine contradicente

Attest Thomas Cheever.

1735	At the Church Meeting, ffebr: 28: it was Unanimously Voted, that the Church should Meet upon the last fryday in March in Order to choosing Ruling Elders.
March: 16:	A Child of Ebenezer Kendal baptized, named Asa. Same day a Child of David Whittemore baptized, named Allie.
March: 28:	The Church mett according to their Appointment, to choose Ruling Elders: When they brought in their Votes. Capt. Samuel Watts, & Deacon William Halsey were Chosen by the Majority of Voters. At the same time Mr Jacob Halsey was Chose to ye Office of a Deacon, by a Major Vote
May: 11:	Abigail Halsey, daughter of Jacob Halsey, was admitted to full Communion. Same day a Child of Benjamin Floyd baptized, named Abigail.
June: 8:	A Child of Capt: Samuel Watts baptized, named Belcher.
17	A Church Meeting according to appointment, to consider a letter received from the Church of Christ in Hopkinton desiring this Church to send their Pastor & other Delegates to meet with the Delegates of some other Churches to give them advice in a matter of difficulty referring to a Number of Bretheren of fframingham Church who desire to joyn with the Church in Hopkinton upon the account of the Congregational Principles: after the letter was read, the Church referred the matter to farther consideration till next Lords day then I acquainted the Church, that Joannah Tuttle had been with me to desire to

make her peace with the Church, on account of her sin of Fornication &c, and that I had [app]ointed[22] her to attend the Church on the sixth of July next, Our Sacrament day in order [the]reunto, the Church approved of my doings herein without any opposition. Then the [Chur]ch proceeded to the consideration of their choice of Mr Jacob Halsey to the Office [of] Deacon their last Meeting, because same manifested great uneasiness about that Vote, desiring the Church to reconsider it; after considerable arguings pro and con; When it was put to the Vote, Whither the Church did abide by their former Vote, it passed in the Affirmative by a great Majority of at least two to One: Then the Church proceeded to make Choice of Deacon Chamberlane, Mr Samuel Tuttle, & Mr Nathanael Oliver to treat with Capt: Samuel Watts, & Deacon William Halsey about their accepting the Office of Ruling Elders to which they had been Chosen, and report their answer to the Church as soon as Conveniently might be. After Mr Jacob Halsey declared his unwillingness to serve in the Office of Deacon, but he was desired to take the matter into farther consideration, and so the Meeting was concluded.

Attest Th: Cheever.

The Church was stayed, & concluded not to comply with the desire of Hopkinton Church.

17 A Child of Samuel Floyd baptized, named Noah.

18: Joannah Tuttle, who had fallen into the sin of Fornication, having been with me in Order to giving satisfaction to the Church attended at this time according to my Direction. After her Confession was read to the church; when the Question was put, Whither they was satisfied with what she Offered; so as to restore her to their Charity & Communion, the Church Unanimously declared their acceptance. Attest. Thomas Cheever.

— 17 A Child of Thomas Eustace baptized, named Thomas.

1 A Child of Elias Whittemore baptized, named Rachel.

8 I stayed the Church, & read the 2^d letter from the church of Christ in Hopkington desiring this Church to send their Elders & other Messengers to meet with the Elders & Messengers of several other Churches in an Ecclesiastical Council, on the 3^d Wednesday in September next, to Consider & advise them in the case of some Members of Framingham Church who desired to be received into the Church of Hopkington; the Church consented unanimously with the desire of Hopkington Church;

but it was desired that Our Ruling Elders should be Ordained before that time; accordingly it was Voted that Our Ruling Elders should be Ordained the fourteenth day of Septemb; & then they Nominated Mr Nathanael Oliver & Mr Benjamin Floyd to attend that Service with my self & Elder Watts

Sept: 14: This day, according to the former agreement of the church, Capt. Samuel Watts, & Deacon William [39] Halsey were Solemnly Ordained to the Office of Ruling Elders in this Church of Christ.

17 My self with Elder Samuel Watts, Mr Nathanael Oliver, & Mr Benjamin Floyd according to former appointment, went to Hopkington, where we Mett with ye Elders & Messengers of the Church of Berwick of Boston Old South, & of the Old & New-North Churches, & of Mr Loring at Sudbery; After a full hearing of all that was offered on both sides, the Council after serious & deliberate consideration of the whole case, Unanimously advised the Church of Hopkington to receive those Members

—— 21 A Child of Joseph Whittemore baptized, named Nathan.

I acquainted the Church with the issue of the Council at Hopkington. Then I read a letter from the 2^d Church of Christ in Maldon to this Church to entreat such an act of Communion that they would send Delegates with their Rev^d: Pastour & Elders, in conjunction with the Churches of the Old & New-North in Boston, of Charlstown, the first Church in Maldon, the 2^d Church in Brantry, the Churches of Scituate, Pembrook, & Hannover, to Assist in the Ordination of the Rev^d: Mr Joseph Stimpson to the Pastoral Office over them; the 24th day of Septemb. The Church complied with their request, & chose Mr Jacob Halsey, Mr Samuel Tuttle, Mr Samuel Floyd, & Mr Thomas Pratt to attend that Service.

—— 24: This day the Elders & Messengers of the Churches mett in Council at Maldon, and after their Covenant was read; and the Result of the Council of three Churches by whom they were imbodied into a distinct Church state was read, and after the Consideration & debate upon what was Offered by the Rev^d: Mr Emerson & a Committee of his Church in Objection to the Proceedings to Ordination The Council Voted that they were a Church of Christ & to be acknowledged as such, and that what had been Objected was not Sufficient to hinder the Proceeding to Ordination; Accordingly they immediately Went to ye Meeting house: Where ye Rev^d: Mr Stimpson was Ordained after ye usual way.

Oct: 27: At a Church Meeting according to appointment for choosing a Deacon. Mr Jacob Halsey was chosen to ye Office of a Deacon by a great Majority of Voters. At the same time by a Vote of the Church the Ruling Elders were desired to sit in the Pulpit. Also it was Voted Unanimously that Mr John Brintnall be desired to sett the psalm, & to sit in the foreseat.

1735/6:

  March: 7:   A Child of Benjamin Whittemore baptized, named Abraham.

  —— 21:   A Child of John Leath baptized, named Elizabeth. A Child of Steven Kent baptized, named Elizabeth.

  April. 11:   A Child of Ensign Thomas Pratt baptized, named Mary.

  —— 18.   A Child of Mr John Brintnall baptized, named Thomas.

  May. 16.   A Child of John Halsey baptized, named William.

  Aug: 1:   A child of Elder Samuel Watts was baptized, named William.

1736/7

  Feb: 20th.   A Child of Samuel Floyd baptized, named Joseph.

  March. 6.   A   Child of Daniel Watts baptized, named Rachel.

  June. 19.   Mrs Abigail Halsey, wife of Elder William Halsey, was admitted to full Communion.

  July. 31:   A Child of Elder Samuel Watts baptized, named Edward.

  —— ——   Same day a Child of Thomas Eustace baptized, named William.

  August: 28:   A Child of Ensign Thomas Pratt baptized, named Joseph.

  Sept: 6.   A Child of Elder William Halsey baptized, named Ebenezer.

1737/8

  Jan: 1st: A Child of John Halsey baptized, named Mary.

  Feb. 26.   A Child of Benjamin Whittemore baptized, named Amos.

  June. 18:   A Child of Samuel Pratt baptized, named Caleb.

  —— -25:   A Child of Samuel Floyd baptized, named Ezra.

  August. 6.   A Child of Elder Samuel Watts baptized, named Isaac.

  Septemb: 10:   A Child of Benjamin Floyd baptized, named Elizabeth.

  —— 17:   Samuel Maxwel was admitted to full Communion.

  —— 24:   I acquainted the Church with a letter from Mr Welsteed's Church, desiring of their Rev^d: Pastor and Elders with other Delegates, to joyn in Counsel with the Elders & Messengers of Severall other Churches, upon Wednesday 27th of this instant Septemb, ye day appointed for the Ordination of Mr Ellis Gray: ye Church consented, and Voted to send the two Deacons, viz Deacon Chamberlane & Deacon Halsey, Mr Nathanael Oliver, Mr John Floyd, & L^t: Nathan Cheever to attend that Service.

  27:    This day the R^d Elders & Messengers of Eleven Churches viz: all in Boston with Roxbury and Charlstown, mett in Council; & ye Rev^d: Mr Ellis Gray was Ordained to ye Pastoral Office.

Oct. 12:	A Child of Daniel Watts baptized, named Daniel.

1739.
April. 22: A Child of Benjamin Dix, member of a Church in Watertown, baptized, named Mehetabel.

—— 29. Abigail Eustis, wife of Thomas Eustace was admitted to full Communion. ~~And at yᵉ other ca~~

May: 13: Mary Halsey, wife of John Halsey, was admitted to full Communion.

—— 20. A Child of Edmond Dix, member of a Church in ,²³baptized, named Josiah.

June. 17: Mary Parker Wife of John Parker was admitted to full Communion.

July: 8: A Child of Thomas Eustace baptized, named Abigail.

——— Same day Sarah Halsey, Wife of Samuel Halsey was admitted to full Communion.

——— Same day, Hannah Chamberlane: and Susannah Chamberlane were admitted to full Communion.

July. 22. A Child of Samuel Halsey baptized, named Martha. [40]

Same day a Child of John Parker baptized, named Ezra.

Novemb: 4: A child of Samuel Floyd baptized, named Rachel.

—— 11 A Child of John Halsey baptized, named Hannah.

—— 18. A Child Samuel Halsey baptized, named Abigail.

Decemb: 16. James Stower was admitted to full Communion, & his Child baptized, named Elizabeth.

1740
May. 4ᵗʰ A Child of Stephen Dent baptized, named Stephen.

—— 28 Anne Taylor was admitted to full Communion.

Octob: 5. A child of Abel Robison, (member of Mʳ Sparhawks Church of Salem) baptized, named Mary.

——— 12 A Child of Nathan Cheever baptized, named Joshua.

1741:
March. 28 Hugh ffloyd was admitted to full Communion.

April: 12 A Child of Samuel Floyd baptized, named Nathanael.

Same day a Child of Hugh Floyd baptized, named William.

July. 5ᵗ: Hannah Chamberlane dismissed at her desire to yᵉ Church in Hopkington.

—— 19 A Child of Thomas Eustice baptized, named Mary.

August. 9: A Child of Elder Samuel Watts baptized, named Hannah.

Sept: 13. A child of John Halsey baptized, named Susanna.

Octob: 4: A Child of Daniel Watts baptized, named Katharine.

Novemb: 8: Mary Newhal was admitted to full Communion.

—— 22.   A child of Hugh Floyd baptized, named Steven.

1741/2:
Jan: 17.   A Child of Stephen Kent baptized, named Jacob.

Febr: 14:   A Child of Samuel Halsey, baptized, named Phebe.

March: 15.   A Church-Meeting appointed to deal with Mr Elisha Tuttle for his Withdrawing from the
Communion of the Church, which he had done a considerable time, he declared the
reason was, he apprehended that he was Slighted by the Church and they did not show
that Regard to him which they did to the Other Brethren, and he thought severall
of them were prejudiced against him &c: and mentioned some words and actions of
some of the Brethren which he took as evidence therof, these things made him
so uneasy in his Mind that he thought it not fitting to Come and sitt down at
the Lords table with them &c. After considerable debate, and the answers given by
those Brethren to what Mr Tuttle Objected, and declaring they had no personal Prejudice against him, and should be glad he would return to his Duty: Mr Tuttle
Owned that he had done wrong in his Absenting himself so long without endeavouring to remove those Prejudices; and promised that for the future he would attend his Duty in Communion with the Church as long as should be for his edification: hereupon the Brethren declared themselves satisfied therewith, and M^r
Tuttle said, he did thankfully accept it. Attest Thomas Cheever Pastor.

—— 28:   Damaris Tuttle, daughter of Mr Edward Tuttle, was admitted to full Communion.

April. 18.   A Child of James Stowers baptized, named James.

——- 25   A Child of Abel Robison baptized, named Susanna.

Sept: 19   Mrs Sarah Marble was received to full Communion.

Oct: 17   Benjamin Tuttle was received to full Communion.

Nov: 21   A Child of Samuel Floyd baptized, named David.

1742/3
Feb: 6.   A Child of Ambrose Blaney a Member of Lynn Church, baptized, named Mary.

March: 6.   A Child of Edmund Dix baptized, named Joseph.

June 26^t: Susanna Richardson at her desire was dismissed to the 2^d Church of Christ in Woburn.

Oct: 30.   A Child of Joseph Halloway baptized, named Joseph.

Decemb: 25. A child of Mr Hugh Floyd baptized, named Andrew.

January 1st. Elder Watts Negro woman was received to full Communion and baptized, by the name of Phillis.

1743:44:
———— 15   A Child of Thomas Eustis baptized named Chamberlane.

———— 29   A Child of John Halsey baptized, named Mary.

Feb: 12.   A Child of Samuel Floyd baptized named Nathan.

———— 26   A Child of Samuel Halsey baptized named William.

April: 29   A Child of Steven Kent baptized named Benjamin.

Septb: 16   A Child of Nathanael Oliver junr: baptized named Nathanael.

———— 23   A Child of Daniel Watts baptized, named John.

Decemb.   A Child of Samuel Tuttle Member of the 2d Church in Maldon, baptized, named Anne.

1744/5
Jan. 20. A   Child of Samuel Halsey baptized, named Esther.

Jan. 27: A   Child of James Stowers baptized, named Sarah.

1745:   [41]
April: 7.   A Child of John Sargeant, (who Married Susannah Chamberlane) baptized named Susannah.

———— 14   A Child of Edmund Dix baptized named Hannah.

June. 16.   A Child of Joannah Tuttle, by William Lamson, baptized, named William.

Sept: 1.   A Child of Ambros Blaney baptized, named Aaron.

———— 29.   Three Children of Elder Samuel Watts's Negro Woman Phillis, baptized, Cato, Balindon, & Violet.

To the Revd: Mr Thomas Cheever Pastour of the church of Christ in Chelsea.

to be Communicated: Revd: Honoured & Beloved.

Taking into Consideration the various Rebukes of Divine Providence upon

us of late with respect to Mr Fisk &c. and being willing to Exercise a Godly [watch]

over our Selves, & to confess our faults to our fellow Professours, as it may

appear to us to be our Duty. We would now in this explicit manner freely

acknowledge, that We were greatly Wanting in love to and Concern for those

Once called the Aggrieved Brethren of Our Church, in the time of our Controversy

with them, and did not use the Means proper to Quiet and satisfy them: viz: by

Consenting to Meet, as a Church. And were [far] from paying due Regard to the venerable
Councils that came to Salem in that time, We now believe came out of love, and
with a Sincere Aime to do the best service they could: We also Acknowledge Our
fault in speaking Slightly of Councils, and the Constitution that we now profess to hold, viz: that called Congregational. We entreat, that all our Sister
Churches & Christian Brethren would forgive Overlook & Pray for us their
Brethren in the faith of the gospel: Tim Pickering & Abijah Eustis: in
the name and at the Desire of the first Church in Salem. particularly those that [were]
in Communion in the time of the late Controversy.

I read this letter to the Church before the Congregation, Octob: 20: 1745: and propounded
to the Church, that if they did accept the acknowledgement therein made by the
s^d first Church in Salem, so as to restore them to their Communion and all the
priviledges and acts of Communion, which the Communion of Churches do
allow and require they should Manifest it by the Usual Sign of uplifted hands
which they did: Attest Thomas Cheever Pastour.

Dec: 8: A Child of Thomas Sarjeant; a Member of Mr Emersons Church of Maldon, baptized, named Tabi

—— 29 A Child of Benjamin Brintnal, a Member of Maldon South Ch^h. baptized, named Elizabeth.

—— A Child of Sarah Slack Widow baptized, named Elizabeth.

ffeb: 9. A Child of Thomas Eustis baptized named Abigail.

   Mrs Sarah Slack Admitted to full Communion Decemb: I^t

1745/6

March: 2^d A Child of Samuel Floyd baptized, named Benjamin.

April 13. Sarah Whittemore daughter of Mr Benjamin Whittemore received to full Communion.

June. 8. A Child of John Halsey's baptized named Lois.

July. 13. A Child of Steven Kent baptized, named Carissa.

Novemb: 9 A Child of Samuel Tuttle, Member of ye 2^d Church in Maldon, baptized, named Joannah.

March: 15: 1746: A Child of Thomas Sergeant baptized, named Thomas.

May 17 A Child of Pelatiah Whittemore, a Member of Maldon South Church baptized, named John.

May 24. A Child of Edward Dix baptized, named Nathan.

Nov 15 A Child of James Stowers baptized named Abigail.[24]

Chelsea Sep[r]. 24. 1747

[42]

At a Church meeting duely appointed, at the house of the Rev[d]: M[r] Thomas Cheever Pastor of said Church, and moderator of said meeting.

The Rev[d]: M[r] Cheever proposed to the Church his desire that Nath[l]: Oliver Jun[r]: might be appointed Scribe to make & keep a record of the Churches proceedings Which was Voted in the afirmative, nem[e] Contrad[e].

Then it was proposed that wednesday the 7th of October next be appointed a day of fasting and prayer to implore the direction of Almighty God in the choise of a minister as collegue with the Rev[d]: M[r] Cheever; which was Voted in the affirmative.

Voted, Mes[s]: Sam[l] Floyd & Nath[l]: Oliver Jun[r]: in the name of the Church invite the Rev[d]: Mes[s]: Appleton, Emerson, Abbot, Hobby, Prentiss and Cleveland to assist in & at said Solemnity.

Voted - - - Elder Hosey make provision at his house for the Entertainment of said Gent[n]: and at the Churches Charge.

Voted - - - Elder Watts, Elder Hosey, & Nath[l]: Oliver Jun[r]: settle the Church's acc[t]: with Deacon Hosey and report thereon at their next meeting.

Voted the same Com[ee]: request the Donation of M[r]: Hugh Floyd deceased of his Execut[r]. and if they receive the same in Cash or plate to give a discharge therefor.

Voted - - - The Rev[d]: Mes[s]: Appleton and Abbot be desired to preach the Sermons on the intended fast.

Voted - - - This meeting be adjourned to the first monday after the above fast, at Elder Hosey's house at 3 o'Clock afternoon to receive the above reports, and transmit any other businesss that may properly be laid before the Church.

Die Sabbati Sep[r]: 27.

After divine Service the Rev[d]: M[r] Cheever inform'd the Church that the Rev[d]: Gent[n]: appointed to attend the fast propos'd could not oficiate on said day but would endeavor

Chelsea Sep'r 24. 1747

At a Church meeting duely appointed at the house of the Rev'd Mr Thomas Cheever Pastor of said Church, and Moderator of said meeting.

The Rev'd Mr Cheever proposed to the Church his desire that Nath Oliver Jr might be appointed Scribe to make & keep a record of the Churches proceedings Which was Voted in the affirmative, Nem'e Contrad.

Then it was proposed that Wednesday the 7th of October next be appointed a day of Fasting and prayer to implore the direction of Almighty God in the choice of a Minister at collegue with the Rev'd Mr Cheever; which was Voted in the affirmative.

Voted Messrs Sam'l Floyd & Nath'l Oliver Jun'r in the name of the Church invite the Rev'd Mess'rs Appleton, Emerson, Abbot, Holby, Prentice and Cleveland to assist in & at said Solemnity.

Voted ... Elder Hasey make provision at his house for the Entertainment of said Gent. and at the Churches Charge.

Voted ... Elder Watts, Elder Hasey, & Nath'l Oliver Jun'r settle the Church's acc't with Deacon Hasey and report thereon at their next meeting.

Voted the same Com'e request the Donation of Mr Hugh Floyd deceas'd of his Exe'rs and if they receive the same in Cash or plate to give a discharge therefor.

Voted ... The Rev'd Mess'rs Appleton and Abbot be desired to preach the Sermons on the intended fast.

Voted ... This meeting be adjourned to the first monday after the above fast, at Elder Hasey's house at 3 o'Clock afternoon to receive the above reports, and transact any other business that may properly be laid before the Church.

Die Sabbati Sep. 27.

After divine Service The Rev'd Mr Cheever informd the Church that the Rev'd Gent'n appointed to attend the fast proposed could not officiate on said day but would endeavour it on Wednesday the 14th of October: Then the Church Voted to postpone said Solemnity till said day and adjournd the Church meeting to the monday following.

Die Lunae Oct. 19

The Church met by adjournment at the house of Mr Nathan Cheever, inasmuch as the Rev'd Pastor could not travell so far as Elder Haseys at whose house the Church were adjourned to this day.

The Committee on the Churches acc't reported that the Church was indebted for Elements two pounds thirteen Shillings & fivepence old ten. and the account for the poor stood £ in favour of the Church Eight pounds ten Shill. and fourpence, that there was also in the deacons hands an English Shilling & a new England Sixpence.

Said Committee also reported that they thought proper that the heirs of Mr Hugh Floyd deceas'd should themselves purchase a peice of Plate with their fathers Donation, and present the same to the Church. Which Reports were severally accepted.

Elder Hasey then presented his acc't of charge on the late fast which was allowd. And w'ch was £ ... 2 old ten.

It was proposd to discharge the Same by subscription, accordingly there was subscribed £ old ten. more than discharged Elder Haseys acct. and which Sum was delivered to Deacon Hasey, and he was desired to the Church therefor.

It was mov'd and seconded that the Church should at this meeting proceed to the choise of a Collegue with the Rev'd Mr Cheever. The Question being put, It pass'd in the Negative. Then,

Voted that the towns Comittee be desired to request and agree with the Rev'd Mr William McClenachan to preach for the term of two months on further probation.

Then the Rev'd Moderator, after prayer, adjourned this meeting Sine Die.

it on wednesday the 14th of october: Then the Church Voted to postpone said Solemnity

till said day ~~and adjourn'd~~ and adjourn'd the Church meeting to the monday following.

Die Lunæ Octr. 19.

The Church met by adjournment at the house of M^r. Nathan Cheever, inasmuch as the

Rev^d: Pastor could not travell so far as Elder Hoseys at whose house the Church was ad:

journed to this day.

The Comittee on the Churches acct^s. reported that the Church was indebted for Elements

two pounds thirteen Shillings & five pence old ten^d. and the account for the poor

stood C^r n favour of the Church Eight pounds ten Shill^s. and four pence, that there

was also in the deacons hands an English Shilling & a new England Six pence.

Said Comittee also reported that they thot proper that the heirs of M^r. Hugh Floyd

deceas'd should themselves purchase a paire of Plate with their fathers Donation, and

present the Same to the Church. Which Reports were severally accepted,

Elder Hosey then presented his acc^t of Charge on the late fast; which was

allowd. and w^c. was £ 9 - - - 2 Old ten^r.

It was propos'd to discharge the Same by subscription; accordingly there was

subscribed £ 9 - - - Old ten^r. more than discharged Elder Hoseys acc^t and which Sum

was delivered to Deacon Hosey, and he was desired to C^r the Church therefor.

It was mov'd and seconded that the Church shou'd at this meeting proceed to the

choice of a Collegue, with the Rev^d. Mr Cheever. The Question being put; It pass'd

in the Negative. Then,

Voted that the towns Comittee be desired to request and agree with the Rev^d.

M^r. William McClenahan to preach for the term of two months on further

probation.

Then the Rev^d. Moderator, after prayer, adjourn'd this meeting Sine Die.

Die Lunee March 8. 1747.8 [43]

At a Church meeting at the meeting house appointed to see if the Church wou'd

proceed to the Choice of a Colleague with the Rev^d. Mr Cheever, or what the Church wou'd act with respect to the Supply of the Pulpit under the advanced age and weakness of their rev^d. Pastor.

After some debate it was thôt proper to take the advise & opinion of some Judicious neighbour ministers respecting the ministerial Qualifications of the Rev^d. Mr William McClenachan; and that he be desired to supply the Pulpit for a further term as the town's Com^ee. shou'd agree with him.

Accordingly the following Letter was draughted And Mes^s. Hugh Floyd with Nathl. Oliver Junr. appointed a Comittee to wait on the Rev^d. Mr William McClenachan for his Consent, and then to present the Same to the Gent^n. to whom it was directed. Upon his assent the Com^ee. proceeded.

Chelsea March 8. 1747.8.

The Church of Christ in Chelsea
to the Rev^d. Mes^s. Nathl. Appleton

William Hobby & Ellis Gray }	After hearing the rev^d. Mr William McClenachan for the Space of near ten months and that to very general satisfaction in this

town; Our Church this day met to see what they shou'd do with regard to the Supply of the Pulpit for the future, or whether they shou'd proceed to the choice of said Gent^n. as Colleague to our Rev^d. & aged Pastor M^r. Cheever; and after mature Consideration the Church voted to postpone such matter till after M^r McClenachan had been approved of by you, in conjunction with any other, one or two other Gent^n. he shall appoint both with regard to his Principles and other abilities for the work of a Gospell Minister.

These therefore in behalf of the Church request you'l do us the favour to attend such service with all convenient Speed, at such time and place as Mes^s. Hugh Floyd and Nathl Oliver Junr.; the Church's Comittee shall find most agreeable to you and him.

By order of the Church

N^l Oliver Junr. Scribeat

Then this meeting was adjournd Sine Die.

The same Day the abovesaid Com^ee. waited on the Rev^d. M^r W^m. McClenachan with the above transcript and he freely expressing his assent & consent to the Church's

procedure, nominated the Rev^d. M^r W^m. Welstead & And^w. LeMarcies, and said he wou'd

wait on such Gent^n. at any time and place they should assign.

Accordingly on this day the eleventh instant the above Com^ee. waited on

the rev^d. Mr Appleton with the above letter and acquainted Mr Welstead with the Churches

desire shewing him a Coppy thereof, and from the united concurrence of those

Gent^n. delivered to the said Comittee it appeared to them an unusual procedure and

declined to undertake in such an afair, at the same time gave it as their advice to the

Church to apply in the same manner to the association of Ministers in the town of

Boston, all which the said Com^ee. comunicated to the Rev^d. Mr Cheever, who on the

fourteenth instant march stop't the Church and appointed wednesday the seventeenth

instant a Church meeting at his own house to take the abovesaid matter more

fully into Consideration.

March 17.

At a meeting of the Brethren of the Church of Christ in Chelsea at the house of

the Rev^d. Mr Thos: Cheever Pastor & Moderator of said meeting.

Upon Consideration of the Refusal of the Gent^n. requested by this Church

to examin The Rev^d. M^r W^m. McClenachan expecting his ministerial Qualification

Agreed unanimously that the Rev^d. M^r W^m. McClenachan, if he sees meet wait on   [44]

the associated Pastors of the Town of Boston at their next meeting and ofer himself to

Examination respecting his ministerial Qualifications — and then Voted this meeting

be adjourn'd till this Church receive an answer from said association.

March 29

The Church met at the house of the Rev^d. Mr Thos: Cheever, and having received a

Vote from the rev^d. associated Pastors of the town of Boston, expressive of their disinclination

to comply with the Churches desire that they wou'd give this Church their thots of the

ministerial Qualifications of the Rev^d. M^r W^m. McClenachan, as such a practice was

unusual and they were unacquainted with said Gent^n.

After some debate — Voted to meet on monday the 18th. of april next to see if the Church wou'd give the Rev^d. M^r W^m. McClenachan an invitation to settle among us as Colleague with the rev^d. Mr Thos: Cheever — said meeting to be at ye meeting house at Nine o'Clock in the forenoon, to which time this meeting stands adjourned.

~~Voted also the Select men be desired to issue their warrant for a town meeting at two o'Clock afternoon of said day~~

April 10. 1748

The Church met at the meeting house by adjournment, and after prayer the Rev^d. Moderator viz Mr Cheever proposed that the Church shou'd bring in their written Votes for a Pastor Colleague with him; By which Votes, it appeared that the rev^d. Mr William McClenachan was chosen by a great majority.

Voted the Select men of the town be desired to issue their warrant to call a town's meeting as soon as may be, to see if the town wou'd concurr with the Church in their Choice of the rev^d. M^r W^m. McClenachan, and which if they did, to choose a Comittee to join with the ruling Elders in waiting on said Gent^n. for his Answer.

May 3

At a Church meeting at the meeting house by appointment, It appearing that the town by a very great majority, had concur'd with the Church in their Choice of the rev^d. M^r W^m. McClenachan, and that he had accepted their call as Pastor elect Colleague with the rev^d. Mr Thos: Cheever;

Voted Wednesday the 21st of September next be appointed a day set apart to inaugurate said Gent^n. into said office; and that the following Churches be sent to to join in Council for said purpose Viz the Churches under the pastoral Care of the following Gent^n. Viz the Rev^d. Mes^s. Jno. Webb & And^w. Elliot, W^m. Welstead & Elis Gray, Samuel Mather and Samuel Cooper, of Boston. The Rev^d. Mr Nathl. Appleton of Cambridge, The Rev^d. Mr Eben^r. Turell of Medford, The rev^d. Mr Joseph Emerson of Maldon, The Rev^d. Mr Nathl. Henchman of Lynn, The rev^d. Mr William Hobby of Reading, The Rev^d. Mr John Davidson of Nutfield, and the rev^d. And^w. Le Mercier of Boston.

Voted also the following letter be directed to the abovesaid Sev[l]. Churches and that it
be signed by the Ruling Elders in the name of the Church

To the Rev[d]. &c[a]

S[r]. It having pleased the glorious head of the Church, after, as we
hope, our humble supplications to him, on a day of fasting and prayer for his guidance
in a matter of such importance, to direct us by a very great majority both of Church and
town to invite the rev[d]. M[r] William M[c]Clenachan, late of Blanford to the Pastoral Ofice
among us; and to incline him to accept said Invitation; We have agreed on wednesday
the twenty eighth day of Sep[r]. next, God willing to fix him in said ofice among us in
Conjunction with the Rev[d]. M[r] Thomas Cheever. We therefore desire you with such delegates
of your Church shall think proper to send, to conurr with other Elders and messengers
of several Churches in Exercising such acts of comunion as the nature of such Solemnity
may require. We Subscribe yours in the faith and order of the Gospell.

> Samuel Watts
>
> William Hasey

} Ruling Elders

September 12. 1748   [45]

To the Church of Christ in Chelsea

Brethren

As there is a meeting of some of the Church and Town at Nath[l]. Olivers
Jun[r]. at 3 o'Clock this Even[g] in order to receive some advices come to hand respecting The Rev[d].
M[r]. M[c]Clenachan; We therefore humbly desire all the brethren of said Church to meet there also
for the End aforesaid; and there pass such Votes as they shall think proper.

We are yours in the faith and fellowship of the Gospell

> Sam[l]. Watts
>
> W[m]. Hasey

} Ruling Elders

Wednesday morn[g] 11. o'Clock.

These may certifie We notified the members of the Church in Chelsea to meet at time and place above mentioned, except M[r]. Nathan Cheever who is out of town.

Attest

Jacob Hasey

Thomas Pratt

} Members of said Church.

At a Church meeting the day above at
the house of Nath[l]. Oliver Jun[r] - - -

The above notification and return being read
and finding all the members present excepting M[r]. Nathan Cheever and M[r]. Hugh Floyd
who was Sick, The hon[e]. Sam[l]. Watts Esq[r]. as Senior Elder was moderator.

Voted all the papers referring any ways to the person Character of Circumstances of
the rev[d]. William M[c]Clenachan should be laid on the table, that authentick Coppies
be taken, and the originals return'd to the possessors of 'em.

The Moderator demanded of Deacon Jacob Hasey or any others who might be
possesd of any such papers to gratifie the Church in the above Vote.

Deacon Jacob Hasey said he had in this possession all the papers above referr'd to
but wou'd not lay 'em on the table nor sufer any Coppies to be taken of them
which the Church tho't unreasonable in him: and after some debate

Voted to postpone the intended Installment of the Rev[d]. M[r]. William M[c]Clenachan
till the second Wednesday of October next.

Voted also that the ruling Elders acquaint the severall Churches sent to in
order to attend such Solemnity with the above Vote.

Then the Moderator adjourn'd this meeting Sine Die.

Wednesday. Oct[r]. 12

The Venerable & Rev[d]. Council sent to by the Church in Chelsea consisting
of Eleven Churches met at Chelsea at the meeting house. In order to install the
Rev[d]. M[r]. William M[c]Clenachan into the Pastoral Office over said Church as Colleague
with the rev[d]. M[r]. Thomas Cheever. The Rev[d]. M[r]. Nath[l]. Appleton was chosen Mod[r].
of said Council.

Decon Jacob Hasey Mes^s. Elisha Tuttle, Samuel Floyd, Nathan Cheever and Thomas Pratt oppos'd the installment of the said Gent^n. exhibiting by way of memorial ~~many~~ sundry allegations against him both with regard to his ministerial qualifications in point of Learning, & his moral Character of all which The said William McClenachan acquitted himself before a very large assembly in publick hearing so far to the satisfaction of said Council that by their result they discharg'd him of every Charge exhibited, excepting that once they found him guilty of indecent Passion & uttering unbecoming words: Yet that the Council might not be thot too sudden in fixing a Pastor where there had arisen such a diference in the Church and that the above Gent^n. who called themselves aggrieved Brethren might have time to be better reconciled to their said Pastor Elect, said Council advised the Rev^d. M^r. William McClenachan to continue his acceptance of the Churches Call and adjournd the Council to the third tuesday of December next.

Chelsea Nov^r.27.1748

[46]

The Rev^d. M^r. Cheever stop't the Ch^h. & appointed a Ch^h. meeting to morrow at 9 o'Clock forenoon at the meeting house to see if the Church wou'd send their request to the Council met here on the 12th. of Octr. past, in order to install the Rev^d. W^m. McClenachan; And to do any other busness that may be thôt proper.

28

The Ch^h. met as above appointed, and Voted The Council met here on the 12th. of Octr. past be desired to convene according to their adjournment in order if they see fit, to install the Rev^d. W^m. McClenachan as Colleague Pastor with the Rev^d. M^r. Thomas Cheever; And that the Elders Watts & Hasey read the Churche's request herefor to the Rev^d. Moderator of said Council.

Voted, The Ruling Elders, the rev^d. W^m. McClenachan, Mes^s. Thomas Pratt and Hugh Floyd take the Ch^h. Covenant into Consideration, and make what additions or amendments agreeable to the substantials of the Platform that they think just and report thereon.

Voted this meeting be adjourn'd to monday next at 9 o'Clock in
the forenoon to receive the report of the above Comittee and to pass thereon
as the Ch^h. shall think proper.

Voted the select men be desired to convene the town on said Day to
see if they will defrey the necessary Charges of said Council.

Decr. 5

The Church met accordingly and considering but few were present
it was agreed to adjourn the meeting till 4 o'Clock Afternoon at the
dwelling house of the Rev^d. M^r. McClenachan.

Post Meridien

The Church met agreeable to their adjourment, The hon^r. Elder Watts
being Moderator;

The Com^ee. appointed on the Church Covenant reported that
it is their opinion there be no alterations in the Covenant; But that with
respect to that article in the Covenant, wherein, referring to the platform
'tis declar'd, <u>Unto which for the Substance we declare our adherence</u>

They are of Opinion that Ruling Elders are, agreeable to the Platform,
Essential Oficers in a Congregational Church; and that no teaching Elder be
admitted as Pastor of this Church unless he submit to such oficers in ye Ch^h.

They are also of Opinion that the negative power does not pertain to
the teaching, or ruling Elders distinct but to a majority of the Eldership.

They are further of Opinion that the infant Seed of Parents owning the
Covenant consented to by this Ch^h. be subjects of Baptism, altho such
parents have not seen their way clear to join in full Comunion with the
Ch^h. And that such baptized persons be so far accounted members of
The Church, as to be watched over by the Church, and to be
subject to the discipline of the same.[25]

Voted To accept this report, and that the substance thereof be added

[47]

to the standing Covenant or government of this Church.

To which Mes^s. Jacob Hasey and Nathan Cheever entered
their dissents; and insisted the same be recorded: To which the Church
assented.

Whereas the Town Voted eighty pounds old ten^r. to defrey the
Charge of the Council to be convened on the 12th. Instant, and submitted
the same to the Church to lay out for the entertainment of said council.
Voted, Elder Hasey, Capt. Nathl. Oliver, and M^r. Benjamin Tuttle be a
Comittee to make provisions &c^a. accordingly.

Dec^r.12

The Venerable Council met at the house of Capt. Nathl. Oliver
and adjourned to the 20th Instant.

20

Said Council met according to their adjournment, and after a long
debate Voted to install the Rev^d. William McClenachan to morrow
in the forenoon being the 21st. When the Rev^d. M^r. W^m. Hobby began
the Solemnity with prayers; The Rev^d. M^r. McClenachan preached.

The Rev^d. M^r. Prescott gave the Charge and the Rev^d. M^r. Henchman
gave the right hand of fellowship.

Jan^y: 10

The Church met by agreement at the House of the Rev^d. M^r.
McClenachan.

M^r. Nathan Cheever desired a Dismission from this Church to
the 2^d. Church in Maldon And —
Voted, That whereas said M^r. Cheever has for several years belonged to this
Church, and enjoyed special ordinances here; but fore some time past has

absented himself from our comunion; and once and again has declared he

can't be easy without a Dissolution of his membership with us, We, in

point of prudence consent to grant his request; and that he be

accordingly dismist.

14

M^r. William Oliver own'd the covenant, in order to have a Child baptized.

Voted, That the Sacrament of the Lord's supper shall be celebrated   [48]

on the last sabbath of every month in the year; Excepting December

and January, and to be omitted those two Months, by reason of the

Shortness of the Days & severity of the season.

Voted, That the Sabbath before the sacrament, the teaching or ruling

Elders shall propose to the Church and Congregation whether there

shall be a Lecture any Day in the week before the Sacrament; and

take their voice therein.

Voted, That it shall not be a term of Comunion, That Persons to be

admitted into the Church shall exhibit a written relation, so termed,

as has heretofore been the practice of this Church.

Voted, That Divine Service, for the future, upon all fast Days be

performed with singing of Psalms, as upon Lord's Days.

Voted - - - Elder Hasey and Nathl. Oliver jun^r. Settle the Church's acc^ts.

with Deacon Jacob Hasey, who refuses any longer to act in his Ofice

and receive the Utensils belonging to the Church till further Order

Then the Rev^d. M^r. McClenachan dismiss'd this meeting.

Jany 20

The Rev^d. M^r. McClenachan stop'd the Church, and read a

letter from the Rev^d. M^r. Cleaveland, Pastor of the South Church in

Maldon, signifying the desire of M^r. Benjamin Brintnal, to be

dismissed from said Church, and recomending him to this Church

Then he propose'd him to the acceptance of the Church, and

Voted - - - To receive said M[r]. Brintnall to this Church's particular Comunion. M[r]. M[c]Clenachan also inform'd the Church that M[r]. Jacob Hasey refused to oficiate as Deacon; and wou'd not deliver the utensills of the Church to the Comittee before appointed to receive them, but said he wou'd wait till the Church had another Deacon to receive them.

Voted, Elder Hasey be specially impowered to demand and receive said Utensills, and possess them till the further order of this Church.

Voted - - - That Monday 27th. Instant at 3 o'Clock P:M: there be a Church meeting at the meeting house.

27

[49]

The Church met as the members agreed. After Prayer Elder Hasey reported he had with much persuasion received the utensills of the Comunion Table. He also brôt a letter from Deacon Hasey, Signed Jacob Hasey, Abigail Hasey his wife, and Abigail Hasey jun[r]. his Daughter signifying their earnest Desire this Church wou'd dismiss them from the special comuni on of this Church, and recomend them to the second Church in Maldon. Upon which,

Voted, Elder Hasey and Nath[l]. Oliver Jun[r]. wait on said persons and urge they withdraw their desire, and report next Lord's Day after Divine Service.

Elder Hasey reported the Comittee had settled the Church's Accounts with Deacon Jacob Hasey, and found him indebted to the Church on the account of providing for the Comunion Table Six pounds, eight Shillings and eleven pence Old ten[r] and on Account of Collection for the poor eight pounds ten Shillings and four pence Old ten[r], which Sums, together with an English Shilling, and a new England Six pence amounting to thirteen Shillings and nine pence Old ten[r], he had received, as also the Church's account Book. Whereupon

Voted - - -The above report be accepted, and that Elder Hasey

Keep said Sums in his hands, with the said Book till the

further order of the Church.

The Rev^d. M^r. McClenachan proposed to the Church's

Consideration whether they would relinquish the use of the

present Version of the Psalms, in Divine Service and for the future

Sing Doctor Watts's version of the Psalms; after considerable

debate it was agreed this matter shou'd subside for the span of a

month, and in the mean time, the members wou'd examin said

Version; and the Elder's converse with any of the Congregation

that shou'd be dissatisfied, and indeavour their Satisfaction.

February 2^d. [50]

The Rev^d. M^r. McClenachan stop'd the Church.

Elder Hasey reported that he, with N^l: Oliver jun^r. had

waited upon M^r. Jacob Hasey, and urged he withdraw his

desire of a Dismission from this Church, but that he insisted

thereon, insisting he cou'd not edifie under the publick

worship. As did his wife and daughter. Upon which,

Voted - - - M^r. Jacob Hasey M^rs. Abigail Hasey, and Abigail

Hasey jun^r. be dismis'd from this and recomended to the

second Church in Maldon.

Deacon John Chamberlain acquainted the Church

with his desire of resigning his place as a Deacon, being

obliged thro^h. the infirmities of old age to be often absent from

duty &c^a. Upon which,

Voted - - - Deacon Chamberlain have the thanks of this Church

for his past services; and that he be released from his Ofice.

9.

The Church were desired to tarry after divine service
when the Rev^d. M^r. McClenachan read a letter from the Rev^d.
M^r. Samuel Cooper signifying the Desires of Capt. N^l. Oliver
and M^r. Daniel Watts, that their particular relation to the
Church of Christ in Brattle Street be transferred to this Church
in which said Persons were heartily recomended to the holy
fellowship of this Church.   Whereupon,

Voted - - - Capt. Nathl. Oliver, and M^r. Daniel Watts be admitted to
the Pastoral Care of this Church.

The Rev^d. M^r. McClenachan inform'd the Church that
there was a necessity of a Church meeting soon and requested it
might be held at his dwelling house — Accordingly —

Voted - - - The Church meet at the house of M^r. McClenachan on
Monday the 17th instant at 2 o'Clock afternoon.

E. Die

M^rs. Rachel Floyd was admitted a member in full Comunion.

16   [51]

M^r. Joshua Sale jun^r. was admitted to full Comunion.

17

The Church met as appointed at the house of the Rev^d.
M^r. McClenachan who proposed to the Church the Desire of
M^rs. Lewis that she own the evill and profess her sorrow in
cohabiting with her husband M^r. Nathan Lewis before they
were married.

M^rs. Lewis appeared and made a satisfactory Acknowledgement

Voted to restore M^rs. Lewis to our Charity and the enjoyment of
all Church Priviledges.

Voted, That the Church stock for the poor together with

what shall be collected on the next fast day be appropriated to
the use of M^rs. Marble and M^rs. Mary Breeden; That
Capt. Oliver receive the same, and distribute two thirds of
said moneys to M^rs. Marble, and the remainder to said M^rs. Mary
Breeden.

  M^r. McClenachan acquainted the Church that he
was obliged to be absent a week or ten days on some busness
to the eastward and desired the Church wou'd indulge his
absence if necessarily detain'd one or two Sabbaths; and in the
mean time requested the Church wou'd think on two suitable
persons to supply the place of Deacons: He then dismised
this meeting with a Blessing.

Anno 1749

March 27 — The Rev^d. M^r. McClenachan stop'd the Church
 and requested they wou'd appoint a Church meeting for some
 purpose under consideration and to do any other busness that
 at such meeting might be necessary. Accordingly,

Voted, The Church meet at the meeting house on Wednesday
 the 30th instant at 2 o'Clock afternoon for the purposes
 aforesaid.

E. Die, M^r. Samuel Vial owned the Covenant, for baptism of a Child.

March 30. 1749

[52]

 The Church met by appointment; After Prayer, The Rev^d.
M^r. McClenachan propos'd to the Church whether they wou'd
alter the Version of Psalms in comon use & for the future sing
D^r. Watts's version at Divine service.

  Elder Hasey desired the consideration thereof might be
continued a further time. Whereupon,

Voted, to postpone that matter for the space of two months, and if
no material objection to the use of said Version shou'd be
ofered in that term, agreed to the use thereof.

Voted To continue the Consideration of the Choice of Deacons
till a further time.

Voted, Tis reasonable that those members who attend Church
meetings on secular matters, and yet absent themselves from
special Ordinances shou'd make satisfactory acknowledgment
or their Votes shou'd not be accounted of in this Church.

   After a blessing this meeting was dismis'd.

April 16

The Rev^d. M^r. McClenachan stop'd the Church and read a
Letter from the second Church in Maldon, dismissing and also
recomending Samuel Tuttle and Anna his wife from said
Church to this Church signed Aaron Cleaveland Pastor.

Voted, to receive said members into the pastoral Care and fellowship
of this Church.

May 19

M^rs. Sarah Hill was admitted to full Comunion.

June 22

At a Church meeting duely notified last Sabbath, after prayer
M^r. McClenachan acquainted the Church he had received no
objection from any members of the town or Church against the
use of D^r. Watts's Psalms in publick worship but what he thôt
were obviated, Upon which, Nem^e. Cont^e.

Voted, This Church will for the future, use said Version at Divine
Services.

July 2

The Rev^d. M^r. McClenachan stop'd the Church and acquainted
them that M^rs. Mary Hasey, having become inhabitant and unstable,
desires a dismission from this Church and that she be recomended
to the Church in that Town,[26] Upon which,

Voted, That her request be granted.

September 15

The Church met at the meeting house by appointment
to choose two Deacons; After Prayer The Rev^d. M^r McClenachan
desired the Members to bring their Votes for two Deacons,

And it appeard Messrs David Watts and Benjamin
Brintnal were chosen to that ofice.

26

Being a Lecture The Rev^d. M^r. McClenachan in his
Sermon gave a Charge to the Deacons lately chosen, and in the
name of the Church desired they would for the future oficiate
as such oficers, being duely elected.

Novr. 19

The Rev^d. M^r. McClenachan stop'd the Church and read a
Letter from M^r. John Sale Junr. signifying his conviction of the
evill, and his sorrow for cohabiting with his wife before marriage
Whereupon,

Voted, to accept the same, as ample satisfaction and that the
said M^r. Sale be restored to his Church priviledges.

Decr. 18

The Church met at the meeting house by appointment.
The Rev^d. M^r. McClenachan read a Letter from the Rev^d. M^r. Salton
Pastor of a Church in Mensfield acquainting this Church that

he understood Prince negro Servant of M^r. Jacob Hasey had
ofer'd himself to the comunion of this Church, That the said
Prince had laid himself obnoxious to a Suspension in their Church
by leaving his duty with them and joining with the disorderly
Separates,   Whereupon,

Voted, not to admit said Prince to the comunion of this Church till
he had given Satisfaction to the said Church in Mensfield.

Decr. 21. 1749   [54]

The Rev^d. M^r. McClenachan stop'd the Church and read an
acknowledgment from Phillis Servant to the hon^l. Samuel
Watts Esqr. wherein she own'd the Sin, & profes'd her Sorrow in
cohabiting with her husband Before marriage; Upon which,

Voted,   To accept the same, and restore her to her Church
priviledges.

29

Capt. John Sale was admitted to full Comunion.

January 12

M^r. John Brintnal was admitted to full Comunion.

20

The Church met at the house of the Rev^d. M^r. McClenachan
by appointment; and propos'd to M^r. Samuel Floyd as an
Executor to his father M^r. Hugh Floyd, that it was high time
the donation of said M^r. Hugh Floyd deceas'd of ten pounds
~~lawfull~~ money shou'd be paid; who inform'd the Church that
he would consult his Brother, the other executor to his father's
Estate, and procure a peice of Plate agreeable to the intent of
the Donation.

May 17. 1751

M^rs. Sarah Sale was admitted to full Comunion.

July 23

M^rs. Elizebeth Stower was admitted to full Comunion.

Sepr. 3

M^r. John Tuttle Owned the Covenant in order to have
his child Baptized. M^rs. Deborah Brintnal was admitted for
full Comunion.

August 3. 1753

M^rs. Mary Wait was admitted to full Comunion.

Decr. 17. 1754 [55]

The Rev^d. M^r. McClenachan stop'd the Church and appointed
monday the 18th instant a Church meeting to consider a matter of
importance he had to lay before them.

18

The Church met by appointment. The Rev^d. M^r. McClenachan
desired the Church would dismiss him from his pastoral relation
to this Church and insisted thereon, Upon which,
Voted, Unanimously not to dismiss him.

25

The above said M^r. McClenachan having disolved his relation
to this Church by leaving them contrary to the above Vote was
received confirmed and partook of the Lords Supper under the
establishment of the Church of England, By the Rev^d. D^r.
Timothy Cutler.

January 13

The Church met by appointment to see what might be propos'd
to be done respecting a supply of the Pulpit; The hon^l. Elder Watts
being Moderator. After some debate on the destitute State
of a minister, it was unanimously agreed to leave the
consideration thereof to the Town.

January 12. 1756

The Church met by appointment, to choose a minister
Elder Watts was Moderator.
It appeared that M^r. Aaron Putnam was Chosen by a
Majority of Votes.

March 15

The Church met to consider what was proper to be done
upon the refusall of M^r. Putnam to accept the Church's and town's
Choise of him as their Pastor elect, when it was agreed to leave it
to the town to choose a Com^ee. to wait on M^r. Putnam and urge
his acceptance, notwithstanding his refusal; and proposed a
Subscription be had thrô the town to preferr to him on supposi
tion his refusal might be owing to his not being chosen more
unanimously.

Mem^m: The town sent their Com^ee. to Pomfrett to wait on M^r. Putnam
with a general Subscription satisfying a desire he wou'd settle in their
town; who notwithstanding finally refused.

July 3^d. 1756   [56]

The Church met by appointment to consider their Covenant
and to see what they wou'd do respecting a minister.
And considering few were present, adjourn'd till to morrow after

divine Service.

4

The Church stop'd according to their adjournment; and having

chosen Cap^r. Nathl. Oliver Moderator in the absence of Elder Watts,

Voted — This Church abide by their original Covenant with the

explications agreed to by this Church, on the 5th. of Decr. 1748.

That therewith the Covenant be fairly transcribed, and subscribed

by all the present members of this Church.

Voted — Unanimously, that all past Votes relative to the dismission of

M^r. Nathan Cheever be reconsidered; and that said M^r. Nathan Cheever

be restored to his membership with this Church, provided he will

subscribe the Covenant.

Voted – M^r. Samuel Floyd be added to the Town's Com^ee. for supply

of the Pulpit, and that said Com^ee. wait on M^r. Norton and acquaint

him 'tis the Church's desire he would preach with us a month or six

weeks longer upon probation. Then adjourn'd to next Sabbath.

11

The Church stop'd agreeable to their adjournment; The Covenant

was read and signed by several members, some others desired a perusal

of it as they said they did not thoroughly understand it, as it now stood

which was unanimously agreed to.

It was moved the Church do something respecting the Choise

of a Minister.

M^r. Floyd and others reported that M^r. Norton said he thôt he had

been preaching some time under the Idea of probation; and

his busness wou'd not permit his tarry in this town any longer.

Which past over without any Vote thereupon.

Voted to leave a further Supply of the Pulpit to the town's Comittee

And dismist this meeting.

Decr. 27

The Church met at the meeting house in order to chuse

a Minister, The hon^l. Elder Watts being Moderator, It

appeared M^r. Joseph Jackson was unanimously chosen. Then

Voted, This choice be transmitted to the town for their Concurrence.

Decr. 29

[57]

M^r. Joseph Jackson desired the Church wou'd tarry after the

Blessing, which being pronounced, he retired; after which

Deacon Brintnall read a Letter from M^r. Jackson to the Church

and Town, signifying he wou'd not accept the Choise this Church and

town had made of him as their Pastor elect.

July 17. 1757

Elder Watts stop'd the Church and desired they wou'd come into

some measures respecting a settlement of a Minister, especially as he

understood M^r. Phillips Payson was generally liked, in the Town

Whereupon,

Voted - - - The Com^{ee}. for the supply of the pulpit desire the said

M^r. Payson to preach four Sabbaths from this date on Probation.

24

Elder Watts stop'd the Church and Congregation and acquainted

them that the Com^{ee}. had waited on M^r. Payson who said he cou'd

not tarry to preach any longer upon probation upon which

Voted - - - unanimously to appoint Thursday the 28th instant at

3 o'Clock afternoon a Church meeting to see if they will give

M^r. Phillips Payson an Invitation to settle in the ministry in the

Town.

28

The Church met at the meeting house agreeable to appointm^r.

And unanimously declared Viva voce That 'tis their minds M^r.

Phillips Payson be invited to take the Pastoral Care of this

Church, which being transmitted to the Town, they did on

the same day unanimously concurr with the Church in the

Choise of the said M^r. Payson.

Sepr. 18

Elder Watts stop'd the Church, and desired they wou'd consider what

they thought might be proper to be done consequent upon M^r.

Payson's answer of acceptance of the Church & town's choise of him

as the town's minister which lay before them. Upon which

Voted — That the Com^{ee}. appointed by the town, to wait on M^r. Payson

to know what time will be agreeable to him to instate him in his

Ofice as Pastor among us, be desired to discharge said Trust, to morrow

and bring his answer before the Town's meeting.

Voted — Also to morrow at 5 o'Clock afternoon there be a Church meeting

at the meeting house to consider and determine such matters, as shall

then properly be Laid before them.

Sepr. 19   [58]

The Church met agreeable to their appointment, Elder Watts

being Moderator, and unanimously,

Voted - - - Wednesday the 26th of October next be appointed to Solemnize

the Ordination of M^r. Phillips Payson to the pastoral Ofice over this

Church and Town.

Voted - - - Also That the Rev^d. Doctor Sewall's and the Rev^d. M^r. Eliots Church

of Boston; The Rev^d. M^r. Appleton's of Cambridge, M^r. Payson's of

Walpole, M^r. Rogers's of Littleton, Mes^s. Emersons and Willis's of

Maldon, M[r]. Swifts of Acton, and M[r]. Robie's of Lynn be sent

to, to instate M[r]. Phillips Payson in the pastoral Ofice over this

Church and Town, to which he has been unanimously Chosen, and

which he has accepted.

Voted - - - Mes[s]. Samuel Floyd, Benjamin Brintnal, & Nathl. Oliver

Junr. be a Comittee to provide Entertainment &c[a]. for the Venerable

Council, & other Gent[n]. on the ensuing Ordination Day.

25

Elder Watts stop'd the Church and proposed to them that M[r].

Payson thôt there was a Clause in the Church Covenant relative to

Ruling Elders which he could not fully assent to, Whereupon,

Voted - - - The Church meet to morrow at 3 o'Clock afternoon, at the house

of M[r]. Hough, to consider thereon and that M[r]. Payson be desired to

attend the Church at said meeting.

26

The Church met at time and place, with M[r]. Payson, who related

his dificulty on the paragraph in the Church Covenant, wherein it

is suggested that Ruling Elders are of Scripture warrant, which he was

not fully satisfied of; yet declared he wou'd be passive in whatever

the Church thôt proper to act thereupon.

After some debate M[r]. Payson was desired to mend a Clause on

that part of the Covenant, relative to Ruling Elders that he cou'd freely

subscribe to; which he did in these words Viz:

At least so far to submit to such Oficers as that they should

exercise what Power the Church ~~should~~ has see fit to invest them with.

Which clause the Church readily come into, and thereon

Voted - - - The Covenant be transcribed adding said Clause, and that the

Church meet next Sabbath, after divine Service to receive the same.

Octr 23rd

The Church stop'd but considering several members were absent, it was thôt best to continue the consideration of signing the Covenant to a further time.

15

The Church met after divine Service and having read the covenant, all that were present subscribed the same.

M^r. Pason came into the Church meeting, and requested that all matter of grievance or ofence respecting any members shou'd subside or be made up before he took upon himself the pastoral Care of the Church, and then withdrew.

Which matter the church took into Consideration, And Voted - - - That this Church look upon all such of their numbers who have or shall subscribe the Church Covenant, having had the same distinctly read unto them; any matter or cause of grievance heretofore subsisting among them notwithstanding.

It was moved and seconded that the members wait upon M^r. Elisha Tuttle with this Vote and endeavour his reconciliation.

Which was readily comply'd with; The Church Covenant was distinctly read to him; all the members present, being majority of the Church, united in their desires he would sign the Church Covenant, and for the future attend his Duty and Priviledge. Whereupon said M^r. Tuttle subscribed the Covenant, The article relative to Ruling Elders excepted.

26

The Church met the Venerable Council sent to in order to ordain M^r. Phillips Payson, at the house of Nathl. Oliver Junr.

M^r. Payson signed the Church Covenant; He then with the

Church waited upon the Venerable Council.

The Rev^d. M^r. Daniel Rogers mentioned a dismission of the particular membership of M^r. Payson with an hearty recomendation of him to this Church; from the Church at Littleton.

The Rev^d. M^r. Appleton, Mod^r. of the Council, declared [60] The Council were satisfied as to the principles and other ministerial abilities of M^r. Phillips Payson, and were ready to proceed to his Ordination.

The Church then waited on said Council to the meeting house to solemnize the same.   Where

The Rev^d. M^r. Rogers began the solemnity with Prayer.

The Rev^d. M^r. Payson of Walpole preached a Sermon, suitable to the occasion.

The Rev^d. M^r. Appleton gave the Charge.

The Rev^d. M^r. Emerson gave the right hand of fellowship.

The Rev^d. M^r. Swift closed the service with prayer.

After which a Psalm being sang, The new ordain'd Pastor Viz - - - The Rev^d. M^r. Phillips Payson jun^r. dismis'd the assemb;y with the usual blesssgings.

Deo opt: max: Laus et Gloria

Notes

1. Preceding this entry, the copy reads: "Octob:19:1715. This day the Church was Gathered at Rumny marish, & Mr Thomas Cheever was Ordained their Pastour."

2. The end of this and a number of lines following on this page, as well as the beginnings of several lines further down, are affected by MS damage; words in brackets supplied from MS copy, pp. 1-2.

3. The next sentence and a half appears only in the copy; the top of MS p. 2 is damaged at the top.

4. Original MS resumes.

5. The top of MS p. 2 is shorn, and the right side of the page is damaged; bracketed text taken from MS copy, pp. 4-5.

6. This word is written in shorthand.

7. This word is written in shorthand.

8. An illegible shorthand notation follows.

9. MS damage.

10. On Tuttle, see introduction, p. 19.

11. "Scilicet," Latin for "plainly," or "namely."

12. *I.e.* on MS p. 15.

13. Robert Sturgeon of Ireland, sett. Watertown, 1721-22, at a short-lived independent church, dismissed by ecclesiastical council, then served churches in Connecticut and New York.

14. James McGregore (1677-1729), emigrated from Ireland 1718, removed to Londonderry (Nutfield), N.H., pastor of Presbyterian Church of Derry, 1719-29.

15. Page cut off for next three lines.

16. MS damage at lower right corner of page; bracketed words supplied from MS copy, pp. 34-35.

17. MS damage on lower left-hand corner; words in brackets on this and following lines supplied from MS copy, p. 35.

18. Cambridge Platform, ch. X, "Of the powr of the Church, & its Presbytery." The council may be referring to sec. 11: "From the premisses, namely, that the ordinary

powr of Government belonging only to the elders, powr of priviledg remaineth with the brotherhood, (as powr of judgment in matters of censure, & powr of liberty, in matters of liberty) It followeth, that in an organick Church, & right administration; all church acts, proceed after the manner of a mixt administration, so as no church act can be consummated, or perfected without the consent of both." Quoted from Williston Walker, *The Creeds and Platforms of Congregationalism* (New York, 1893), 220.

19. A later comment beside this name reads, "Now Elizabeth Halsy, & living in the poor house. Her memory is yet good. June 14. 1825."

20. *I.e.* Malden (David Parsons), Andover (John Barnard), Marblehead (Edward Holyoke), Peabody (Benjamin Prescott), Cambridge (Nathaniel Appleton), Weston (William Williams), Sudbury (Wayland) (William Cooke), and Rumney Marsh.

21. Damage to the right margin of MS p. 37 obliterates words or parts of words through the remainder of this paragraph and the following one; words are supplied from MS copy, pp. 67-68.

22. The first word in this and the following two lines partially lost due to MS damage; words supplied from MS copy, p. 69.

23. Cheever left a blank space to fill in the name of the church, but never did.

24. This entry is written in very shaky handwriting, and is the last Cheever made; subsequent entries were written by Nathaniel Oliver Jr.

25. On the liberalization of the Rumney Marsh church, see introduction, p. 33.

26. The town is not specified.

Index

Spellings of family names vary. Check variant spellings to find all entries for specific people and for family members. Cross-references in the index indicate variant spellings. Dates in parentheses following names refer to the year in which the person appears in the church records.

Abbot, Rev. Mr., 301
Abbott, James, 143, 194
Abbott, Sarah, 194
Aburn, Abigail, 118
Acton, Mass., 325
Acts, Book of, 254
Adams, Benjamin, 198
Adams, Mary, 135, 138, 175
Admission to churches.
    See Church admissions and membership
African slaves. *See* Blacks
Alcoholism. *See* Drunkenness
All, Margarett, 138
Allen, Joseph, 286
Allin, Margaret, 129
Amherst, Mass.: dismissals of Reading
    church members to, 152, 153, 182, 200,
    218*n*85; Wilkins as minister in, 219*n*103
Andover, Mass., 257, 329*n*20
Anglican Church, 53, 320
Antinomian Controversy, 51
Appleton, Rev. Mr. Nathaniel: and fast day
    at Rumney Marsh church, 301; and
    Leicester's problems, 268, 329*n*20; and
    McCalachan as ministerial colleague in
    Rumney Marsh church, 304, 306, 308;
    and ordination of Hobby, 139; and ordi-
    nation of Payson, 324, 327
Appleton, Nathaniel (Reading), 144
Archer, John, 289
Arminianism, 185
Arnold, Elizabeth, 88, 104
Arnold, Joseph, 115
Arnold, Mary, 110
Arnold, Rebecca, 106
Arnold, William, 98, 108
Ashfield, Miriam, 111
Attleburrah, Mass., 156

Atwol, Rachel, 113
Awakenings, 37, 45-47, 50, 188, 190-191

Bacheldor, Elizabeth, 111
Bacheldor family. *See* headings beginning
    with Bacheldor; Batchelder; Batcheldor
Bacheller, Abigail, 140
Bacheller, David, 146
Bacheller, Elizabeth, 176
Bacheller, John Jr., 152
Bacheller, Nathaniel, 142, 174
Bacheller, Nathaniel Jr., 195
Bacheller, Samuel, 174
Bacheller family. *See* headings beginning with
    Bacheller; Bachellor; Batcheller
Bachellor, Henrie, 97
Bachellor, John, 96
Bachellor, Sarai, 97
Bachellor family. *See* headings beginning
    with Bacheller; Bachellor; Batcheller
Bachelor, David, 83
Baldwin, Elizabeth, 119
Baldwin, Timothy Sr., 116
Baldwin, William, 189-190
Balindon (black), 299
Bancroft, Abigail, 105, 125
Bancroft, Caleb, 150, 151
Bancroft, Captain, 179, 184, 188, 190, 191
Bancroft, D., 168
Bancroft, David, 141, 185
Bancroft, Ebenezer, 96, 103
Bancroft, Edmund, 142
Bancroft, Elizabeth (1670), 83
Bancroft, Elizabeth (1687), 97
Bancroft, Elizabeth (1706, 1712), 111, 115
Bancroft, Elizabeth (Mrs. Joseph), 150
Bancroft, Ensign, 160, 163
Bancroft, Hannah, 149, 152, 156

24; excommunication for, 17-18, 36, 107-108, 189, 193; as problem of Congregationalists, 36; Reading church disciplinary cases on, 36, 37, 91-92, 106-108, 175, 177, 178-179, 183, 188-189, 191-193, 211; Rumney Marsh church disciplinary cases on, 32, 286-287, 288
Dudley, Mass., 176
Duntlin, Hannah, 103
Dunton, Brother, 67
Dunton, Rebecca, 104
Dunton, Ruth, 103
Dunton, Samuel, 103
Dunton, Sarah, 86
Dutton, G., 79
Dutton, Joseph, 103
Dutton, Rebeccah, 98, 101

Earthquakes, 45, 217*n*63
East Haddam, Conn., 176
Eastham, Mass., 178, 193, 218*n*84, 218*n*91
Eastis, Thomas, 227
Eaton, Abigail, 110, 111
Eaton, Abigal, 152
Eaton, Captain, 145, 146, 184, 190, 191, 195, 199
Eaton, Charity, 152
Eaton, Daniel, 85
Eaton, Daniell, 96
Eaton, Dorcas, 86, 111
Eaton, Elizabeth (1678), 90
Eaton, Elizabeth (1684), 93
Eaton, Elizabeth (1697), 106
Eaton, Elizabeth (1702, 1705), 109, 111
Eaton, Elizabeth (1756), 150
Eaton, Elizabeth (1762), 152
Eaton, Elizabeth (Mrs. Joseph Jr.), 138, 177
Eaton, Eunice, 149
Eaton, Grace, 104
Eaton, Hanna, 87
Eaton, Hannah (1697), 106
Eaton, Hannah (1701), 108
Eaton, Hannah (1713), 116
Eaton, Hannah (1716), 118
Eaton, James, 151
Eaton, Mrs. John, 69

Eaton, John (1648), 69
Eaton, John (1684), 96
Eaton, John (1710s), 113, 118
Eaton, John (1720/21), 124, 159
Eaton, John (1727/1728), 134, 170
Eaton, John Jr. (1670), 84, 101
Eaton, John Jr. (1677), 86
Eaton, John Jr. (1687), 98
Eaton, Jonas (1648), 67
Eaton, Jonas (1659), 73
Eaton, Jonas (1672), 85
Eaton, Jonas (1687), 98
Eaton, Jonas (1735), 140
Eaton, Mrs. Jonas, 67
Eaton, Jonathan (1679/80s), 90, 98
Eaton, Jonathan (1703), 109
Eaton, Jonathan (1706), 112
Eaton, Jonathan (1720/22), 127
Eaton, Jonathan (1736), 141
Eaton, Jonathan (1747), 36, 188
Eaton, Jonathan (1760s), 202, 212
Eaton, Mrs. Jonathan, 127
Eaton, Joseph (1672), 85
Eaton, Joseph (1680), 90
Eaton, Joseph (1701), 108
Eaton, Joseph (1712), 115
Eaton, Joseph (1738), 178
Eaton, Joseph Jr., 138, 177
Eaton, Joshua, 90, 97, 108
Eaton, Lidia, 132
Eaton, Lille, 153
Eaton, Lilley, 54
Eaton, Lois, 151
Eaton, Lydia, 119, 127
Eaton, Martha, 93
Eaton, Mary (1648), 70
Eaton, Mary (1672), 85
Eaton, Mary (1684), 96
Eaton, Mary (1687), 97
Eaton, Mary (1693), 104
Eaton, Mary (1708), 112
Eaton, Mary (1712, 1715), 115, 116
Eaton, Mary (1719), 120
Eaton, Mary (1720/21), 127, 159
Eaton, Mary (1735), 140
Eaton, Mary (Mrs. Joseph; 1720/21), 124

children of, 245, 296; and charges against Skinner for stealing, 231; in church member list, 227; and communion vessels, 228; as deacon of Rumney Marsh church, 15, 243, 274; election of, as deacon, 243, 244; election of, as ruling elder, 293, 294; and fast day, 301; and financial accounts of church, 245, 256, 278, 301, 303, 312, 313-314; and hymns for worship, 316; and installment of Thatcher in Boston, 242; and Jacob Halsey's dismissal to Malden church, 313, 314; and Leicester's problems, 268-269; and McClanachan as ministerial colleague for Cheever, 307, 309, 311; and North Reading's problems, 257; ordination of, as ruling elder, 295; and ordination of ministers of other churches, 263, 266-267, 277; as ruling elder of Rumney Marsh church, 15, 26, 293, 294; and Salem's problems, 282, 286; signing of Rumney Marsh church covenant by, 226; and utensils of communion from Deacon Jacob Halsey, 313; and Watertown's problems, 246, 252-253; wife of, admitted to full communion, 296

Halsey family. *See* headings beginning with Halsey; Halsy

Halsy, Abigail (Mrs. Jacob), 227

Halsy, Asa, 226, 227, 230

Halsy, Mary (Mrs. Asa), 226, 230

Halsy, Sarah, 227

Halsy family. *See* headings beginning with Halsey; Halsy

Hamlet, Rebecca, 104

Hanover, Mass., 295

Harndel, Elizabeth, 112

Harndel, Susannah (Reading), 116, 165

Harndel, Susannah (Rumney Marsh), 227, 276

Harndell, Elizabeth, 117

Harndell, Mary, 86

Harnden, Richard, 97

Harrington, Edward, 247

Hart, Adam, 104

Hart, Elizabeth: disciplinary cases of, 17, 35, 70, 71-72; in membership list, 67

Hart, Samuel, 107, 117, 128

Hart, Sarah, 107, 112, 128

Hartshorn, Abigail, 146, 151

Hartshorn, Benjamin (1670s-1680s), 89, 99, 101

Hartshorn, Benjamin (1730), 138

Hartshorn, David, 108

Hartshorn, Elizabeth (1670, 1687), 99, 101

Hartshorn, Elizabeth (1728), 135

Hartshorn, Hannah, 105

Hartshorn, James, 150

Hartshorn, Joseph, 110

Hartshorn, Martha, 117

Hartshorn, Mary, 147

Hartshorn, Rebecka, 108

Hartshorn, Sarah, 104, 105, 110

Hartshorn, Susan, 104

Hartshorn, Susannah (1720s), 129, 165

Hartshorn, Susannah (1751), 148

Hartshorn, Tabitha, 150

Hartshorn, Thomas (1648), 67

Hartshorn, Thomas (1723), 165

Hartshorn, Thomas (1763), 203

Hartshorn, Mrs. Thomas, 67

Hartshorn, Timothy Sr., 125

Hartshorn, Mrs. Timothy Sr., 125

Hartshorn, Timothy Jr., 111, 115, 125

Hartshorn family. *See* headings beginning with Hartshorn; Hartshorne

Hartshorne, David, 96, 98

Hartshorne, John, 84

Hartshorne, Joseph, 89, 98, 101

Hartshorne, Martha, 98

Hartshorne, Rebecca, 98

Hartshorne, Sarah, 88

Hartshorne, Sister, 70

Hartshorne, Susannah. *See* Deverix, Susannah

Hartshorne, Thomas, 85

Hartshorne, Timothy, 90, 98

Hartshorne family. *See* headings beginning with Hartshorn; Hartshorne

Harvard, Mary, 108

Hasey family. *See* headings begining with Halsey

Hastings, Elizabeth, 107, 157

Hastings, Joseph, 109, 157

Hathorn, Joseph, 289